POLITICS OF MODERN MUSLIM SUBJECTIVITIES

D1072735

THE MODERN MUSLIM WORLD

Series Editor: Dietrich Jung of the Center for Contemporary Middle East Studies, University of Southern Denmark

The modern Muslim world is an integral part of global society. In transcending the confines of area studies, this series encompasses scholarly work on political, economic, and cultural issues in modern Muslim history, taking a global perspective. Focusing on the period from the early nineteenth century to the present, it combines studies of Muslim majority regions, such as the Middle East and parts of Africa and Asia, with the analysis of Muslim minority communities in Europe and the Americas. Emphasizing the global connectedness of Muslims, the series seeks to promote and encourage the understanding of contemporary Muslim life in a comparative perspective and as an inseparable part of modern globality.

Migration, Security, and Citizenship in the Middle East: New Perspectives
  Edited by Peter Seeberg and Zaid Eyadat

Politics of Modern Muslim Subjectivities: Islam, Youth, and Social Activism in the Middle East
  Dietrich Jung, Marie Juul Petersen, and Sara Lei Sparre

POLITICS OF MODERN MUSLIM SUBJECTIVITIES

Islam, Youth, and Social Activism in the Middle East

Dietrich Jung, Marie Juul Petersen, and
Sara Lei Sparre

POLITICS OF MODERN MUSLIM SUBJECTIVITIES

First published in 2014 by
PALGRAVE MACMILLAN®
in the United States—a division of St. Martin's Press LLC,
175 Fifth Avenue, New York, NY 10010.

Where this book is distributed in the UK, Europe and the rest of the world, this is by Palgrave Macmillan, a division of Macmillan Publishers Limited, registered in England, company number 785998, of Houndmills, Basingstoke, Hampshire RG21 6XS.

Palgrave Macmillan is the global academic imprint of the above companies and has companies and representatives throughout the world.

Palgrave® and Macmillan® are registered trademarks in the United States, the United Kingdom, Europe and other countries.

ISBN: 978–1–137–38064–7 (hc)
ISBN: 978–1–137–38063–0 (pbk)

Library of Congress Cataloging-in-Publication Data is available from the Library of Congress.

A catalogue record of the book is available from the British Library.

Design by Newgen Knowledge Works (P) Ltd., Chennai, India.

First edition: January 2014

10 9 8 7 6 5 4 3 2 1

To our interview partners
Who so generously allowed us insight into their lives
May their visions for a better society come true

CONTENTS

PREFACE

This book is the final result of a longer collaborative effort. In early 2006, Marie Juul Petersen dropped into my office with a project idea on Islamic civil society organizations in Jordan. Together we developed a research proposal that we submitted to the Royal Danish Ministry of Foreign Affairs. At this point in time, I was a senior researcher at the Danish Institute for International Studies (DIIS), an independent research institute, however, with very close ties to the ministry. Under the umbrella of the "Partnership for Dialogue and Reform" (*Det Arabiske Initiativ*), the ministry has aimed at strengthening dialogue, understanding, and cooperation with the Arab world through collaboration with and support of a broad variety of civil society organizations. It was within this framework that we were able to get funding for our project on Islamic civil society organizations together with financial and institutional support by DIIS. In August 2006, Sara Lei Sparre joined us and we elaborated our research plan for the two case studies on social welfare organizations in Jordan and the new religious youth organizations in Egypt. The fieldwork, then, was conducted in November/December 2006 and from March to June 2007.

Given the funding background of this project, the first aim was to provide the foreign ministry with a scholarly report on Islamic social welfare and youth organizations in Egypt and Jordan. This analytically guided documentation of our project was published as DIIS Report 13/2007: *Islam and civil society: Case studies from Jordan and Egypt*. However, right from the beginning, we had the additional academic ambition of writing a scholarly book based on our field data. Already the first reading and discussion of our notes and interviews indicated the promising potential of the material. The data gave a unique view on the ways in which these organizations provide fields for societal negotiations and individual processes of modern identity construction. More strikingly, the social processes we could observe seemed to be quite similar to those about which I have read in sociological accounts of modern subjectivity formation in Europe. Apparently, both people in the Middle East and Europeans have been referring to more general, global social imaginaries in shaping different types of modern subjectivities. Given my strong interest in the sociology of modernity, I decided to aim at writing a book on the politics of modern Muslim subjectivities through the lenses of contemporary analytical devices, which have been provided by the so-called Western social theory.

This book was eventually written from February to July 2012 at the Centre for Studies in Religion and Society, University of Victoria, Canada.

In January 2009, I had moved from DIIS to the University of Southern Denmark, taking up a chair in contemporary Middle East Studies. My first sabbatical, then, gave me the chance to turn the above-mentioned ideas into a book manuscript. Thus, our field data were for a couple of years in the drawer, before I again had the chance to read and analyze it under a socio-logical gaze. Contemporary university life is not really conducive to produce academic monographs. The increasing pressure in teaching, administrative work, competing on funding resources, and benchmarking of all kinds of activities represent major obstacles to focused research. The various tasks of a university professor lead to an enhanced departmentalization of time that does hardly allow for the necessary phases of concentration and reflective writing. Without the sabbatical granted by my university and the relaxed and intellectually inspiring atmosphere at the Centre for Studies in Religion and Society, this book probably would have never been written. I am very grate-ful to the staff of the Centre and its director, Paul Bramadat, for offering me this opportunity. Moreover, by renting me and my family their house at Swan Lake, the Henderson family provided us with an excellent place to stay in Victoria at which parts of the book were written when I had to escape the office once in a while.

It is only normal that this course of events left its marks on the book. First, the data on which its case studies rest to a certain extent have been dated, in particular, with respect to the revolutionary processes that we have observed in the Arab Middle East since 2010/2011. The so-called Arab Spring has certainly impacted the new reading of our data. Yet in linking it closely to fundamental theoretical questions, the importance of this time-lag appears to me of minor relevance. Secondly, although still being in close contact, the three authors of this book have not been institutionally linked to each other since the end of 2008. Once being research assistants, Marie Juul Petersen and Sara Lei Sparre meanwhile have completed their PhD theses at University of Copenhagen. Therefore, and in order to keep the book in one voice, I have written the final manuscript of the book. The two case studies, however, are largely based on the original draft chapters of my coauthors. This shared authorship of the book has caused some problems with regard to the case studies. Originally, Marie Juul Petersen has conducted most of the field work in Jordan, whereas Sara Lei Spara has been in Egypt, also for her PhD thesis after our project at DIIS came to an end. In order to avoid shifting voices in the book, we decided to present the whole material in the plural, that is, to say we decided to write the whole text in the third person plural. Field purists might criticize this sacrifice of "authenticity" to style, but we think it is in this way the book reads best. It goes without saying that my coauthors have carefully read and discussed the whole manuscript with me, which also in this sense is the final result of a joint project.

DIETRICH JUNG
Copenhagen, Summer 2013

Acknowledgments

First and foremost, our gratitude goes to the many members and volunteers of the Jordanian and Egyptian organizations who open heartedly shared their ideas, expertise, and experiences with us. This book would not have been possible without their trust and time. We also want to thank our research assistants Doaa al-Awaysheh, Hala Imam, and Mohamed Hayek for their indispensable help. They not only assisted us with translation, but also facilitated our access to the field and provided us with invaluable insights into daily life in Jordan and Egypt.

During and after our fieldwork, many other people kindly offered their assistance, insights, and advice in order to advance our research. These include a great number of researchers, university professors, journalists, and governmental representatives from various countries. In particular, we would like to express our gratitude to Mona Atia, Mogens Blom, Egbert Harmsen, Fathy Abou Hatab, Barbara Lethem Ibrahim, Julie Pruzan-Jørgensen, Klaus Schlichte, Catherine Schwerin, and Morten Valbjørn. In addition, we are grateful to the insightful comments of three anonymous reviewers and to Farideh Koohi-Kamali and Sara Doskow from Palgrave MacMillan in New York, who have been extremely supportive in transforming this research project into a book.

Finally, we would like to thank a number of institutions for directly facilitating this project. These include the Centre for Studies in Religion and Society, University of Victoria, Canada, as well as the Institute for History and the Faculty for Humanities at the University of Southern Denmark. Furthermore, we are in debt to the Royal Danish Ministry of Foreign Affairs and the Danish Institute for International Studies for funding and facilitating the initial research project on Islam and civil society organizations in Jordan and Egypt, which laid the groundwork for this book.

Introduction: "We Have a Collective Vision to Build Our Society"

When launching the research project for this book in 2006, we did not imagine what kind of consequences the spirit behind the above quote from one of our informants would have. Like the overwhelming majority of the Middle East studies community, we were surprised by the events subsequently labeled the "Arab Spring." There is no doubt that the various uprisings across the Arab Middle East were driven by a multiplicity of different visions. Yet they were united by the fundamental goal of getting rid of regimes that have stifled the development of Arab societies and the personal life expectations of their people for decades.[1] The Arab Spring was motivated by a deep dissatisfaction with the general living conditions in the region. In Egypt and beyond, we have also witnessed the rage of a defeated, frustrated, and often humiliated middle class (cf. Amin 2011, 85). Consequently, the cry for democratic politics is closely intertwined with visions of the "good life" and attempts to successfully construct meaningful modern selfhoods. In addressing the politics of modern Muslim subjectivities, we perceive the Arab Spring as an historical event that made visible a much more fundamental social transformation. How to understand this social transformation?

In order to address this general question in a scholarly way, it is first necessary to develop a theoretical framework and an analytical tool kit for organizing our observations. For this undertaking, the huge corpus of social theories on modernity would be an obvious source. Yet social theorists have usually referred to the history of the so-called West.[2] The conceptual apparatus of sociology largely builds on Western historical experiences and its appropriateness in applying it to non-Western societies, therefore, has been severely questioned. Moreover, social theorists such as Michel Foucault, Anthony Giddens, or Charles Taylor often assume that their respective concepts only have analytical relevance with regard to "Western" or "developed" societies. In applying a novel analytical framework based on a selective choice from contemporary social theory, our analysis of the politics of modern Muslim subjectivities aims at showing the flaws in these assumptions that are grounded in the idea of the specificity and exclusiveness of Western modernity. Contrary to the aforementioned theorists, we contend that a critical application of their concepts can tell us something about ongoing social transformations in Muslim societies.

The idea of a specific Western kind of modernity finds, to a certain extent, its mirror image in the field of Islamic studies. In this field, scholars often emphasize the allegedly unique features of Islam. This is without doubt true for the orientalist tradition whose essentialist image of Islam was heavily criticized in Edward Said's *Orientalism* (Said 1978). In Islamic studies proper, the orientalist tradition meanwhile has been pushed to the margins, although an influential group of neo-orientalist scholars remains (cf. Sadowski 1993). Contemporary scholarship on Islam has pretty much transformed itself into a discipline whose research is increasingly but not systematically informed by the more recent theoretical and methodological approaches of the social sciences and humanities. Instead of analyzing classical Islamic literature, scholars of Islam have gradually turned toward the study of Muslim modernities, including popular culture, social movements, as well as religious discourses and social practices that characterize the everyday life of Muslims.[3]

In *An Enchanted Modern*, for instance, Lara Deeb explored the "multiple intersections between ideas and practices of modernity and of piety" among Shiite women in Lebanon (2006, 4). On the basis of extended fieldwork, Deeb analyzed religious discourses, symbolic representations, and daily social practices through which her informants try to live an authentic form of Islam, which she called "authenticated Islam." Another case in point is Saba Mahmood's study on the "politics of piety" among the participants of Egyptian neighborhood mosque movements. Borrowing from poststructuralist theory, Mahmood aimed with her study at a critique of some liberal assumptions on which many Western feminist theories so far have rested (2005). Yet with their explicit focus on consistent, perfect, pure, and strictly pious forms of Islamic behavior, these studies tend to neglect the complex contexts and often contradictory forms of everyday life that characterize the social practices of the majority of Muslims (cf. Bangstad 2011; Schielke 2009). Moreover, in its search for differences rather than similarities between Western and Muslim social experiences, recent scholarship on Islamic modernities still builds often on the assumption of a fundamental dichotomy between Western and Islamic societies, representing Muslims as being engaged with modernity as an external and colonizing force (Soares and Osella 2009). Consequently, both social theory and Islamic studies have a tendency to reinforce the idea of an, in principle, mutual exclusiveness between Western and Islamic ways of life.

This book aims at making a contribution to breaking with this circular reinforcement of exclusivist and reductionist perspectives. We will argue that the construction of Muslim modernities also takes place with reference to social imaginaries similar to those which social theory has discerned in European history. In stressing similarities in the formation of modern Western and Muslim subjectivities, we do not discard differences. On the contrary, we claim that our understanding of differences has to be grounded in more precise knowledge of similarities. These similarities are due to the impact of globally relevant social imaginaries, as well as to mutual challenges and opportunities with which the spread of global modernity has confronted people who otherwise relate to different cultural traditions. In heuristic terms, we can use the conceptual tools of social theory to develop a standard against which we interpret differences resulting from historically and culturally contingent paths of social evolution. We will develop this standard in the first part of the book and illustrate it with examples from Islamic history and the modernization of the Muslim world in more general terms. In the second and third parts of the book, our two case studies will serve as means to show the applicability of this standard in analyzing phenomena of social change and individual subjectivity formation in the Middle East. In this way, we hope not only to contribute to a better understanding of the puzzling images with which we have been confronted in our own project and the Arab spring, but also to advance the communication between social theory and Islamic studies.

In the beginning, our study was triggered by a growing dissatisfaction with both the scholarly and popular debates on Islam and the Middle East. In light of the preoccupation with radical Islamist politics, we aimed at a change of perspective. Focusing on social welfare activities, we wanted to explore Islamic organizations that are primarily engaged in social and cultural realms, comprising a puzzling variety of Islamic charity associations, development NGOs, youth clubs, health clinics, and educational institutions. From these segments of civil society, we recruited our informants and, besides their religious orientation, their social engagement was driven by serious concerns about the social conditions in Jordan and Egypt, respectively. They all referred to a number of pressing social problems for which so far the state or initiatives from abroad have not been able to provide solutions. Moreover, in doing voluntary work in Islamic charities, our interlocutors were following individual strategies of the formation of the self. In our fieldwork, we could observe combinations of social engagement and personal identity building relatively detached from high politics, but with a nevertheless strong political connotation.

Making use of a term from the social philosopher Theodore Schatzki, we treat these organizations as "social sites" for the construction of modern Muslim selfhoods in the context of authoritarian politics and severe economic constraints (cf. Schatzki 2002). In which ways do contemporary social structures, civil society organizations and religious traditions condition the formation of modern Muslim subjectivities? Does religion indeed play a specific role in the construction of collective and individual Muslim identities? How do these identity constructions relate to globally relevant social imaginaries? What place have Islamic traditions occupied in both the promotion of specific modern social orders and the personal strategies to successfully establish modern Muslim selfhoods?

We put the focus on Islamic civil society organizations in order to better comprehend the role that religion plays in the ongoing transformation of Middle Eastern societies and in the subjectivity formation of modern Muslims. In this way emphasizing the role of Islam, however, we do not contend that the religion necessarily plays a key role in understanding social structures and agency in the Muslim world. On the contrary, in our field-work we made at least two important observations that bring into question a number of widespread assumptions about religion, civil society, and individual agency in the Middle East. First, the analytical distinction between religious and nonreligious civil society organizations became increasingly blurred when entering the field. There is no clear-cut boundary consistently demarcating Islamic from non-Islamic civil society organizations, and individual engagements are driven by a multiplicity of motivations among which religion is nothing more but one factor. Applying different levels of analysis—systemic, organizational, and individual—we observed religious and nonreligious realms intersecting in complex ways. Secondly, we encountered multiple forms of religiosity difficult to define and often of an ambiguous nature. Religiosity is, in other words, not a straight-forward characterization. Groups and individuals employ religious discourse in a broad variety of ways, thereby interpreting Islamic traditions along a fluid continuum between the extreme poles of radical Islamist ideologies and liberal, pluralistic versions of personal piety. In particular at the micro level, we were confronted with peculiar mixtures of traditional practices and norms with entirely new religious interpretations and sets of values that originate in the logics of diverse social arenas such as democratic politics, liberal market economy, or the modern sciences. In short, with respect to their social practices, collective and individual actors engage in processes of a constant constructing and reconstructing of Islamic traditions according to the social and intellectual environments in which they move. Although a significant element in the social life we observed, Islam does not represent an independent variable for the understanding of Muslim walks of life.

We have organized our book in three major parts. The first part provides the theoretical and historical framework for the following two case studies and presents a number of ideal types related to what we consider to be globally relevant modern social imaginaries. Chapter 1 lays out our general theoretical perspective on modernity and our conceptual apparatus that is selectively derived from social theory. We will make use of concepts such as "multiple" and "successive" modernities, putting them into a broader framework of sociocultural evolution as provided by modern systems theory. Furthermore, we will present three ideal types of modern subjectivity formation that are based on more recent poststructuralist thinking. Given the central role that religion plays in our inquiry, the second chapter relates our theoretical and analytical framework to the concept of "modern religion," which we employ in this book. First, we will define religion from the macro-sociological perspective of modern systems theory as a specific subsystem of modern society, as a "global system of modern religion" (Beyer 2006). Then we briefly discuss modern religious organizations and movements. In terms of micro-sociological analysis, our study goes back to Max Weber's definition of religious social action, exploring religious communication as directed to supernatural actors. Chapter 3 concludes the first part of the book with two excursions on the Islamic reform movement and on the role that Islamic traditions have historically played in constructing modern Muslim subjectivities. This analytically guided historical overview serves as a contextualization for the two case studies in parts II and III. Together, the three chapters of the first part offer the background knowledge that is necessary to understand the crucial concepts applied to our case studies, concepts such as "the Islamic modern," "organized Islamic society," or "postmodern Muslim subjectivities."

In the second part of the book, we present our case study on Islamic charities and social welfare organizations in Jordan, while the third part is a case study on new Islamic youth organizations in Egypt. To be sure, in these case studies, we are not testing theories. The theoretical and conceptual discussions of the first part provide us interpretative and analytical frames for our empirical observations. Moreover, we are perfectly aware of the historical relativity of these concepts and do not ascribe the defining features of modern religion a transhistorical nature. Weber's concept of religious action, for instance, originates in an abstraction from particular nineteenth-century Protestant revisions of Christianity and turns them into an ideal type. In this way, our conceptual apparatus bears imprints of historically particular social environments and their fundamental power relations. Modern religion as both an academic concept and a global social imaginary is, therefore, the result of specific historical processes, yet processes to which we assign global relevance. The relative closeness between core features of Islamic and Christian religious traditions, however, makes it, in this case, comparatively easy to tackle contemporary Islamic practices with the help of these concepts, despite the fact that our abstractions have their origin empirically in the Christian–European heritage.[4]

The case studies observe societal negotiations about different concepts of religiously inspired social orders, what we call the Islamic modern, as well as ways in which welfare and youth organizations constitute social sites for the construction of modern subjectivities among their members. In both studies, we contend that we can interpret ongoing social transformations as a hegemonic cultural conflict among forms of successive modernities. In each case, we investigate this conflict through the analytical prisms of the concepts of first and second modernity by subsequently applying the before-mentioned three levels of analysis. First, we discuss the relationship between state and religion from macro-sociological and historical perspectives. More precisely, we investigate to which extent ideas of an Islamic modern became a part of the social imaginary that has accompanied modern state formation in Jordan and Egypt. In this way, we lay out the global and national contexts in which our informants act. Secondly, we analyze the social organizations and movements in our two studies according to the patterns of religious communication and action on which they built. In doing so, we try to identify to which extent these organizations have a religious character. Given the fact that organizations and movements tend to cross-cut the boundaries of societal subsystems, in this analysis we can only apply the label "religious" as a relative attribute. Thirdly, we take a look at individuals, exploring the form and extent to which they construct their modern selfhoods with reference to religious traditions. While organizations cross-cut the boundaries of functionally defined areas of communication and social action, individuals tend to blur them in idiosyncratic ways. Again, we can only come to very tentative results in our judgment about the meaning of the individual forms of social action we have observed and the ways in which Islamic traditions take part in the formation of modern Muslim subjectivities. We wrap up our findings in the conclusions, put them into theoretical context, and point to future avenues of research.

In selecting civil society organizations associated with charity, social welfare, and youth movements, our case studies follow a path of research that has previously been paved by scholars such as Mine Ener (2003), Janine Clark, and Amy Singer. However, treating them as social sites for the construction of Muslim subjectivities, we do so by adding a new dimension to this kind of research. Clark, for instance, puts her study in the broader discussion about the moderation of Islamist activism. She identifies two major contexts for the explanation of the rise of Islamic social institutions: first, as a response to the weaknesses of contemporary Middle Eastern states to provide public services and, secondly, as an epiphenomenon of the rise of Islamic activism in general. Moreover, she defines the new educated middle class as the central social carrier of Islamic social institutions. Interestingly, however, she concludes that in the case of Islamic clinics in Cairo, for instance, there is "very little that is Islamic" about these organizations (Clark 2004, 41). References to Islamic traditions are apparently knitted into a complex mesh of norms and interests through which this modern middle class based on educational and professional assets tries to pursue its interests and establish societal conditions, which live up to their expectations about the good life. To a certain extent, Amy Singer's study on charity in Islamic societies confirms this conclusion. Defining charity as "voluntary action for the public good," Singer looks at charity as both an intrinsic part of Islamic history and as a universal phenomenon of social life (2008, 8). While she does acknowledge that charity might evolve from sincere religious belief, Singer also emphasizes the interlacement of religious motivations with self-interest and self-promotion. Consequently, she rejects the simple notion of charity as being a response to poverty alone (2008, 222–3). Departing from those conclusions, we are entering new territories in exploring the role of Islamic charities and social welfare organizations in the construction of modern Muslim identities. In particular, we want to understand the role of religion and of global social imaginaries in this complex mesh of norms and interests that characterizes the social practices of charitable organizations in two modern Muslim societies.

The fieldwork for our two case studies in Jordan and Egypt was divided in two parts.[5] Marie Juul Petersen and Sara Lei Sparre conducted a joint exploratory trip to both countries during November and December 2006. The actual fieldwork was then conducted from March through June 2007, when Petersen went to Jordan and Sparre to Egypt. There, they carried out interviews with members of civil society organizations, representatives of governmental institutions, the United Nations, and other international organizations. In total, we conducted about 90 interviews in each country, augmented by participant observations and random interviews with volunteers and employees of the respective organizations. In both Jordan and Egypt, we made use of assistants, all of whom were young university students or recent university graduates. They helped us with a broad variety of practical issues such as the planning and organization of meetings, as well as serving as interpreters and translators if necessary. In terms of language, approximately two-thirds of the interviews in Jordan were held in Arabic, whereas in Egypt more than two-thirds were conducted in English and the rest in Arabic. Our fieldwork was preceded and accompanied by intensive desk studies in Denmark, as well as by interviews with representatives of Danish NGOs working in either Jordan or Egypt and other relevant resource persons who have substantial knowledge of the civil societies of these countries.

Finally, it makes sense to say some words regarding our access to the field and the methodological, practical, and ethical obstacles we were afraid to face. Before entering the field, we asked ourselves whether we would encounter difficulties in accessing Islamic civil society organizations, whether as young female researchers, nonnatives, or as Danes whose country at that point in time was globally known as the scene of the "Muhammad cartoon affair."[6] Most of these apprehensions turned out to be without any foundation. In Jordan, none of the organizations that we approached turned down our requests for interviews, and in Egypt only two rejected them. The majority of our interviewees turned out to be very open, talkative, and eager to participate, appreciating the subject and the approach of our study. Only a few of our informants mentioned the cartoon affair at all, however, without it causing a strained atmosphere in our talks, merely wanting to give their own opinion on this matter. Likewise, we did not face visible obstacles related to the fact of being young female researchers. Sometimes we even got the impression that this fact rather facilitated our research as long as we observed some of the basic gender practices at work. Only in very few instances were we asked to wear a headscarf, yet not in form of an ultimate requirement but in order to mingle with the crowd and feel more comfortable in our participant observations.

PART I

Theoretical and Analytical Framework: Understanding Islamic History with the Help of Social Theory

Modernity is a highly contested concept. Since the foundation of the social sciences and humanities in the nineteenth century, different narratives have competed with each other in their claims to represent the whole of the modern transformation. Scholars have invented a number of different analytical concepts in their attempts to grasp the essence of this continuing stream of social change. These concepts have contested each other, and there is hardly any definition of modernity upon which contemporary scholars would mutually agree. At the same time, modernity almost randomly has been turned into a normative concept. Political parties and social movements have used modernity as a normative category in the justification of their programs for the conscious reconstruction of societies. In popular political debates, political actors have claimed their right to power in the name of being modernizing agents. There is no doubt that the modern history of Islam is also rich with examples demonstrating the various ways in which modernity served in this normative sense and has been used to underpin political action driven by both secular and religious ideologies. In short, modernity is both an analytical concept of human sciences and an emic term in culturally different discourses.[1]

In light of this complex mesh of scholarly, ideological and normative applications of the terms modern, modernity and modernization, this first part of the book will situate our work in the context of contemporary debates about modernity and religion in social theory. In the first chapter we will explain our general theoretical perspective which frames the case studies in the second and third part of this book. Drawing selectively on classical narratives of modernity, theories of multiple and successive modernities, as well as modern systems theory and poststructuralist approaches to the formation of modern subjectivities, we elaborate a number of highly abstract but nevertheless applicable analytical concepts for our case studies. The second chapter puts its focus on the among scholars very controversial conceptualization of religion. We will present a pragmatic working definition of "modern religion" with respect to macro-sociological, organizational, and individual levels. Finally, chapter three comprises two excursions into the modern history of Islam which serve as both an illustration of some of our theoretical reflections and as a historical contextualization for the following case studies. We first give a brief descriptive analysis of the Islamic reform movement which in the concept of an "Islamic modern" laid the foundations for the later construction of Islamic modernities. The second excursion, then, will present a historical overview about the ways in which Islamic traditions contributed to shaping modern Muslim subjectivities. On the basis of these theoretical, analytical, and historical explications, the reader should be prepared to follow the argumentation that we unfold in the subsequent empirical parts of this book.

CHAPTER 1

Modernity, Successive Modernities, and the Formation of the Modern Subject

In light of the contested nature of modernity as an academic concept, the theoretical discussion in this chapter is guided by the general question as to how we can still make sense of modernity. How can we define and understand the related concepts of modernity, modernization, and "the modern"? In classical sociology, the emergence of modern society was discussed as processes of rationalization, differentiation, and individualization. In juxtaposing tradition with modernity, classical sociologists conceptualized modern society as a relatively homogeneous structure of the social that evolved over time and space after a rupture with tradition by gradually increasing its rationality (Reckwitz 2008a, 227–9). Emphasizing the theme of rationalization, post-World War II sociologists constructed modernization theories that proposed the linear and progressive development of societies toward convergence in a universal form of a modern social order. History has proven wrong these universal projections of the modernization theories of the 1950s and 1960s with their assertion of being able to predict the course of social change. Empirically, modernization has generated both convergence and divergence among societies, representing modernity in a multiplicity of culturally different forms; it is to this multiplicity of forms that contemporary theories of "multiple modernities," successive modernities, entangled modernities, or varieties of modernity refer.[1]

On the following pages, we will present a theoretical and analytical framework that builds selectively on different strands of contemporary social theory. We shall start with a very broad definition of modernity in the singular, adopting the perspective of conceptualizing modernity via the experience of social contingency and a set of related fundamental questions, in the first section. This perspective opens up to accommodate a multiplicity of alternative modernities without giving up a common point of reference for the modern condition. Then we combine theories of "multiple" and "successive" modernities that help us to think modernization in nonlinear and culturally fragmented ways. The second section will enhance this theoretical framework by making analytical use of two classical sociological narratives of modernity, the narratives of differentiation and of individualization. In order to develop a language of observation, we borrow elements from modern systems theory and poststructuralist theories. On the macro-sociological level, modern systems theory will help us to observe modernization as a process of differentiation without accepting the reifying tendency of the functionalist tradition to represent society as a given structure. On the micro level, we draw from poststructuralist theories in defining the modern subject, conceptualizing it as having a hybrid nature that is based on competing orders of social and discursive practices. Employing modern systems theory and poststructuralist approaches provides us the means to both critically revise the narratives of differentiation and integration and show their dialectically intertwined nature. Moreover, these two strands of theories will help us to criticize liberal assertions about modern "Western" subjectivity, which have also made a deep inroad into the field of Islamic studies. Finally, this chapter presents three ideal types of modern subjectivity formation. Together with the three forms of successive modernities discussed prior to this, we consider these ideal types as forms of globally relevant social imaginaries to which Muslims also refer in their collective and individual identity constructions.

CONTINGENCY AND SUCCESSIVE MODERNITIES

A review of contemporary works on social theory reveals the concept of social contingency as being directly in the middle of mainstream interpretations of modernity. Meanwhile, a broad range of social theorists conceptualize societal structures as contingent and modernization as an open and emergent social process whose systemic unity is no longer a given. Society is contextualized by different perspectives. Consequently, successful representations of modern society are only established on temporary hegemonies for which once the equation of society and national state was a prominent example (Bonacker 2008, 32–8).[2] In conceptual terms, contingency rests on a double negation: Nothing is impossible and nothing is necessary (Frick 1988, 18; Luhmann 1992, 96). This penetrating idea of "all that is could be otherwise," however, does not exclude the existence of relatively durable historical structures. The resilience of social institutions and the path dependency of their emergence are cases in point. Specifically "modern" is the principal belief in the contingent nature of social life, the acknowledgment of its historically shifting complexities. Individuals and collectives live in constant tension between order and uncertainty, experiencing contingency historically in the chaotic breakdown of previously firmly established orders. In this sense, contingency is a fundamental experience of modern humankind (Wuchterl 2011, 7–11).

In adopting this perspective, we define modernization as a process in which the transformation of contingency into necessity became a central, inner-worldly, heavily contested, and autonomous task for collectives and individuals alike. Identifying the core condition of modernity in social contingency, we understand modernity by posing a set of open questions, rather than relating it to an integrated set of specific modern institutional answers.

These recurring questions are, for instance, about the certainty in knowledge, a just and viable social order, and appropriate forms of collective and individual selfhoods that guarantee the identities of the present in relation to the past and future. What do we know? How should we live? Who are we and where do we come from? Modernity is characterized by the ongoing confrontation with these fundamental questions to which humanity can find only historically temporal solutions (Wagner 2001). Although abstracted from European historical experiences, the inherent logic of this theoretical perspective undermines the authoritative role the narrative of Western modernization has tried to play. The history of the West and its particular modern social institutions is nothing other than historically specific paths of engaging with modern predicaments. Defining modernity through questions instead of institutions contributes, therefore, to an understanding of what was called the "provincialization of Europe," the abandonment of a straight equation of modernization with Westernization.[3]

We consider theories of multiple modernities to be an expression of this provincialization of Europe among contemporary modernization theories. They refute the idea of a convergence of societies, while retaining the premise of a number of common features of modernity, however, combining these features with different cultural programs that frame their historical realization (Eisenstadt 2000). Accordingly, different forms of the modern are the result of relatively stable and historically rooted cultural programs. Through these lenses, scholars observe and compare the emergence of alternative modernities that not only open up the concept for non-Western forms such as Islamic, Chinese, or Japanese modernities, but also do away with the homogenizing view on Europe and the Americas that tends to lump their cultures together in the idea of a single Western modernity as such. The story of Western modernity is then told as that of the multiple modernities of Europe and the Americas (Allardt 2005).

While the concept of multiple modernities rejects the notion of a universal cultural form of modernity, theories of "successive modernities" have replaced the linear developmental model of modernization theories by conceptualizing modernization in terms of ruptures and social breaks. With reference to the work of Ulrich Beck, Anthony Giddens, and Peter Wagner, we can differentiate analytically between three successive stages of modernity: restricted liberal modernity, organized first modernity, and pluralistic high or second modernity.[4] In this distinction, each of these successive stages has evolved from a crisis of the previous stage.

The first form of a restricted liberal modernity was characterized by an elitist top-down application of morally and rationally grounded liberal rules. While liberal rules applied to a distinguished bourgeois minority, the majority of the people were excluded from the liberal order, shaping national societies characterized by massive social inequalities and impoverishment (Wagner 2010, 14). In the second half of the nineteenth century, the inequalities of this liberal order of the excluded masses, together with the all-pervasive experience of contingency, was comprehended as the "first crisis of modernity"

(Wagner 1994). In French thought, this crisis was expressed in catchwords such as social dissolution, egoism, and anomie. French intellectuals were searching for new forms of solidarity, intending to replace postrevolutionary chaos by a conscious program of scientifically informed social reconstruction (cf. Hayward 1960; Lukes 1985). Bourgeois societies in nineteenth-century Europe apprehended modern contingency as a deep social crisis demanding the establishment of new forms of a regulating social order. The solution for this first crisis of modernity was eventually the invention of organized society within the territorial confines of a bureaucratically administered national state (Wagner 1994).

The major pillar of this state-centered modernity of the organized masses in the twentieth century was a collectively shared belief in linear progress, instrumental rationality, and the management of society. Revolving around the institutional containment of organized society in the territorially demarcated national state, this form of first modernity became the classical self-interpretation of Western modernity. However, in a reflexive process in which the systemic consequences of first modernity have undermined the very fundament on which it rests, this well-ordered world of nationally integrated industrial societies has been gradually replaced by the "risk society" of second modernity (Beck 1992, 1997; Giddens 1991). This crisis of the previous model of organized first modernity, the "second crisis of modernity," has led to a dissolution and reconfiguration of societal conventions, as well as to a pluralization of the social practices that have so far characterized first modernity. The move from first to second modernity has been discernible in discursive shifts regarding the construction of state-society relations on a global scale. Discourses about duties and obligations to the state have gradually been superseded by an emphasis on individual rights. The social order of second or high modernity is characterized by the disembedding of political and economic institutions from local contexts and the continuous experience of doubt and multiple choices. As such, organized modernity with its focus on collectivity has gradually been replaced by the more individualist and pluralist patterns of second or high modernity, often also described as postmodernity.

Poststructuralist social theory and postmodern philosophies have further radicalized this ambiguous view of modernity. Developing from within the modern paradigm, they put into question all the certainties of the classical modern worldview, replacing the stability of organized social structures by instabilities, contradictions, and constantly changing meanings, which we can also observe in the discourses and social practices of everyday life (Reckwitz 2008a, 232). The regulated life of first modernity appears from this perspective as nothing more than a passing fantasy. Similar to poststructuralist theories, most of postmodern critique does not represent a radical break with the modern paradigm. Rather postmodern theories attempt a thorough revision of the grand narratives of organized modernity and defend cultural and religious particularities against tendencies toward global cultural homogenization. At first glance, this makes poststructuralist/postmodern reasoning and theories of multiple modernities akin. Contrary to theories of multiple modernities, however, postmodern and poststructuralist approaches do not assume the relative stability and homogeneity of major cultural programs. They reject assumptions that the symbolic borders of cultures are congruent with those of social collectivities, conceiving multiple modernities as fragile, fuzzy, and shifting forms of historically particular social orders. In our study, we adopt this general perspective of viewing modernization as an ambiguous process and the related postmodern understanding of cultures and social imaginaries. We understand modernization in terms of processes of unpredictable social change with ruptures, blind alleys, sometimes circular moves, and cultural and historical variations.

Against this background, we argue that the conceptual instruments of theories of successive modernities may help us to better understand social change in the Muslim world. The combination of theories of multiple and successive modernities with a poststructuralist concept of culture allows us to observe different forms of competing Islamic modernities in which various social imaginaries both contest each other and overlap. The Arab Spring, for instance, we could interpret as a clash between the two essentially different forms of first and second modernity. The authoritarian regimes thereby represent historically specific forms of organized modernities challenged by collective visions among the population that relate to some of the core features of second modernity such as social pluralism and individual rights.[5] The impact of global transitions as epitomized in financial crises, ecological degradation, revolutions in communication technologies, or flows of migration make Middle Eastern states a part of the global risk society, spreading uncertainties that no longer can be managed and controlled by the established means of authoritarian rule. While everyday life has increasingly been conditioned by the corrosive influence of high modernity, the social and political institutions of the region still reflect the organizational premises of first modernity. Evidently, contemporary demands for new institutional forms in Middle Eastern societies are an inherent part of humanity's encounter with modern contingency. Among the revolutionaries of the Arab Spring, we can detect social actors who reject continuously addressing the problem of social contingency by means of an authoritarian form of organized society.

Differentiation, Individualization, and Modern Systems Theory

It was in the transformational period from liberal restricted to organized modernity in Europe that the classical narratives of the sociology of modernity, the intertwined sociological narratives of differentiation and individualization, found their origin. Both narratives are based on the modern idea of increasing autonomy, however, interpreting autonomy in opposite manners. In addressing the fundamental question of social order, the narrative of differentiation refers to the systemic macro level at which modern society appears as a social structure based on the autonomy of functionally complementary social systems. From this macro perspective, the autonomy of social structures represents the core feature of modern society. Narrating modern autonomy at the micro level, individualization stands for the evolution of the idea of a rationalist individual subject whose autonomy excludes any preexisting social institutions. In this reading, social order is not a given autonomous structure, but the result of the interaction of rational individuals. The first narrative suggests a solution to the modern problems of contingency in the form of stabilizing systemic structures, and the strongest historical manifestation of this solution might have been the national state. In the second narrative, it is autonomous but mutually dependent individuals who address modern contingencies by their rational actions. Taken together, these narratives accentuate the modern problem of the relationship between society and the individual, whose claims for autonomy seem to be mutually exclusive. The political discourse of first modernity emphasized the claim for autonomy of national collectivities, whereas in second modernity we can observe the resurgence of the individual against the state.

In our analytical framework, we will make use of the perspectives of both narratives. On the one hand, we will look at Muslim societies from a systemic perspective. The narrative of differentiation provides us with the necessary structural context for our inquiry about the politics of modern Muslim subjectivities. On the other hand, we apply the narrative of individualization at the micro level. On this level, we investigate the ways in which Islamic traditions play a role in shaping modern forms of individual self-understanding. These two levels of analysis with their respective narratives of differentiation and individualization we combine with the periodization of first and second modernities. With the emergence of second modernity, state authorities and political actors have felt progressively compelled to relate to global discourses about civil liberties and human rights. The state-centered structures of organized modernity have been challenged by a new emphasis on the individual, an individualization that finds its justification in a discursive structure superseding national states. Apparently the rise of second modernity goes along with a reconfiguration of interdependence between the narratives of differentiation and individualization. To conceptually clarify this perspective further, we will now borrow a number of analytical tools from modern systems theory and poststructuralist approaches to modern subjectivity formation.[6]

Modern systems theory follows the tradition of Durkheim in understanding society as a structural setting relatively apart from individuals. Adopting the narrative of differentiation, it is directed against social theories in the utilitarian tradition that stress the narrative of individualization in comprehending modern society as a result of a social contract among interest-oriented individual actors. For Durkheim, society was a given social fact to which social actors had to relate. Niklas Luhmann's modern systems theory maintains this direction against utilitarian interpretations of modern society, but decisively breaks with the functionalist tradition regarding the given nature of society (Bonacker 2008, 28–32). According to Luhmann, society represents a fluctuating self-referential (autopoetic) system that produces and reproduces its own structural arrangement. Rewriting the narrative of differentiation, modern systems theory understands the emergence of modern society as a nonteleological process of sociocultural evolution in the course of which functional differentiation becomes the dominant mode of social differentiation. In structural terms, modernization replaces the primacy of segmentation and stratification as the ordering principles of premodern forms of the social by social systems based on functional differentiation (Luhmann 1981, 187).

In a nutshell, Luhmann conceptualizes modern society as an all-encompassing global system of communication in which all world horizons are integrated as horizons of one communicative system. Consequently, he refuses to conceive of society in the liberal meaning as a corporate actor based on relations between individuals and suggests observing it as an all-embracing system of communications. As a consequence, this definition of modern society does not know any cultural or territorial limits, and thus both the Western and the Muslim worlds, for instance, are integral parts of global modernity. Modern systems theory further differentiates modern society into functionally defined, equally self-referential subsystems such as politics, economy, law, education, science, or religion. These subsystems operate according to their own distinct communicative codes, and they are in this way clearly separated from their environments. The self-referential logic of these subsystems is based on specific binary codes deciding the compatibility of communications. The legal system, for instance, operates with the code legal/illegal, science with true/untrue, religion with transcendent/immanent, and economics with to have/to have not. It is through these codes that functional systems draw sharply differentiated boundaries to their environments (Luhmann 1986). The selective mechanism of binary codes transforms contingency into order by autonomously defining elements of a regulated systemic communication. This mechanism guarantees the operational closure of function systems—that communication is identified as juridical, scientific, religious, or economic—through a sharp distinction between systemic communication and communication in its environment (Luhmann 1986, 124, 183).

From an evolutionary perspective, modern systems theory defines modernization as a specific transformation of society's primary modus of differentiation from stratification to functional differentiation. Leaving open the concrete ways in which functional differentiation appears in historically manifested institutions, this theoretical perspective is easily compatible with the idea of multiple modernities. At the systemic level, functional differentiation can be observed as an increase in social complexity, whereas at the micro level it simultaneously generates new semantics of individuality. Stratified societies build on hierarchies in which the individual is a "natural" part of the social whole. In Charles Taylor's words, premodern selves were socially embedded, and individuals could not imagine themselves outside this societal matrix (2007, 149–50). This modern isolation of the individual from society, however, should not be confused with the assertion of the emergence of an independent modern subject. Modern systems theory clearly rejects the image of the sovereign modern individual that has characterized the narrative of individualization in liberal terms. Instead, it conceptualizes the individual as a result of the disembedding consequences of functional differentiation. Historically, individualization can be observed in the semantics of a widening gap between the individual and society. Through the lenses of Luhmann's systems theory, modern society reproduces itself in distinction to the individual; therefore, modern individuality no longer results from inclusion in the social whole but from the exclusion of the individual by society (Luhmann 1989, 159).

Moving from the macro to the micro level, the disembedded modern subject has been engaged in continuing reflexive projects of establishing a coherent and explicit narrative of self-identity in light of social exclusion (cf. Giddens 1991, 76). It is this continuing reflexive project that appears as an ongoing process of individualization. Living in a social environment that no longer ascribes identity, it is the task of individuals to identify themselves in a context of diversity. Identity in a modern setting is the constant production of oneself, taking oneself as the object of a complex, difficult, and idiosyncratic elaboration (Foucault 1988, 41). To be sure, this elaboration is not a matter of individual choice, but of compelling social necessity. When the emergence of the individual is perceived as a result of structural change, the autonomy of the modern subject is recognized as nothing more than a modern fiction. Yet, while modern systems theory gives an insight into the social evolution of this fiction, it does not provide us with analytical tools to understand the ways in which individuals construct this synthesis of the self in the context of authoritative language games, symbolic orders, and social practices (cf. Reckwitz 2008b, 114). For this task, we will dip into the analytical pool of poststructuralist cultural theories.

In the critical analysis of modern subjectivity, poststructuralist theory takes its point of departure in challenging the hegemonic status that liberal concepts of the self have played in the narrative of modern individualization. In liberal terms, the emergence of the modern subject has been constructed as the emancipation of a reflexive, rational, self-interested, and expressive individual from the confines of tradition. Society and individual, the macro and the micro levels of sociology, also appear in this narrative as opposite poles. However, they do so in a very different form. In this liberal reading, the modern subject is not the result of social exclusion, but of a self-conscious, progressive liberation of the individual from social constraints. In short, in the liberal narrative, everybody has their fortune in their own hands. In sharp distinction to this concept of the rational modern subject, poststructuralist theories have emphasized the hybrid nature of modern subjectivities. Moreover, poststructuralist reasoning works with an embodied self, therewith rejecting the Cartesian legacy of the liberal subject to associate reflexive processes of identity formation with cognitive activities alone. In line with their reconstruction of modernity as a sphere of contradictions and uncertainties, they place the process of modern subjectivity formation in an environment of competing orders of social and discursive practices in which the liberal individual represents nothing more than one among other interpretative types of modern subjectivity.

The relative hegemonic status of the liberal narrative also has made an impact on the field of Islamic studies. Some scholars on Islam have interpreted the rational self-interested individual as the form of Western subjectivity as such. Consequently, they juxtapose this hegemonic type of liberalism with culturally different types of an Islamic authenticity. Samira Haj, for instance, tried to analyze the thought of the nineteenth-century Islamic reformer Muhammad Abduh (1849–1905) beyond the conventional categorization between liberal reformers and fundamentalists. According to Haj, the standard literature on nineteenth-century Islamic reform movements pictured Abduh wrongly as a liberal. In contrast to this image, she claims that Abduh was most fearful of the liberal worldview and most concerned about the moral survival of the religiously defined community. He rejected the idea of an autonomous, self-constitutive, and rationalistic individual of liberalism and resisted the specific configuration of Western modernity in which the interest of the individual represented the fundamental social determinant and where religion and morality were banished from the public sphere (Haj 2009, 28). In sharp contrast to utilitarian concepts of the modern individual, Haj views Abduh's main concern in the creation of a civil modern Muslim subject, able to make conscious decisions in the political and social realms, while safeguarding the role of religion as the defining authority on morality (2009, 98, 109).[7]

We fully subscribe to her interpretation of Abduh's concerns. The Egyptian *alim* definitely was not a liberal in the utilitarian sense, but a religious apologist who wanted to demonstrate the compatibility of the Islamic revelation with modern culture. Consequently, he did not view modern reason and rationality as an inner-worldly faculty of the human kind, but as emanating from God. Yet, to make Abduh's critical and apologetic stance against liberalism the central difference between European and Islamic conceptions of modernity is clearly wrong (cf. Haj 2009, 28). This interpretation completely neglects the fundamental struggles in European societies from which the relative hegemony of the ideal of a liberal subject only emerged as a late result. During Abduh's life time, France, for example, experienced a long-lasting confrontation between positivist and religious forces with regard to the role that Christianity should play in the public sphere. This struggle continued until the year of Abduh's death, when the Ferry Laws were passed in 1905, establishing the laicist republic as which we know France today (cf. Bloch 1972). In 1864, to take another example, Pope Pius IX issued his famous Syllabus condemning modern errors such as absolute rationalism, liberalism, or socialism, as well as the separation of state and church, a position of the Catholic Church that his successor Pius X confirmed in 1907 (Schatz 1992).

In the nineteenth and early twentieth century, European understandings of individualism were diverse and the liberal image of the modern subject, on which Haj's study is predicated, had not yet achieved its hegemonic status. While French intellectual life was occupied by the threat of anomie, German intellectuals advocated an individualism of difference, the romantic idea of a unique individuality that was transformed into the collective pretensions of organic nationalism. Even in Great Britain, the affirmation of liberal visions faced severe criticism and shaped at best an ambivalent position toward utilitarian ideas (Lukes 1971). In other words, with respect to its antiliberal position and an emphasis on the moral role of religion, something akin to Abduh's "Islamic" modernity was by no means absent in the European context. Protestant and Catholic apologists tried hard to maintain the defining power of Christian traditions in moral questions.

THREE IDEAL TYPES OF MODERN SUBJECTIVITY FORMATION

In line with the above discussion, we do not define the modern subject in liberal terms, building on the idea of the emancipation of a rational and self-interested individual. Instead, the analytical gaze of our study emphasizes the hybrid nature of the modern subject that is based on competing orders of social and discursive practices. Forms of subjectivity are, then, collectively shared but contested cultural types to which individuals refer in an idiosyncratic way. In our theoretical approach, we build on the work of the German sociologist Andreas Reckwitz (2006). Reckwitz delivered a comprehensive 700-page synthesis of sociological approaches to and historical literature about the formation of modern selfhoods. In his analysis of modern subjectivity, Reckwitz looks from the perspective of cultural studies at specific cultural forms to which individuals relate in a certain historical and social context in order to shape themselves as competent and exemplary individuals. Although Reckwitz constructed his ideal types of the modern subject with reference to a limited cultural history of Europe (France, Germany, and Great Britain) and the United States, we claim that these types are of a more global relevance and therefore also applicable in analyzing Muslim societies. Together with the aforementioned three forms of successive modernities, we consider them to be globally relevant social imaginaries. With our case studies, we try to show that his approach offers new insights into parallels and differences in the formation of modern subject cultures in Muslim and Western contexts.

From Reckwitz's poststructuralist perspective, the modern subject represents the contradicting unity of a self-determining creator and a subordinate object of creation. The formation of modern personal identity implies in this Foucaultian perspective a continuous process of the hermeneutics of the self. In their quest for authenticity, modern subjects interpret themselves in the framework of collectively acknowledged social dispositions consisting of various discursive orders of knowledge, social practices, and cultural artifacts, as well as routinized motivations and affects. The modern subject is not a psychomental system, but an idiosyncratic synthesis of sociocultural forms, a contingent product of symbolic orders and social practices (2006, 34–46).

Similar to Charles Taylor with his thesis of the modern "affirmation of ordinary life," Reckwitz grounds the formation of modern subjectivities in the practices of everyday life. Taylor defined the affirmation of ordinary life as one of the most powerful ideas in modern civilization (1989, 14). Ordinary life, according to Taylor, refers to "those aspects of human life concerned with production and reproduction, that is, labor, the making of things needed for life, and our life as sexual beings, including marriage and the family" (1989, 211). In a similar way, Reckwitz identifies three complexes of social practices in which the subjectification of the modern self takes place: as working subject, as subject of private and intimate relationships, and as subject of technologies of the self (2006, 53). In each complex, we can observe networks of discourses and social practices. The discursive manifestation of specific cultural codes establishes explicit models of subjectivity, whereas social practices provide regulated forms of social action. Social practices are not only necessarily interactive but can also be directed toward objects (material culture) or the self (technologies of the self). These different complexes, however, are not homogeneous in themselves, and they do not have clearly demarcated borders of meaning. Their discursive and social practices interfere. Each complex offers arrangements of institutionalized modes of behavior and symbolic orientation for the autonomous but collectively dependent creation of subjectivity position by individuals (Reckwitz 2006, 51–3).

Reckwitz discerns a sequence of three historically hegemonic types of subject cultures since the nineteenth century that have subsequently dominated the modern period in the West: the classical bourgeois, the peer-group-oriented type of the salaried masses, and the postmodern creative worker and entrepreneur. We claim that the rise and fall of these three types largely takes place parallel to the periodic hegemonic stages of successive modernities.[8] The nineteenth-century bourgeois type coincides with Peter Wagner's stage of a "restricted liberal modernity" that preceded the organized mass society of first modernity (Wagner 2004, 37). The peer-group-oriented type of the "salaried masses" and the third of a creative and consumption-oriented "post-modern" form of subjectivity closely reflect the stages of the organized first and of second modernities, respectively.[9] As successive historical forms, these subject cultures have not just replaced each other, but some features of the previously hegemonic type live on in the later types. Together with new and alternative patterns, they shape hybrid combinations continuously challenging the dominance of the hegemonic form in place. In Reckwitz's study, sociocultural change is not characterized by clear ruptures with the past. Instead, he examines social transformations through the lenses of cultural conflicts over the opening and closure of contingency, that is, about the successful establishment of collectively acknowledged and historically particular forms of subjectivity.

The first form of modern subjectivity Reckwitz defines as the bourgeois subject. The bourgeois gains autonomy as a morally sovereign subject and is predominantly a subject of work. The daily practices of disciplined work became the exemplary place at which bourgeois subjects find their moral formation. In terms of intimacy, marriage developed into the central moral institution, which was partly molded by elements of Protestant culture. The major technologies of the self were related to literacy, thus writing and reading became central practices of self-formation. Diaries, letters, newspapers, and books are media of this hermeneutical self-reflection of the bourgeois. Combining the liberal code of an autonomous reflexive subject with the more conservative values of moral regulation, bourgeois subjectivity formation took place in contradistinction to the cultural codes of both the previously dominant aristocracy and popular culture. In its hegemonic claim to universality, romanticist culture challenged the bourgeois in denigrating bourgeois behavior as an unauthentic and artificial form of life. However, both bourgeois culture and its antagonistic romanticist challenger were not mass cultures, but expressions of the modern social configuration Peter Wagner described as restricted liberal modernity (cf. Reckwitz 2006, 97–274).

With the beginning of the twentieth century, we can observe the gradual erosion of the hegemonic status of bourgeois culture in the West. This erosion was due to three developments turning the restricted liberal society of the nineteenth century into the mass society of the twentieth century. First, the structural transformation of material culture and technology caused a reorganization of time and space, allowing the creation of new forms of mass collectivity. The discursive dissemination of new knowledge by the humanist sciences such as psychology and sociology complemented technological developments with ideas of the social engineering of society. Finally, aesthetic counter-movements discovered the human body as an object for technologies of the self and set creativity as a value against bourgeois morality. Reflecting the macro structures of organized modernity, the hegemony of bourgeois subjectivity was replaced by the peer-group-oriented culture of the salaried masses of first modernity. Having its center in the United States, this form of subjectivity was characterized by the generalization of behavior.[10] In contradistinction to the rationalistic and introverted self of the bourgeois, now an extroverted consumption-oriented group type became the leading model. Bourgeois individual work ethics gave way to collectively binding practices of efficient work coordination of the managerial type. Private life was increasingly characterized by informality among peers, the sexualization of marriage, and an erosion of the sharp distinction between private and public life of classical bourgeois culture. The culture of the salaried masses was also marked by a decisive change in the technologies of the self. The introverted literacy of bourgeois culture was superseded by new practices in which audiovisual media, modes of consumption, the body, and public performances were of growing importance. While turning against the elitist bourgeois as the excluded Other, peer-group-oriented subjectivity nevertheless adopted the ideas of regulation and control of its predecessor, however, in a different form. In line with core features of organized modernity, the subjectivity of the salaried masses combined formalized and efficient coordination of action with practices of consumption that took on the character of self-gratification. The subject of first modernity claimed to be all-inclusive, advocated social adaptation, and transferred the aesthetics of romanticist critique into a commodified field of consumption (Reckwitz 2006, 275–440).

Parallel to the shift from organized to second modernity, Reckwitz observes the hegemonic rise of a third form of modern subjectivity now antagonizing the peer-group-oriented "average culture" of first modernity. This postmodern type of subjectivity formation advocates a self whose imaginary is related to individualized patterns of consumption and creative action. Postmodern subject culture combines the type of the creative worker with the entrepreneur, rejecting the tropes of rational calculability, bureaucratic organization, and technical coordination that characterized the managerial imaginary of first modernity. Similar to the shift from bourgeois culture to first modernity, the transformation of the means of communication plays an important role in the rise of postmodern subjectivity. While the printing press was revolutionized by the new audiovisual media during the first part of the twentieth century, the post-Second World War period has experienced another technological revolution through digital media. They facilitate highly individualized forms of work that replace the bureaucratized working culture of organized modernity. In postmodern working culture, the model is the self-reliant, dynamic, and creative entrepreneur who is engaged in a number of shifting projects. At the same time, digital technologies offer the creative subject of second modernity new means for the hermeneutics of the self that are characterized by their digital, individual-consumptive, and body-oriented characters. Intimacy, finally, turns into a medium of expressive subjectivity. Intimate personal relationships and sexuality are no longer confined to the nuclear family and become to a growing extent characterized by communicational, emotional, and experimental practices (Reckwitz 2006, 441–630).

Like the two other transformations in modern subjectivity formation, the postmodern turn does not mark a radical break with previous forms of modern subjectivity either. Rather the postmodern self resembles an eclectic amalgam of the autonomous pretentions of the bourgeois with the counter-images propagated by romanticist and aesthetic movements of the nineteenth and early twentieth century. Furthermore, it maintains the consumer orientation of the subjectivity formation of first modernity, however, giving it a new individualized and aestheticized face. Analyzing contemporary society, we can detect elements of all three ideal types. In fact, the three types of the modern—the classical bourgeois, the organized, and the postmodern type—are part of constant cultural conflicts about the adequate representation of modernity (Reckwitz 2006, 635).

In our case studies, we shall apply Reckwitz' three forms of modern subjectivity and the related forms of successive modernities as ideal types, that is, as heuristic tools based on coherent abstractions from empirical observations. They represent for us both analytical instruments and globally relevant social imaginaries, in other words, a global context within which contemporary collective and individual identity constructions take place. Alternative or multiple modernities are then different ways in which these contemporary construction processes relate to a global horizon. In comparison to the mainstream European trajectory, it appears that religion seems to play a rather different role in the historical formation of modern Muslim subjectivities. Only in the conception of moral intimacy of classical bourgeois culture does Reckwitz briefly indicate the impact of religion (Protestantism) on modern Western subjectivities.[11] In Muslim societies, however, the mainstream scholarly literature in the West has pointed to the significant role that references to Islamic traditions have played in modern history. Also in Muslim intellectual traditions, we can find strong parallels to this Western emphasis on religion in Islamic history in the broad range of the so-called Islamist or neo-fundamentalist ideologies.[12] Since the early twentieth century, the development of Islamist ideologies has revolved around the very same themes of difference to the West, claiming that Islam is more than a mere religion but represents a holistic civilization. In the conceptual language of Ernesto Laclau, Islam/religion has developed into a more general hegemonic concept in defining Muslim societies across time. From this perspective, we perceive Islam not to be a fixed cultural program; rather it represents an "empty signifier," a chronically indeterminate discursive nodal point for the imagined unity of an increasingly hegemonic discourse of Islamic modernities. In juxtaposing the religious nature of Muslim modernities with the allegedly secular character of European modernity, this nodal point has been turned into the central "Constitutive Other" through which both Islamic and European identities were constructed in the course of the twentieth century. In order to analytically grasp the role of religion in the formation of modern selves, the next chapter will present some conceptual clarifications regarding the ways in which we understand and define religion in this book.

CHAPTER 2

Modern Religion, Religious Organizations, and Religious Social Action

In public debates, the meaning of the term "religion" appears to be almost self-evident, whereas in the social sciences and humanities defining religion is a highly contested matter. Indeed, from a scholarly perspective, it is far from evident what should be understood by religious, religiosity, and religion. In order to examine the role of Islamic traditions in contemporary Muslim societies, however, we necessarily have to rely on some concepts with which we are able to grasp religion in its structural dimension as well as in the various forms in which it is a part of individual and collective social action. This chapter will, therefore, answer the question as to how we can reach a conceptualization of religion with which we are able to observe religious phenomena. We first shall present some general conceptual reflections about religion that have guided our study. We begin with a brief discussion of different ways to define religion, situating our own concept within the context of this scholarly discussion. Then we introduce our approach to conceptualizing religion embedded in the general theory of modernity that we have outlined so far. We specify our analytical angle on religion with reference to the three levels of analysis at the macro, meso, and micro levels. The macro dimension of religion we try to capture with the help of modern systems theory, defining modern religion at the societal level as a relatively autonomous social subsystem. At the meso level, which mediates between the systemic and individual levels, we look more closely at the role that religion plays in organizations and social movements. Regarding the micro level, observing individual religious action, we go back to the sociology of Max Weber and his definition of religious action.

DEFINING RELIGION: A HISTORICALLY CONTINGENT CONCEPT

In the sociology of religion, two definition types have been prevalent so far: substantive and functional. Substantive definitions mostly rely on references to the supernatural, and to dimensions of human existence that are above and beyond the empirical realm of human experience. Applying dichotomies such as sacred/profane, superhuman/human, or transcendent/immanent, they conceptualize religions as sui generis phenomena. As a distinctive realm of beliefs and social practices, substantive definitions construct religion as independent from the economic, political, and social spheres of life. Substantive definitions give an answer to the question "What is religion?" Functional definitions, in contrast, define religion within a framework of societal problem solving, rather asking "What does religion do?" They conceptualize religion as a means of social integration and systems of meaning, subordinating the religious sphere to society in general. While substantive definitions have a rather exclusive character, functional approaches tend toward inclusiveness. In principle, functional definitions can open the meaning of religion to all kinds of ideologies, institutions, and movements that could facilitate social integration, as well as provide cognitive understanding and moral guidance.

In recent decades, both functional and substantial definitions of religion have come under severe critique. This criticism is primarily directed against the allegedly unconsidered cultural foundations on which these two sociological definitions of religion have rested. Emile Durkheim, for example, perceived religion in his functional approach as "a unified system of beliefs and practices relative to sacred things, that is to say, things set apart and forbidden" (Durkheim 1995, 44). In defining religion by the distinction between profane and sacred, according to his critics, Durkheim took the major building blocks of his definition from the historical development of Christianity. Together with more general theoretical shifts in the social sciences, this criticism has sparked new attempts to define religion differently from the functionalist and substantive approaches.

With this shift, constructivist and poststructuralist theories have made their inroads into the sociology of religion. They refute the assumption of religion being an anthropological constant or a societal necessity. Instead, they view religions as socially and historically constructed phenomena that are "in a constant process of framing and re-framing." From a constructivist perspective, religion "is a social construct that varies in meaning across time and place" (Beckford 2003, 2, 7). Approaching religion in a constructivist way, an increasing number of scholars reject the idea of considering religion as a transhistorical and transcultural phenomenon. They advocate the understanding of religious symbols and institutions in dependence on their formative historical and social contexts. Religions are then observable as changing social practices that have been authorized with discursive reference to specific religious traditions (cf. Asad 1986).

In order to grasp religious phenomena in this study, we take these assumptions of constructivist approaches as our point of departure. We view religion as a historically and socially contingent category, however, a category that in the contemporary world has assumed a specific modern meaning. Modern religion is defined by its interrelatedness with other social institutions—state, science, education, law, and so on—that we in general associate with modern society. Contemporary forms of Islam, therefore, represent results of continuing processes of the reframing and reinvention of Islamic traditions conditioned by cognitive and institutional patterns of modernity. In our field studies, we observed Islam as a set of religious traditions to which historically specific forms of practicing Islam relate. The various concrete features of these practices result from ongoing societal negotiations and contestations about the appropriated ways of Islamic behavior.

Choosing a constructivist approach, however, does not make substantive and functional explanations entirely irrelevant. Rather this approach historicizes elements of these explanations such as the ideas of religion's supernatural character or its integrative power, giving them a historically and socially relative meaning. Moreover, approaching religion from a constructivist position does not rule out conceptualizing it with a certain kind of "universal" applicability. Talal Asad argued that there cannot be a universal definition of religion because this definition is itself a social and historical construct (Asad 1993, 29). Contrary to this radical constructivist position, we do claim that it is possible to apply a "universal" concept of religion within the limits of a historically and socially specific epoch of modernity. Like other isomorphic institutions of contemporary "world culture" (Meyer et al. 1997)—states, economies, education systems, and so on—a generalized concept of religion that informs global discourses about religion does exist. It is precisely due to this implicit knowledge on religion that in everyday life we do not face the same problems grasping religious phenomena as it appears in the field of scholarship. Furthermore, all concepts and definitions are historically specific results of discursive processes. Applying abstract definitions is not an attempt to capture the essence of things, but merely a provisional procedure to transparently organize thoughts (cf. Lincoln 2003, 2). Universality and historicity are, therefore, not mutually exclusive.

To be sure, the modern concept of religion is by no means transhistorical. However, it represents a hegemonic idea about religion in a specific epoch. The modern concept of religion has the quality of an ideal type against which we can empirically observe a multiplicity of religious forms. Even if the origin of this ideal type may be identified in the Protestant reconstruction of Christianity, as many critics rightly mention, theoretically this particular historical origin does not undermine the validity of the concept. Spread in the context of international power relations, this "Protestant concept of religion" attained the quality of a globally applied means of transcultural negotiations about religion in the modern world. The universalization of the particular Protestant interpretation of Christianity is a typical instance of what Roland Robertson perceived to be a general feature of globalization: The relationship between the global and the local is characterized by the circular universalization of particularisms and the particularization of universalisms (Robertson 1992). The universality of the concept is a matter of general recognition and not of its specific origin. What, then, are the features of this general concept of modern religion?

In defining modern religion, we put some elements of the substantive and functional definitions of religion into a constructivist framework. Making use of these scholarly traditions does not necessarily mean endorsing their philosophical foundations. The idea of the universal concept of religion closely linked to both substantive and functional definitions can be related to the deist notion of Enlightenment thinkers, who explained different religions as the emanation of a "natural religion" (cf. Pals 1996, 6–7). Yet from this speculative philosophical origin, these definitions have traveled into the legal, political, and scientific frames of an emerging modernity. They became an influential means of orientation in the modern world that have emancipated themselves from their own history of ideas. It is common knowledge that there is something like religion "out there." We do not assert the existence of an anthropological constant of natural religion, but the discursive relevance of a specific concept of religion as a shared point of reference.

In the functionalist tradition, the modern concept of religion is closely linked to the sociology of knowledge, viewing religion in terms of being a source of cognitive, normative, and moral orientations. According to this tradition, the social function of religion has been related to moral codes, foundational worldviews, and cosmologies. Religion is an inherent part of knowledge in its broader sense, which, manifested in traditions, institutions, and languages, transcends individuals and provides them with social meaning (cf. Luckmann 1963). In short, religion has frequently been associated with "the most basic self-evidences that inform our approach to the world" (Beyer 2006, 1). However, the alleged premodern monopoly of religious institutions over this social function of orientation has been eroded under modern conditions. Modernity is characterized by the fact that modes of thinking, feeling, and judging are no longer shared by everyone (Taylor 1989, 17). This dissolution of rather homogeneous collective worldviews was reflected in the tendency of classical sociologists such as Max Weber or Emile Durkheim to generally conceptualize premodern social formations as inherently religious. In juxtaposing modern and premodern worlds, religion was perceived as representing in the premodern world the central source of both "meaningful frameworks for the apprehension of reality and of a set of moral constraints on social conduct" (Poggi 2001, 62).

In modern society, however, different bodies of religious and secular knowledge compete with each other, and meaning has lost its predominant foundation in revealed traditions. The previous unity of knowledge, ethics, and aesthetics has been replaced by separated fields of communication and action, dominated by functionally differentiated specialists such as scientists, legislators, and artists. The holistic claims of religious worldviews have been challenged not only by secular scientific knowledge and nonreligious ethical systems alone, but also by other religions. Secularization in its societal dimension, the separation of state authority from religion, has engendered religious competition based on the constitutional precepts of religious freedoms. Consequently, at the systemic level, religion has lost its holistic character, while religious individuals may claim to maintain it or not. In the following, we understand the formation of the modern concept of religion as a characteristic pattern of modern society as world society. In macro-sociological terms, religion emerged as a clearly identifiable sector of society in the broader context of the transition from stratification to functional differentiation as the predominant mechanism of social differentiation. The conceptualization of religion must be embedded in a theory of society at large for which modern systems theory offers us a number of useful concepts.

RELIGION AND MODERN SYSTEMS THEORY: THE MACRO LEVEL

In the theoretical framework of modern systems theory, religion features as one among many functional subsystems of global society that are autonomous in terms of being self-referential but not independent in their operations.[1] On the basis of the code transcendent/immanent, religious communication has gained relative autonomy. It is precisely this operational closure of religion as a function system that sharply distinguishes it from the rest of society and furnishes it with a sui generis character. At this point, functional and substantive approaches to religion apparently meet. The progressive functional differentiation of society has drawn boundaries that gave religion specific "substantive" features. In this way, religion gains its exclusiveness in its communication with the supernatural. Modern religion has gained this autonomy at the expense of accepting the autonomy of other systems such as the state, education, the economy, or law. From this macro-sociological perspective, secularization does not mean the disappearance of religion. On the contrary, in separating religious communication from other subsystems, religion attains it specific modern contours, establishing it as a specifically defined and therefore autonomous subsystem of modern society. Ironically, secularization as an inherent part of progressing functional differentiation shapes the contours of religion as a clearly identifiable and circumscribed sector of modern society. Only when looking at the past with modern eyes do we see an undifferentiated world permeated by religion "in which the social was grounded in the sacred and secular time in higher times" (Taylor 2007, 61).

In historical terms, we might interpret the *Kulturkampf* (cultural struggle) between the German state under Bismarck and the Catholic Church about education, political representation, and social services as an historical expression of this establishment of functionally defined domains in German society. State and Church were in conflict about the institutional control of education and the double role of individuals as citizens and believers. Comparable processes of societal differentiation have been observable in the Muslim world. There, for instance, the traditionally religious learned, the *ulama* have been in a continuous struggle with the modern state regarding control over juridical and educational institutions. The relationship between the Egyptian state and the role of al-Azhar as a university and an Islamic center of religious learning is a good case in point (cf. Zaman 2002; Zeghal 1999). Among other factors, the absence of a hierarchical institution such as the Catholic Church, however, has certainly constituted a quite different environment for this struggle between religiously and state-governed education in Muslim countries than the German chancellor Bismarck faced in his attempt to impose the supremacy of the national state over Catholic institutions.

In *Religion in Global Society*, Peter Beyer took his point of departure in the perspective of Niklas Luhmann: "Observing religion as one of several differentiated function systems" (Beyer 2006, 3). Beyer combines insights from both Roland Robertson's globalization theory and Luhmann's systems theory in order to analyze religious phenomena in the global context. In his theory of a global system of religion, he observes religion as an emerging system of recursive and self-referential communication based on the general binary code of being "blessed or cursed" (Beyer 2006, 85).[2] According to him, it is this communicative order of a specific circular system of signification and "not the conscious belief of human participants that makes a religion" (2006, 93). Beyer combines social constructivism with elements of functionalist and substantive approaches to religion that have gained their validity due to historical reasons, that is, the very fact that the function system for religion "constructed itself more in a substantive way" (2006, 4). The classical ways of defining religion via substantive or functional approaches are, therefore, themselves inherent parts of the historical construction of modern religion, involving both observers and the observed.

Internally this global system of religious communication is segmented into a variety of religions that derive their particular identities from very different and more specific traditions. Beyer defines the major "world religions" —Christianity, Islam, Hinduism, Judaism, and Buddhism—as different "religious programs" that represent relatively stable patterns of religious communication defining the identity of individual religions. Referring to a specific corpus of traditions, these programs define what a particular religion is, and they are characterized by inner contestations over orthodoxy, orthopraxy, authenticity, and authority (Beyer 2006, 89).[3] From a macrosociological perspective, the modern religious system evolved in conflictive boundary demarcations with other functional systems, developing its own specific code by excluding other fields of communication from its realm. Yet communications are not restricted to functional domains alone. The differentiation of society into function systems is only the most abstract level of analyzing contemporary society at the macro level. Looking at different levels of analysis—social interactions, organizations, and movements (2006, 51)—communication and social action frequently transgress the systemic barriers of the macro-structural setting of modern society; it is on these intermediate levels that religious, political, economic, scientific, and aesthetic communications mesh.

Religious Organizations and Social Movements: The Meso Level

The abstract level of function systems serves us as the conditioning context in which religious organizations and individuals act. While binary codes at the macro level such as blessed/cursed or transcendent/immanent construct the self-reference of the functionally defined subsystem of modern religion, religious programs are the organizing tools in making religion a social reality (Beyer 2006, 88). These religious programs or authoritative sets of religious traditions have been established through religious organizations and movements. In the framework of modern systems theory, organizations are social systems on an intermediate level that generalize motivations and specific forms of social action to a high degree. In this way, they decisively enhance the capacity to coordinate complex social communications in comparison to systems of social interactions that are based on physical presence.

Representing face-to-face relations, interaction systems can only focus on one theme at a time, which strongly limits the complexity of social structures and makes the coordination of social actions very time consuming. Social organizations, instead, are based on formal rules acknowledged by membership that in terms of expectations establish relatively clear social boundaries between members and nonmembers. Organizations establish formalized ways for communication, for the distribution of resources, and for the assignment of social responsibilities. They can be "wide ranging, very complex, and be adapted to a virtually infinite variety of purposes" such as business firms, sports clubs, churches, social welfare organizations, or political parties (Beyer 2006, 51). Situated in between systems of social interaction and functional systems, organizations "can cut across other systemic boundaries, largely ignore these or seek to undermine them" (2006, 52). Consequently, a religious organization can draw political or economic communication into the religious system and vice versa. Islamist organizations are a good example of this attempt to transgress and undermine the boundaries of functionally separated social systems by colonializing their specific communication through religious vocabulary.

In the religious field, the analysis of organized forms of religion provides us with answers to questions about the forms in which religious authority appears in modern societies (Beyer 2006, 107). The various forms of religious organizations—monasteries, temples, churches, congregations, pilgrimage centers, local mosques, charitable foundations, youth clubs, and so on—give religions their recursive presence (Beyer 2006, 108–109). Transformations at this level of religious organization mark another dimension of what has been narrated as secularization. This organizational secularization follows known paths of modernization such as in the bureaucratization of religious institutions, the formalization of membership structures, and the individualization of religious interpretations. Largely, this transformation of the organizational structures of religion reflects the social imperatives of successive modernities. Moreover, this organizational reconstruction of the religious field has been accompanied by the rationalization of religious beliefs, for which Max Weber coined the term of the "disenchantment of modern life." Often misunderstood as a general and linear disappearance of religious beliefs in modern times, Weber's term refers first and foremost to an inner process of religious rationalization, stripping religion of all kinds of magical and ritual belief. The disenchantment of modern life does not eradicate the religious field, but means a consistent rationalization of religious beliefs and the disempowerment of magic (cf. Breuer 2007, 13–23).

Similar to organizations, social movements also represent social systems of a lower order that are adaptable to almost any purpose. In contrast to social organizations, however, social movements are structured around particular issues rather than based on more rigidly formalized membership structures. Social movements mobilize communication and social action around specific themes. Eventually, they might transform into social organizations or they lose their mobilizing power and disappear. Religious social movements profile religion and generate religious communication without being controlled by any kind of central authority. In this way, they contribute to changes in both religious organization and doctrine. In contrast to the situation with religious organizations, however, the participation in religious movements is episodic, occasional, and does not follow a mutually acknowledged pattern of social conduct (cf. Beyer 2006, 110). From a historical perspective, religious movements either disappeared or developed into organizations if not newly established, formally acknowledged religions through their association with powerful institutionalizations of other function systems such as the state. In particular, the orthodoxification of religious traditions, the formation of authoritative religious programs as officially recognized religions, has often taken place with the support of state authorities. In cases such as the Islamic Republic of Iran or Saudi Arabia, coalitions of state authorities and religious scholars transformed their interpretations of Islamic traditions into technologies of domination in order to achieve their respective ideal forms of an organized Islamic society.

RELIGIOUS SOCIAL ACTION: THE MICRO LEVEL

While functional systems, organizations, and religious movements represent the institutionalized macro and meso levels in our analysis, individual social action is the third level on which we try to observe contemporary processes of shaping modern Muslim subjectivities. At this level, religious traditions can inform technologies of the self and become part of the self-reflexive creation of individual identities. In this process, meaningful forms of individual selfhood are oriented toward collectively acknowledged imaginations of the "good life." The successful construction of personal identities with respect to these imaginations essentially relies on a moral discourse based on the binary code between good and bad. Although often linked to religious norms and values, this moral discourse is not necessarily a religious moral discourse at all. Under modern conditions, religion only represents one possible source among others for this orientation in a wider moral space. The worship of God can but need not be the "highest good" in the construction of modern selfhoods (cf. Taylor 1989, 62). In sharp contradistinction to the marginalization of religion in Reckwitz's ideal types of modern subjectivities, however, religion actually can and does offer a significant symbolic reservoir for the formation of modern selves. The moral code good/bad often serves as a secondary code for religions (Beyer 2006, 88). In parts 2 and 3, we will observe how Islamic traditions have been utilized by contemporary Muslims in constructing modern Muslim subjectivities in religiously defined moral spaces.

The micro level of religious social action was one of the concerns of Max Weber, whose insights still seem useful for the purpose of our study.[4] According to him, religions provide an important means of achieving salvation and redemption (1915, 490–92). Weber declares religious ethics to resemble a "cosmos of obligations," which offers corporative and individual actors moral guidance in the form of collectively shared belief systems (1915, 430). In systematizing "all the manifestations of life," religions represent in Weber's sociology one of the major sources of the development of particular worldviews and ways of life (1915, 451). Evidently, Weber also assigns religions a central role in providing cognitive and normative means of orientation. References to religious traditions help us to understand the world, to rationalize our complex experiences, and to put them into a "meaningful cosmos" (Weber 1948, 281). In short, also from a Weberian perspective, religious traditions can play a major part in the shaping of a modern meaningful selfhood.

In the above quotes, Weber deals with religion as a part of the sociology of knowledge. However, the functionalist voice of these quotes does not have any methodological implications. In concordance with his general definition of sociology, he approached religion as a particular type of social action. In Weber's sociology of religion, the explanation of the social must start with the specific meaning that the believers associate with their actions. With this methodological prerequisite, Weber defined religion as an autonomous but not independent realm of social action; a concept of religious autonomy that scholars have traced back to his early engagement with liberal Protestant theology (Graf 1987, 124). In the general context of his sociology of religion, Weber viewed both religiously and magically motivated actions as rational and essentially worldly oriented forms of social action (Weber 1915, 399).[5]

Within the conceptual framework of salvation, Weber associates the ends of religious actions basically with two spheres, an inner-worldly and a transcendent realm. First, religious action aims at the transformation of specific states or conditions of being; for instance, the release from suffering such as illness, economic deprivation, and suppression. Secondly, it is directed toward the transcendental realm relating, for instance, to the final Day of Judgment as in Christian and Islamic traditions. For the latter, the idea of *thawab*, the expectation of rewards for good deeds on the Day of Judgment, is a good example from the practices of contemporary pious Muslims (cf. Deeb 2006, 103, 195; Nakash 1994, 145; Schielke 2009, 528). In everyday practices, however, Weber observes salvation as predominantly oriented toward this-worldly aims. Given this predominance of worldly aims, Weber identifies the distinctiveness of religious action with regard to other forms of social action, not in its ends. Therefore, he defines religious action by its means and in the specific kind of actors with "whom actors believe they interact." Religious action interacts and communicates with supernatural forces, and the religious realm is linked to the ordering of relations among them and human beings (Sharot 2001, 22–3).[6]

In Weber's sociological work, two very different perspectives appear simultaneously and in a rather abrupt way. On the one hand, he insists on a certain form of "methodological individualism," comprehending the social from the perspective of meaningful individual actors; on the other hand, he presents us in the bulk of his work with the systemic logic of the social and the analysis of social macro structures such as the state, capitalist economics, or the belief systems of world religions (Breuer 2007, 358). While we employ his theory of social action on the individual level, the latter perspective, emphasizing social macro structures, can easily build a bridge to the Luhmannian approach on which we have based our two other levels of analysis. In the light of Beyer's theory of the modern global system of religion, we can read Weber's essay as an analysis of the autonomization of religion vis-à-vis other modern function systems. Weber's essay *Zwischenbetrachtung*, which was published partly in English under the title *Religious Rejections of the World and Their Directions* (Weber 1948, 323–59), essentially reflects the drawing of functionally separated systemic borders of communication in modern society. He discusses the relationship between religion and the world by juxtaposing religious ethics with the ethical demands of other spheres of social life such as the arts, economics, politics, or modern science. The "substance" of religion, that is, the human search for salvation (1915, 353), increasingly becomes alienated from all other spheres of life, and the essence of religion appears to be found in other-worldly relationships and concerns (1915, 357). In the language of Luhmann or Beyer, Weber describes the emergence of an autonomous religious system whose communication has been reduced to the binary code of immanent/transcendent or blessed/cursed. In competition with the formation of other function systems, the social relevance of religion has been enormously limited, but simultaneously it gained a much more pronounced visibility.

To sum up, for the purpose of this study, we work with a definition of religion that has three dimensions. From a macro-sociological perspective, modern religion represents an autonomous but not independent functional system of communication based on the binary code blessed/cursed (transcendent/immanent). This code distinguishes modern religious communication from other forms of communication of societal subsystems such as political, economic, scientific, and so on, which constitute the social environment of the religious system. Moreover, the modern system of religion integrates various authoritative sets of religious traditions as "religious programs" into the global system of religion. As a subsystem of modern society, religion has attained a specific modern form; as a functionally defined subsystem of modern society, it remains relevant in a macro-sociological perspective, but at this level it has lost its holistic claim of representing society as a whole.

On the institutional level, we perceive organizations as religious if they show in their organizational logic regarding membership structure, rules of action, and/or purpose a dominance of religious communication. In a similar way, religious social movements rally around issues characterized by religious communication. At this intermediate level, we can define religious communication with regard to two criteria: its primary code and its addressee. While the first relates to the binary distinction between blessed and cursed, the second relates to communication with supernatural actors. Empirically, religious communication often appears as a moral discourse that derives its normative and evaluative elements from religious traditions legitimized, again, by transcendental relations. Both organizations and movements have been instrumental in the reorganization of the religious realm in the modern world. However, as they tend to cross-cut the boundaries of functionally separated systems of communication, they are also prone to lose their original rationale. As a consequence, religious organizations and movements may or may not remain of a religious nature.

Finally, we follow Weber's definition in conceptualizing religion on the individual level as religious social action. Religious agency, then, is characterized by the interaction with supernatural forces and aims at individual salvation in ordering the social relations between them and among human beings. On this level, also in the modern world, religion can serve as a holistically applied worldview that does not only mold moral spaces. However, this worldview might not necessarily correspond to the authoritative interpretations of religious traditions that are represented at the macro level. The increasing autonomy of the modern individual has been rationalized in another narrative of the secularization theory. Often interpreted as the privatization of religion, we can observe a more eclectic approach in individual beliefs. Organized religion has given way to individual strategies of designing autonomous forms of religious beliefs with reference to different traditions. Again, secularization does not necessarily mean a disappearance of individual religiosity, but rather a transformation of the ways in which individual religious actors behave.

CHAPTER 3

Islamic Reform and the Construction of Modern Muslim Subjectivities

Like in Europe, Muslims also responded to modernity with a broad variety of attitudes including traditionalist rejections and secularist affirmations of modern ideas and institutions. In the second part of the nineteenth century, Islamic reformers tried to reconcile modern culture with Islamic traditions between these extreme poles. This apologetic Islamic reform movement created a historically specific and still enormously influential type of an Islamic modernity. In our analysis, nineteenth-century Islamic reformers laid the discursive foundations for subsequent types of social imaginaries according to which the authenticity of collective and individual modern Muslim identities has been constituted in close reference to Islamic traditions. Comparable to what Prasenjit Duara called the "East Asian modern," this reform movement constructed an "Islamic modern" in building on a characteristic "circulation of practices and signifiers evoking historical authenticity in the region" (Duara 2004, 3). Contrary to the East Asian modern, however, this Islamic modern has a strong religious connotation.[1] During the twentieth century, then, Muslim intellectuals and the broader public increasingly discussed different and mutually contested ideas about an Islamic modern. The Islamic reform movement bestowed modern communications about politics, education, science, or the economy with authenticity by drawing them into the system of religious communication.

To be sure, this Islamic modern has not been without alternatives. On the contrary, it has strongly been contested, transformed, and developed in different directions. In particular, secular Arab nationalism, and socialist and fascist ideas, as well as local nationalisms such as the Egyptianism of the interwar period and Kemalism in Turkey have been in fierce competition with Islamic modernities. For a large part of the twentieth century, not Islamist ideologies but different forms of nationalisms dominated the modern imaginaries of the Middle East. During their lifetimes, the nineteenth-century Islamic reformers could not achieve discursive hegemony, but they succeeded in establishing a modern discourse that linked the authenticity of modern Muslim culture to a reinterpretation of religious Islamic traditions and a religiously defined past. The reform movement was instrumental in mobilizing religious communication and social action around specific Islamic themes that became a fertile ground for the emergence of various religious and political organizations in the twentieth century. Moreover, in a close interplay with international political developments and discursive interlacements with orientalist scholarship in Europe and the Americas, this discourse on Islamic modernity achieved a relative hegemony toward the end of the twentieth century.

In initiating a thorough revision of the core vocabulary of Islam in light of modern questions, the nineteenth-century Islamic reformers created an intellectual reservoir from which subsequent Islamic thinkers have drawn. They imbued a series of Islamic concepts such as *ijtihad*, *jihad*, *sharia*, *shura*, *tawhid*, or *umma* with entirely new meanings. Transforming the language of religious traditions into the semantics of an authentically modern Islam, these religious reformers "liberated" Islamic concepts from their classical context. In doing so, they developed a conceptual tool kit for the Islamization of modern institutions and ideas (cf. al-Azmeh 1996). It is this modern semantics of Islam that speaks to us through the various ideologies of Islamist movements and which has been used both consciously and unconsciously in the articulation of subsequent forms of modern Muslim subjectivities. The following two excursions into the history of modern Islamic reform briefly show in which ways we can interpret these changing forms of an "Islamic modern" with the help of the analytical tools that we described before.

Excursion 1: Islamic Reform and the Concept of the Islamic Modern

The mainstream academic literature associates the beginnings of the modern intellectual history of Islam with the lives and works of Jamal al-Din al-Afghani, Muhammad Abduh, and Rashid Rida. Under the label of the modern Salafiyya movement,[2] these three reformers mark a chain of teachers and disciples whose ideas can be considered to be paradigmatic for the nineteenth century Islamic reform movement in general. Eloquent in various languages and versed in both Islamic and European philosophy, Afghani's lifelong concern was to liberate the Muslim lands from European colonialism. The experiences of European expansionism and modern state formation point the way to understanding his biography. His restless traveling and agitation served basically one purpose, to advocate for Muslim unity against specifically British imperialism. Transforming the theological concept of divine unity (*tawhid*) into an ideology of political unity, he invoked the Westphalian norms of national self-determination and political sovereignty of Muslim peoples in his striving for independence from the colonial yoke.

In contrast to Afghani's "paramount concern with Imperialism" (Euben 1999, 99), Muhammad Abduh's life ambition was directed toward the revitalization of Egyptian society through the means of religious and educational reforms (Livingston 1995, 216). In his life and work, Abduh predominantly followed paths that we can associate with the modern tales of intellectual transformation and religious rationalization. Abduh was convinced of the civilizing potential of Islamic traditions. Understanding them rationally as universal principles, he perceived them as perfectly compatible with the bodies of knowledge that were offered by the modern sciences. Combining his erudition in the Islamic sciences with his knowledge of European thought, Abduh propagated the harmony of Islam with modern science and education. In the educated and morally autonomous religious Muslim subject, he saw the solution to the social ills of Egyptian society (Sedgwick 2010).

Finally, Rashid Rida took up the reform aspirations of Abduh and combined them with Afghani's struggle for independence and Arab/Islamic unity. Inspired by his teacher Abduh, Rida first propagated the combination of science, technology, rationalism, and political constitutionalism with the moral and ethical values of Islam. With respect to the latter, both Abduh and Rida viewed the obedience to a properly interpreted *sharia* as a means against the "material seductions of capitalism" often seen as the vices of Western culture in general (cf. Tripp 2006, 34). In their critique of the materialist nature of Western culture, these Islamic thinkers combined antiimperialist attitudes with elements of the romanticist denigration of classical bourgeois subjectivity as an unauthentic, artificial, and materialistic culture. Consequently, their construction of the authentic Muslim bourgeois subject partly relied on the negativity of Europe's own antagonist in romanticism. In his later years, however, Rida shifted toward more rigid understandings of Islamic reform, merging the ideas of modern Salafism with the traditionalist and puritan outlook of Hanbalism as epitomized in the Wahhabi religious doctrines of Saudi Arabia. Abolishing Abduh's approach of gradual reform and selective collaboration with Britain, Rida became a founding intellectual behind the idea of a more principal antagonism between Islam and the West (Tauber 1989, 124–7).

In light of colonial domination, these reformers agreed with Western observers on the, in principle, miserable and feeble social conditions of the Muslim world. Applying an inverse narrative to the one of European progress, they interpreted Islamic history as a history of decline. In their reading, however, it was not the religion of Islam that caused this decline as many European observers have suggested. On the contrary, for these Islamic reformers, the political, cultural, and economic subordination of the Muslim world to Europe was due to an incompetent political and religious Muslim leadership who deviated from the true path of Islam. Therefore, their reform attempts were not only directed against colonial domination, but also found central targets in the indigenous political leadership and the traditionalist Islamic clergy. Islam was not the problem, but a return to the pristine principles of Islam was the solution. In short, in religion they identified the key resource for a conscious and authentic modern reconstruction of their societies.

Related to the exemplary role of the Prophet and early Islam in general, this modern narrative of decline was in line with traditional interpretations of Islamic history as a retreat from the ideal Muslim community, which demanded a continuum of renewal (*tajdid*), revival (*ihya*), and reform (*islah*). Thus, following a well-established template, the reform movement was able to link the transformation of the present to an ideal past and to a desired future, reframing Islamic history in accordance with the modern reorganization of time as a linear process. The modern watershed to premodern Islamic reform movements, however, was the fundamental experience and recognition of the inferiority of Muslim societies to European power. The colonial subordination of Muslim lands shattered the deep-rooted self-confidence that characterized the worldview of premodern Islamic reformers. Therefore, a simple return to the pristine age of the Prophet and his companions, the period of the rightly guided elders of Islam (*salafiyyun*), seemed not enough anymore. At this point of history, modern Salafi thinkers combined the reorientation toward the religious ideal with a critical reception of cultural elements and institutions of modern Europe. The nineteenth-century reform movement was no longer a mere form of Islamic revival. With their apologetic intentions, these reformers aimed at an entirely new synthesis of Islamic traditions with modernity; they desired the establishment of an authentic Islamic modernity (cf. Haj 2009, 8, 72; Hunter 2009, 10).

In retrospect, we can identify at least six important innovations by the Islamic reform movement that became central points of reference in the subsequent reorganization of Islam as a modern religion and for the construction of various forms of an Islamic modern. First, there is the fusion of the theological concept of *tawhid* with the modern notion of a civilization. On the basis of this conceptual innovation, Muslim intellectuals began to represent Islam as a comprehensive civilization and reconstructed Islamic traditions in terms of an all-encompassing socioreligious system.[3] Second, demanding the right to free reasoning (*ijtihad*), the reform movement undermined the interpretative monopoly of the *ulama* over Islamic traditions without being able to establish alternative modern structures of an authoritative system of religious learning. In the course of the twentieth century, Islamic traditions became subject to the random, trivial, and populist interpretations of religious and political actors who in their reading of the traditions did not have any hermeneutical means at their disposal. Third, in justifying the adoption of Western ideas and institutions by assigning them an Islamic pedigree, the reformers initiated a practice of relating any claim to authenticity directly to Islamic traditions. In this way, they made Islam an independent variable in the representation of everything that claims to be authentically modern. In their response to the functional imperatives of modern society, the Islamic reformers assigned the religious discourse the primary status of representing Muslim society as a whole. Fourth, in making references to the *sharia* a centrepiece of legal and societal reform, they contributed to its legalization in the modern sense of positivist law at the expense of its previous discursive and deliberative nature. Fifth, by reinventing the classical doctrine of *jihad* within the modern framework of social activism and national liberation, nineteenth-century reformers opened an avenue for the uncontrolled appropriation and utilization of this important religious institution by modern political actors. Finally, by turning Islamic unity into an antiimperialist ideology, Jamal al-Din al-Afghani, in particular, took part in the translation of a historical political antagonism into a cultural dichotomy between Islam and the West. Enhanced by both the Islamic authenticity regime and Western stigmatizations of Islam, this dichotomy gradually assumed a hegemonic role in representing the mutually excluded Other in processes of Islamic and Western identity building. Until today, references to the imagined entities of Islam and of the West play a central role in the mutual expression of total negativity. As "empty signifiers," Islam and the West serve in Muslim and Western identity building as discursive nodal points that remain chronically underdetermined while simultaneously representing the imagined unity of self and other (cf. Laclau and Mouffe 2001).

The modern Salafiyya movement was both a radical break with the past and a continuation of Islamic tradition. In this way, the Islamic reformers of the nineteenth century shaped the intellectual fundament on which later constructions of Islamic modernities rest. The movement was not restricted to the Arab Muslim lands, but similar reformist streams appeared in the Ottoman Empire and South Asia. Moreover, the ideas of Islamic reform developed in close interdependence with Western thought and the rise of the human sciences, and only through this global interdependence could the Islamic model of an authentic modern achieve this relative hegemony that is behind the essentialist images of Islam purported by both Western orientalists and Islamist ideologues (cf. Jung 2011). The various interpretations of this type of an Islamic modernity also show that there is not an Islamic modern as such. We do not observe the combination of modernity with a stable cultural program of Islam as at least some theories of multiple modernities would suggest. Rather, we are witnesses to the various ways in which Islamic thinkers have tried to answer the questions of modernity within the discursive traditions of Islam. In these answers, Islamic traditions do not resemble a coherent cultural program, but a pool of more or less authoritative religious concepts, symbols, and practices whose meanings are subject to continuous processes of reconstruction and reinterpretation. Since its inception in the second part of the nineteenth century, the Islamic modern has been receptive to the social alterations that we have associated with the rise of successive modernities.

EXCURSION 2: FORMS OF MODERN MUSLIM SUBJECTIVITIES

Afghani's and Abduh's call upon Muslims to return to the pristine Islamic principles in giving answers to the modern challenges was predicated on the social imaginary of an educated, socially active, and morally grounded individual. These modern Muslim subjects should achieve their autonomy through a combination of work discipline, education, and reflected-upon religious observance. For Abduh, Islam encouraged hard work and personal sacrifice in daily life (Ibrahim 1999, 71). He perceived both blind following of religious traditions and the uncritical imitation of European culture as forms of blind imitation (*taqlid*), which prevented Muslims from living authentic lives. In principle, every rationally thinking and educated Muslim subject should be able to come to an adequate interpretation of the traditions. Therefore, education in Arabic and the use of writing and reading technologies were core concerns of his reformist agenda. Similar to the bourgeois subject in Europe, the modern Muslim was supposed to employ the means of literacy as a central technology of the self, engaging directly with religious traditions. A modern Muslim was self-disciplined, orderly, productive, rational, and fundamentally a moral subject whose intimate relationships were anchored in family life and the religious community (Haj 2009, 118). In short, nineteenth-century reformers constructed modern Muslim subjectivities along the lines of the bourgeois subject, grounded in the affirmation of ordinary life yet with an emphasis on Islamic traditions as the central source for moral autonomy.

In achieving this moral autonomy based on religious traditions, however, Abduh did not advocate the indiscriminate interpretation of religious sources by every single Muslim. In his model of a modern Muslim, the intellectual elite might have had independent recourse to Islamic traditions as a means of a technology of the self, shaping a modern selfhood grounded in religious morality. Yet for ordinary Egyptians, Islam rather had to be first employed as a technology of domination transmitted through a religiously conscious state system of education. Moreover, Abduh restricted the field of free interpretation to the religious dimensions (*ibadat*) of the *sharia* (Eich 2003, 83). His type of a bourgeois Muslim subject was an elitist construction afraid of the assumed lack of self-mastery of the masses. The liberal elements of the Salafist reforms in the nineteenth century were restricted to a well-educated bourgeois class that resembled the social configuration of Wagner's restricted liberal bourgeoisie in Europe (Wagner 2004, 37). The Islamic modern of the reform movement, therefore, contained an ambiguous combination of technologies of domination with technologies of the self, two dimensions that reappear in various combinations in later forms of Islamic modernities. Contrary to the concept of the European bourgeoisie, however, this idea of an Islamic modern could not claim a position of cultural hegemony within the elite cultures of Muslim societies in the nineteenth century. Struggling simultaneously with the imaginaries of traditionalist *ulama*, aristocratic rulers, secular modernists, and the colonial administration, the religious reformers were not able to synthesize these competing positions into a clear-cut antagonism in order to define their excluded Other. In this sense, the Islamic reform movement failed and could not establish the Islamic modern as the dominant social imaginary of their times.

Before rising toward relative hegemony, the Islamic modern first had to get rid of its elitist confines. This happened with the historical shift from the epoch of classical bourgeoisie to the social dominance of organized forms of modernity. In terms of the reconstruction of the modern Salafist reform agenda, this shift is best exemplified in the evolution of the Muslim

Brotherhood as a social movement and a distinct organization. Founded in 1928 by Hasan al-Banna, a "man of transition" whose lifelong concern was the establishment of a social order based on his understanding of "true Islam" (Krämer 2010, 87, xii), the Muslim Brotherhood best reflects an Islamic version of the peer-group-oriented type of modern subjectivity associated with first modernity.[4] Starting as a benevolent society, it soon became a transnational religiopolitical movement that eventually established itself at national levels in forming distinct organizations in various Muslim countries. Hasan al-Banna moved from rural to urban Egypt and studied at the modern educational institution of the *dar al-ulum*, the then newly established teacher training college in Cairo. His biography and educational background makes him a representative of the new Egyptian urban middle class, the so-called *effendiyya* (Commins 2005, 129). In the Egyptian context, this new urban stratum was characterized by its modern education, nationalist sentiments, ambivalent attitudes to Europe, and activist stances regarding the social and political transformation of the country (Eppel 2009). It was this new middle class together with workers and educated members of Egypt's rural population that became the social carriers of the Brotherhood with its Islamic version of an organized society that dominated the social imaginaries of religiously minded Muslims in the twentieth century.

From Rashid Rida, Hasan al-Banna took the concept of the Islamic state and the preeminent role of the *sharia* in shaping an authentic Islamic order. As a sociopolitical movement, the Muslim Brotherhood further transformed the modern notion of the *sharia* from an independently used reference for the formation of an autonomous moral subject to a collectively binding set of norms and laws according to which society has to be organized. The Muslim Brotherhood clearly emphasized the role of Islamic traditions as a technology of domination by shifting its secondary religious discourse from Abduh's moral code toward the legal distinction between lawful and legally forbidden. For Banna, Islamic law was the prime symbol of moral integrity, cultural authenticity, and national independence (Krämer 2010, 114). The contingencies of modernity had to be managed by the implementation of an Islamic social order through legal means. Hasan al-Banna emphasized the Salafi idea that it is necessary to return to the exemplary order of the "Golden Age of Islam" in order to overcome the political subordination and social crisis of the Muslim world. For him, the Prophet and the first four caliphs truly represented Islam as a faith and a just social order (Mitchell 1969, 210). Only the recourse to these exemplary figures of Islam can guarantee the authenticity of an Islamic present in the past. Consequently, Banna envisaged the excluded Other in the allegedly secularist culture of the West and in its indigenous representatives, the secular Muslim modernists.

In spreading Banna's message, the Brotherhood utilized the technological innovations that facilitated the emergence of the new subjectivity formation of the salaried masses. The Muslim Brothers further addressed pressing political and economic questions, combined bureaucratic institutions with leadership structures reminiscent of Sufi Sheikhs, and employed the organizational templates and forms of mass mobilization that characterized the popular political movements of the interwar period in a global dimension. In short, as a religious organization it tried to penetrate all sectors of society with religious communication. In using badges, implementing dress codes and conducting public ceremonies and prayers, the Brotherhood adopted the extroverted performing modes of peer-group-oriented selfhood. Furthermore, it put new emphasis on the body, in particular, with regard to the training of its paramilitary units. Hasan al-Banna's ideal of a modern Muslim was the manly, virtuous, industrious, temperate, clean, punctual, self-confident, modest, polite, physically active, productive, and spiritual Muslim firmly embedded in community life (Krämer 2010, 111). He constructed a model of Islamic subjectivity that implied a modern form of governmentality in which state authorities organize society according to Islamic principles, serving the state in its technologies of domination and Muslim individuals as authoritatively prescribed technologies of the self.[5]

In recent years, a number of scholars have claimed to observe a move from Islamist to post-Islamist worldviews among Muslims. Asef Bayat, for instance, described this development as a departure from the universalist, exclusivist, and obligation-oriented positions of Islamist ideologies to new modes of more inclusive thinking, acknowledging ambiguity, multiplicity, and compromise in the performance of religious practices and the desired restructuring of society (Bayat 2007, 13). Bayat discerns a "clear shift from the earlier emphasis on Islamist polity to one on personal piety and ethics." Islamist ideologies, according to him, move from clearly defined political projects to forms of "active piety concerned with personal salvation and culture" (2002). Although still contested in substance and fuzzy in appearance, this move might indicate that interpretations of the Islamic modern are entering into a postmodern phase. The model of organized society of twentieth-century Islamism is seemingly contested by the self-reflexive and ambiguous character of a type of second modernity whose uncertainties are increasingly managed on an individual instead of a collective level. The previous emphasis on Islam as a technology of domination is competing with the application of Islamic traditions as technologies of the self, which shall bring about a form of the Islamic modern based on the religious and moral development of individuals. This socially cultural conflict is also visible in the emergence of new forms of modern Muslim selfhood.

Whether we look at anthropological studies on contemporary piety movements (Deeb 2006; Mahmood 2005), transnational Islamist movements (Mandaville 2001; Roy 2002), Islamic intellectual discourses (Dagi 2004), or studies on religious commodities and proper Islamic consumption (Fischer 2008; Starrett 1995), there is a visible tendency of practicing Muslims to view their worlds by individually employing Islamic traditions instead of following the prescriptive and authoritative readings of the religious establishment or of mass movements like the Brotherhood. Together with this "postmodern move," a large market of written and digital commodities has emerged that expresses the enormous demand "for information on how to conduct oneself in accord with Islamic precepts in day-to-day life" (Mahmood 2005, 80). Apparently contemporary piety movements are Islamic expressions of what Charles Taylor called the modern idea of a moral order: the affirmation of ordinary life by defining "goodness in ordinary living, production and the family" (Taylor 2007, 370). The material culture of second modernity provides individual Muslims with a market of competitive "ethical commodities" to organize new social practices in their self-fashioned affirmation of ordinary life. The "managerial" approach of classical Islamist thinking, the rational organization of a universally defined Islamic society based on normative principles found in the legalistic interpretation of the *sharia*, is probably losing appeal. Since the modern Salafist agitation against the interpretative monopoly of the *ulama* in the nineteenth century, we can observe a clear process of individualization within the discursive tradition of Islam. In the course of the twentieth century, the Islamic signifier became more important in Muslim politics of defining authentic forms of modern subjectivities. However, this rise to relative hegemony has been accompanied by an increasing loss of cohesive meaning. This transformation is also apparent in the puzzling ways in which the concept of Salafism is meanwhile applied. Academic definitions and Salafist self-descriptions hardly share a common denominator besides the ideal and authoritative status of the Prophet and the early community of Muslims in their otherwise heterogeneous religious constructions.

From the theoretical perspective of this book, Islam has turned into an empty signifier: References to Islamic traditions have meanwhile taken on a polysemic nature. In light of modern contingencies, they seem to guarantee authenticity without providing any shared meaning. Authorized by the Islamic institution of *jihad*, to take just an example, "postmodern Muslims" can justify fighting with military means for pan-Islamic ideals in Afghanistan, Bosnia, Chechnya, or Iraq (Hegghammer 2010), to pursue their personal "women's *jihad*" for the religious, political, and social betterment of their community (Deeb 2006, 204–19), or to advocate civil disobedience and nonviolent actions against repressive Muslim rulers (Stephan 2009). While Islamic traditions remain authoritative, they tend to become almost entirely open in meaning. In shaping postmodern Muslim identities, Muslim believers combine them randomly with diverging political ideologies, self-styled Islamic imaginaries, digitalized technologies, and consumptive practices (cf. Cooke and Lawrence 2005). In moving from first to second Islamic modernity, the figure of the supreme guide of the Muslim Brotherhood is challenged by the televised charismatic preacher, and the pious dress code of the sisters of Islam must compete against various new forms of Islamic fashion (Haenni and Tammam 2003).

We suggest analyzing this shift of the Islamic modern from an Islamist to a post-Islamist phase by combining the sociological narratives of modernization as differentiation and individualization. Sociologists of religion assert that a central element of secularization is the growing autonomy of believers in shaping their religious practices themselves (Spickard 2003). In functionally differentiated societies, the individual does not necessarily reject religious beliefs as such, but believers want to get rid of the bonds of organized religion and to utilize religious traditions in shaping their daily social practices in an idiosyncratic way. By referring to the ideal type of a modern, self-conscious, and creative individual, religion offers to them the means of achieving a good life through consciously applied and autonomously selected technologies of the self and not by implementing the prescribed interpretative templates of a religious and/or political elite.[6] Traditionalist and reformist *ulama*, Islamist ideologues, and Western observers have probably had a tendency to be blind to this development, wrongly perceiving secularization as a Western wholesale enterprise to destroy Islam. In putting their focus on organized forms of religion, they might have marginalized the increasing number of modern Muslims for whom religious practices may or may not be a part of their daily juggling with the communicative logics of the political, economic, or scientific rationalities with which a functionally differentiated society confronts them (cf. Jeldtoft 2011). The remainder of the book will look more deeply into the ways in which contemporary Muslims relate to Islamic traditions in their efforts to construct meaningful patterns of modern Muslim selfhoods. The two case studies on Jordan and Egypt will examine how changing forms of the Islamic modern linked to the more general social imaginaries of successive modernities have been central points of reference for both individual and collective attempts to give specifically Islamic answers to the core questions of modern life.

PART II

Politics of Muslim Subjectivities in Jordan

Much scholarly literature on the relationship between religion and politics in Jordan perfectly reflects academic and popular mainstream discussions, which put their focus on "political Islam." In particular, studies on the Muslim Brotherhood and its political arm, the Islamic Action Front (IAF), play a prominent role in this literature.[1] To be sure, increasing tension between the monarchy and the Brotherhood as well as the rise of militant Salafist organizations in Jordan are important issues for academic analysis. When exploring the role of religion in Jordan's social and political life, we must understand the world of "formal politics," the struggles among the royal family, the state apparatus, the IAF, representatives of Jordanian tribes, and other political parties. Formal politics provide the historical and structural context to which the often more fuzzy and rather opaque social processes relate, which we describe as the politics of modern Muslim subjectivities. From this perspective, the preoccupation of the scholarly mainstream with political Islam is understandable. However, it is important not to confuse formal politics with politically relevant social action as such.

While on fieldwork in Jordan, we often addressed issues regarding Islamist political parties such as the IAF and the Wasat Party in our conversations with people. A few of our interlocutors commented on the Islamic credentials or political aspirations of these parties, some perceiving them as potential forces of change and others seeing them as just as corrupt and inefficient as the rest of the political system. Most of them, however, responded with a remarkable indifference, claiming that they did not know any of these parties.[2] In sharp contrast to this indifference with regard to political parties, we found a high awareness about the social activities of other, seemingly nonpolitical, kinds of Islamic organizations in Jordanian society. Apparently, organizations such as Al-Afaf, which organizes mass weddings for poor people, the Muslim Brotherhood's Islamic Centre Charity Society (ICCS), and the small, local women's association selling bread in the neighborhood are better known—and more respected—than parties on the formal political scene. The majority of our interlocutors, including staunch secularists, were aware of these Islamic charities and expressed positive attitudes toward them, appraising their efficiency, transparency, and goodheartedness. Many knew somebody who worked in an Islamic charity and quite a few had themselves volunteered in one.

Islamic charities have a long historical record in Jordan.[3] The first explicitly Islamic organization, Al-Maqasid Al-Hijaziyya, was established in 1931, one year later followed by the Circassian Brotherhood. Islamic charities differ enormously in size and organizational type. Some, such as the ICCS, are professional organizations with branches throughout the country; others are small local associations run by volunteers from the basement of a mosque. They engage in different kinds of activities from the organization of mass weddings to the distribution of school bags and clothes, provision of financial assistance, job training, health care, and Islamic education. While these Islamic organizations might be hardly visible in formal politics, they represent important sites for contemporary negotiations about Jordan's social order as well as for the individual construction of modern Muslim subjectivities. Despite their apparent social significance, however, the field of Islamic welfare in Jordan has rarely been on the radar of academic research.[4]

In examining four different Islamic charities and welfare organizations, this part of the book seeks to contribute to filling this gap in academic research. We shall present our analysis in three chapters. Beginning at the macro level, we first situate these organizations within the broader structural and historical context of Jordanian politics. Chapter 4 outlines the institutional and discursive structures setting the boundaries for collective action by Islamic charities. Contrary to its media image, the Hashemite monarchy is no less an authoritarian state than most of its Arab neighbors have been. The regime strongly controls, manages, and restricts public discourses and forms of collective action in Jordanian society. Consequently, the state plays a crucial role in framing the religious arena and tries to maintain a monopoly over symbolic reproduction with respect to officially acceptable interpretations of Islamic traditions. We will argue that, from the beginning, the Jordanian rulers promoted the idea of an Islamic modern as an essential part of their state- and nation-building efforts. However, this official version of an Islamic modern had an inbuilt contradiction regarding the ways in which it has been represented on the domestic and the international scene. Internally, it represented a means of granting authoritarian politics religious legitimacy. Internationally, the monarchy displayed Islam as a means of individual and collective moral autonomy. Moreover, in their strategies to define and control religion in Jordan, the state elite entered into an ambiguous relationship with the Muslim Brotherhood, moving from close cooperation to growing contestation and open conflict. In the course of this change, the shift from cooperation to conflict has been accompanied by an increasing divergence between the perceptions of the regime and the Muslim Brotherhood as to who represents the principal antagonist, the excluded Other, in their respective visions of Jordan's Islamic modern. We claim that the alliance between monarchy and Brotherhood deteriorated alongside societal transformations, which we interpret as the erosion of the Jordanian model of an organized

Islamic society through discourses and social practices that are elements of second modernity.

While Chapter 4 analyzes the struggle about the very nature of Jordan's Islamic modern at the macro level of Jordanian state formation, Chapter 5 investigates this struggle on the meso level, with a particular focus on the institutional organization of Islamic charities and social welfare organizations in the country and their respective religious rationales. What does Islam mean in the organizational and discursive structures of these charities? How do they generalize religious motivations and frame specific forms of social action? To which model of successive modernities do their organizational practices relate? With the analytical help of modern systems theory, we can discern that political concerns have gradually been superimposed on the religious rationale, which originally defined the organizational nature of many of the Islamic charities in Jordan. The eminently political struggle about the Islamic modern is mirrored in the informal politics and membership policies of Jordanian welfare organizations.

Finally, in Chapter 6, we zoom in on the individual level and examine in which ways these organizations serve as social sites for the construction of different forms of modern Muslim subjectivities. In this chapter, we turn the focus of our investigation to the employees and volunteers in Jordanian welfare organizations and the various ways in which they use them in constructing their individual forms of being modern Muslims through discursive and social practices. In doing so, we show the ways in which elements of our three types of modern subjectivity formation mesh and mix in these idiosyncratic forms of Muslim selfhood.

CHAPTER 4

State and Islam in Jordan: The Contested Islamic Modern

The Modern Jordanian State: Making the Impossible Possible[1]

On November 11, 1920, Sharif Abdullah arrived from Medina by train in the British mandatory territory of Transjordan. Previously serving his father, King Hussein of the Hijaz, as foreign minister, Abdullah announced in the border town of Maan his will to redeem the Syrian Arab Kingdom whose short life had ended with the French advance into Damascus on July 24, 1920 (Salibi 1993, 49). At this point in time, prospects to transform the Transjordanian territorial remnants of the Arab Kingdom into a modern national state were pretty bleak. Under Ottoman rule, the territory was never an administrative unit and because of its tribal social nature (almost) impossible or difficult to be governed by Istanbul. Moreover, the territory was part of the British mandate and therewith under colonial rule. Given these conditions, state building required strategies for both internal nation building and external efforts to gaining international recognition as an independent state. The crucial balancing act for Abdullah was to cultivate a sense of national unity among independent tribes and to achieve the support of London to establish a sovereign national state. Although formal independence from Great Britain was achieved in May 1946, the very difficult internal nation-building process was further aggravated by the first Arab–Israeli war in 1948–1949. Following his long-standing territorial ambitions, King Abdullah eventually succeeded in incorporating the West Bank into the Transjordanian state in 1950. Together with the influx of Palestinian refugees, this territorial expansion created a state made up of "two peoples," Transjordanians and Palestinians (Robins 2004, 134). From this point onward, societal cohesion was not only challenged by tribal fragmentations but also by fundamental socioeconomic and cultural differences and a rival form of nationalism aspiring to the foundation of an independent Palestinian state (cf. Cohen 1982).

In this situation, resorting to Islam as a means of achieving political legitimacy and national integration was an obvious choice. In the foundational phase of the state, "the gravity of the Hashemites in Arabian politics (...) and their mantle as Islamic leaders, recognized descendents of the Prophet, probably strengthened Abdullah's appeal" (Alon 2007, 39). This initial combination of Arab nationalism with Islam has since then been nurtured by the royal family as a powerful tool in Jordanian nation building and in legitimating its right to rule (Noyon 2003, 81). Articulating domestic politics within the discursive framework of an Islamic modern consequently became an inherent trait of the modern Jordanian state.[2] Of course, the relatively successful state- and nation-building process in Jordan cannot be reduced to the religious variable alone. On the one hand, in integrating the tribal structure with its customary codes and conventions into the new state structure, Abdullah was following a different strategy in comparison to most of his Arab neighbors. Instead of coercively subjugating the tribes, the Jordanian rulers established a process of continuous negotiation of state policies with them, largely contributing to the comparatively strong, although not to be taken for granted, loyalty of tribal leaders to the monarchy (cf. Alon 2007). In these policies, state authorities effectively used the military as a vehicle for the pacification and political integration of Jordan's tribal society (Vatikiotis 1967). On the other hand, the Jordanian state would hardly have survived without Abdullah's close association with Britain and the general support, which the kingdom has been able to achieve at an international level (Wilson 1987, 2–3). From its inception in the 1920s, the Jordanian state has been acting as a notorious political rent seeker. The royal family was extremely successful in using the strategic interests of subsequent international powers, namely, Great Britain and the United States, in order to receive economic benefits and security guarantees, which have been crucial in the survival of Jordan as an independent state.

Central to the state discourse on Islam in Jordan is the representation of the king as the incarnation of Jordanian religious identity and national unity. It places the king far above society with its tribal, ethnic, societal, and political divisions, even above the state apparatus and the government. As a member of the Hashemite family, for centuries the ruler of Mecca and the guardian of the holy sites in Mecca, Medina, and Jerusalem, the king claims a unique and unquestionable religious legitimacy. This linkage of the Hashemite family with the holy places of Islam has continuously been invoked by Jordanian rulers. In a speech to the nation in 1993, for instance, King Hussein put it in reference to the assassination of King Abdullah at the Al-Aqsa mosque in 1951:

> We Hashemites have borne a special historic honour through our distinctive connection with Jerusalem. For it is the site where Allah took his Prophet for a journey by night. And the resting-place of Hussein I. The soil of Al Aqsa Mosque has been moistened by the blood of my martyred grandfather, founder of the Kingdom Abdullah bin al-Hussein.[3]

The close relationship of king, state, and Islam finds its legal expression in the country's constitution, ratified in 1952, and the National Charter, which formally introduced multiparty politics in 1991. The constitution not only proclaims Islam as the state religion,[4] but also stipulates in Article 28c the Islamic adherence of its ruler: "No person shall ascend the Throne unless he is a Moslem, mentally sound and born by a legitimate wife and of Moslem parents."[5] Furthermore, the constitution states that the legal system of the country should be partly based on the *sharia*, implemented by religious courts.[6] The National Charter reemphasizes the role of Islam as state religion, as well as the essential role the concept of an Islamic modern plays in national identity construction. Echoing the language of the nineteenth-century Islamic reform movement, the fifth principle of the charter states:

> Arab Islamic civilization, open to world civilization, is the defining aspect of the national identity of the Jordanian people. It constitutes one of the bases of its unity, independence and progress in the face of division, dependence and cultural intrusion in all its forms. It is also a wellhead of innate values which Jordanian society seeks to strengthen, through science, learning, education and good example.[7]

In this way, the authentic sovereignty of the Jordanian state has been anchored in an Islamic past collectively actualized in an Islamic present and future. That the legitimacy of the Jordanian king and modern state structures more generally are closely connected to religion means that political stability depends on a certain popular acknowledgement of the regime's interpretation of Islamic traditions. If the authenticity of the Islamic modern promoted by the regime is contested, the legitimacy of the political order is put in question, and Islam employed as a technology of domination by the regime can turn into a means of political opposition. Therefore, the management of Islamic discourses and practices must remain under state control. This is achieved—or sought to be achieved—through various political and institutional strategies subordinating the religious field to state control. In making the administration of mosques, the issuance of religious opinions (*fatwas*), and the collection of religious alms (*zakat*) state affairs, the regime tries to assure control over religious communication. The country's more than 2,000 mosques are part of the state system and their imams are state employees, subject to ministerial guidance and supervision. During the 1960s and 1970s, for instance, the state distributed topics for Friday prayers to the imams and made it mandatory for them to provide written copies of their speeches (Wiktorowicz 2001, 57). In the educational realm, the state introduced new school curricula with the aim to modernize religious education according to its vision of "moderate Islam," which should be disseminated through religious lessons in schools (Balba, Connelly, and Monahan 2008, 38). The nature of this kind of moderate Islam is, for instance, presented in the "Amman Message" of King Abdullah II from November 2004. In this message, calling for tolerance and unity in the Muslim world, the king presents his vision of Islam, based on the authority of a number of well-known *ulama*. The message emphasizes the role of the religious establishment in maintaining the internal "checks and balances" developed by Islamic jurisprudence in order to refute the illegitimate interpretations of

Islamic traditions by radical Islamist movements. It pictures Islam as a tolerant religion compatible with issues such as human rights, women's rights, or freedom of religion. The king further calls to spread this message through the media, teaching, and the training of imams.[8] Finally, the regime has implemented numerous legal restrictions on collective action, aiming at the close monitoring of Islamic activism through state agencies.

Although the Jordanian state has been quite effective in its control over religion, images and ideas of Islam in Jordan are not shaped and disseminated by state agencies alone. The modern history of Jordan is also a history of continuous challenges to the official Islamic modern by tribal leaders, Arab nationalist (in particular Nasserist and Baathist) parties, informal Islamic movements, militant Salafi groups, and—last but not the least—the Muslim Brotherhood. In particular, the latter has played a significant role in shaping publicly acknowledged images of Islam in Jordan. Throughout the years, the Brotherhood has been engaged in an ambiguous relationship with the regime, moving from mutual support and a joint management of religious discourse toward contestation and conflict. Presenting a brief history of this relationship, we will sketch out the specific historical trajectory, which the Jordanian modern has taken, making religion a political battlefield for the representation and organization of modern Jordanian society.

Shaping the Islamic Modern in Jordan: The State and the Muslim Brotherhood I

The Muslim Brotherhood in Jordan was founded in November 1945, making it as old as the state. In 1936, Abu Qura, a wealthy merchant, met with representatives from the Egyptian Brotherhood on one of his trips to Palestine, where he was distributing funds in support of the strike against British rule and Zionist settlement. A few years later, in 1943, he went to Egypt to inquire about the possibilities of opening up a branch of the Brotherhood in Jordan and was immediately appointed two assistants to help him in his efforts. Since then, however, the Egyptian and the Jordanian branches of the Brotherhood have traveled along quite different paths. In Egypt, the Muslim Brotherhood increasingly became antagonistic to the state and experienced long periods of severe state repression against its members and institutions. In Jordan, the Brotherhood is a legally established organization that flourished and developed in a close relationship with the regime. In contrast to the Egyptian Brotherhood, the Jordanian Brotherhood has never attempted to overthrow the king, espoused violence, or operated politically underground. Apart from its support for a military struggle in Palestine, the organization refrained from any political activities and mobilization of popular protests against the Jordanian regime (Wiktorowicz 2001, 5).

The Jordanian Muslim Brotherhood was granted legal status as a charitable society in January 1946 by King Abdullah I. In the beginning, the organization focused primarily on Islamic education, social welfare, and cultural activities, with the stated aim of contributing to the development of a new

Arab culture (Harmsen 2008, 137). In this sense, it was an obvious ally in the regime's attempt to create a modern national state organized around the idea of an Islamic society. It was a religious organization that could serve a national political purpose. Furthermore, in the early days, the social base of the organization consisted primarily in property owners and merchants who were all interested in the sociopolitical stability of Hashemite rule and profited from the economic policies of the government, which was protecting private property. Until the late 1980s, relations with the king and the state apparatus were generally good, although not without periods of tension and suspicions.[9] The king for his part recognized the organization's popular support and appeal to religious sentiments and appreciated its sociocultural version of Islam, whereas the Brotherhood accepted the political legitimacy of the regime and the status of the king as a direct descendant of Muhammad and supreme ruler of the country. At the same time, the two sides found a common enemy in those ideological forces who opposed their idea of an Islamic modern: Communism, pan-Arabism, and Baathism. In rejecting the role of Islam in Jordan's national authenticity regime, these movements represented an existential threat to the religious and political rationales of both the Brotherhood and the king. They perceived these secular ideologies as the preeminent excluded Other in their state- and nation-building efforts. From the perspective of the Brotherhood, the stark secularism of these movements threatened its vision of an Islamic society, and many were afraid that a secularist government would treat the Brotherhood as President Nasser had done with the movement in Egypt (Wiktorowicz 2001, 97). In the eyes of the regime, the republican forms of rule promoted by these nationalist and socialist forces posed a danger to the monarchical structures of Jordanian political authority, as well as to the religious legitimacy that the Hashemite dynasty enjoyed.[10]

These threats by Arab nationalist forces became imminent after the relatively free elections in October 1956, which resulted in a victory for the opposition. Although not pleased by the election's result, King Hussein turned to Suleiman al-Nabulsi, the leader of the oppositional National Socialist Party (NSP), to form a government. In the context of the Suez crisis and the concomitant wave of Arab nationalist sentiments, however, King Hussein and Nabulsi soon collided on foreign policy issues, in particular, King Hussein's interest in cooperating with the United States (Anderson 2005, 172). In January 1957, US President Eisenhower announced the so-called Eisenhower doctrine, offering support to states that faced aggression from communist states and movements—apparently a reaction to the political situation in the Middle East, which in the aftermath of the Suez Crisis was increasingly impacted by Cold War rivalries. Furthermore, the Nabulsi government included representatives of the Baath party and the communists, giving relatively free reign to leftist activities in the country. On April 10, 1957, King Hussein dismissed the Nabulsi cabinet, but the confrontation with his Arab nationalist opponents was not yet over. After an alleged attempted military coup and further calls of leftist and secular nationalist forces to popular demonstrations and a general strike, the king declared martial law on April 25,

1957. The dissolution of political parties and the restriction of the freedom of press ended Jordan's brief experiment with democratic pluralism (Singh 2002; Robins 2004, 101).[11]

Sharing a good part of the regime's political concerns, the Muslim Brotherhood had changed sides during these turbulent weeks. While considered a part of the opposition in the 1956 elections, now the Brotherhood openly supported the introduction of martial law; a position the king appreciated and rewarded. The regime and the Brotherhood went into a symbiotic relationship in which Muslim Brothers achieved privileged positions in society for their support in bolstering the state's religious legitimacy. While many civil society organizations and all political parties were prohibited from organizing during the years of martial law, the Brotherhood was allowed to establish local branches, facilitating its spreading throughout the country. In 1963, the king granted the Brotherhood permission to establish the Islamic Centre Charity Society (ICCS). In making the best use of its favorable position, the ICCS would open schools, hospitals, health clinics, and community centers throughout the country, offering education and health care, as well as financial and in-kind support to the poor and needy. As one of very few nongovernmental providers of social welfare services, the Brotherhood had a unique possibility of promoting its own discourses and practices of Islamic traditions and strengthening its social networks and support base in the population during the years of martial law (cf. Boulby 2000).

The Muslim Brotherhood also enjoyed a privileged position with regard to the political system. While political parties were banned and electoral processes stalled during the years of martial law,[12] the Brotherhood gained political influence in other ways. Leading Muslim Brothers were appointed ministers, holding different kinds of state portfolios relevant for constructing the contours of Jordan's Islamic modern. Ishaq Farhan, for instance, was minister of education in five consecutive cabinets from 1970 to 1974 and served later as president of the University of Jordan (Clark 2004, 87). Through positions in the ministry of education and other public institutions, the organization was able to shape the educational system in a religious direction, introducing a strong Islamic component into the state curriculum (Harmsen 2008, 141). In addition, due to its privileged position, the Brotherhood could freely promote the organization's own educational institutions, such as the Islamic College and the Dar al-Ahram School. Likewise, several members of the Brotherhood worked as minister of religious foundations, exerting the organization's influence on the country's religious institutions. Given the supervisory authority of the ministry over the country's religious infrastructure, the Muslim Brotherhood was able to impact significantly on the Islamic discourses that characterized religious communication in Jordanian mosques. This influence was additionally strengthened by Muslim Brotherhood members' heavy involvement in the religious system at a local level, working as imams or muftis (Wiktorowicz 2001).

All the above examples clearly demonstrate the unique position the Brotherhood held during the years of martial law. Rather than asserting its own interpretations of Islam, the regime allowed the Muslim Brotherhood to spread its religious communication, giving the organization access to key sites for the construction of Jordan's Islamic modern, namely, in the country's emerging civil society, the educational system, and religious institutions. Representing a world of a restricted, elitist liberal interpretation of Islamic traditions predominantly directed to an international audience, the royal institutions delegated the domestic dissemination of Islamic modernism to the Muslim Brotherhood. As such, the Brotherhood came to play a crucial part in shaping, expressing, and controlling public Islam according to its own, peer-group-oriented, collectivist model. This meant that for ordinary Jordanians, the country's Islamic modern was largely defined by the Brotherhood's ideas of an organized Islamic society.

In exchange for this privileged position, the king and the regime expected loyalty and support from the Brotherhood—which they almost always got. As mentioned above, the Brotherhood openly and clearly declared its support for the king in his confrontations with Arab nationalists in 1957, resulting in the introduction of martial law. A perhaps greater test to the friendship was the 1970–1971 civil war, or the so-called Black September, when the regime was existentially threatened by a military conflict with Palestinian nationalist organizations, a conflict that resulted in the death of more than 3,000 Palestinians (Barari 2008, 234). While open support of the regime was an impossible and unrealistic demand, taking into consideration the Brotherhood's strong Palestinian constituency, the Muslim Brothers did at least refrain from taking sides. Likewise, the Brotherhood was careful not to criticize the king during the so-called bread riots in 1989 and 1996, which erupted over the reduction of state subsidies for basic goods. Instead of targeting the core of political decision making in Jordan, namely, the royal palace, the Brotherhood diverted its critique toward the cabinet, being careful not to undermine the political authority of the king (Wiktorowicz 2001, 97f). Thus, while the Brotherhood did not necessarily refrain from taking a moderate stand against government policies, this critique was always combined with loyal support of the monarchy (Harmsen 2008, 138).

Summing up, the relationship between the king, the state apparatus, and the Brotherhood was, during the years of martial law, characterized by a mutual sense of trust, dependency, and cooperation. At least in principle sharing the general vision of a modern Islamic order in Jordan, the Brotherhood used to support the strategies and policies of the regime and, in exchange for this support, was allowed to promote its own interpretations of Islamic traditions, as long as these did not directly challenge the religious legitimacy of the king.

COMPETING ABOUT THE ISLAMIC MODERN: THE STATE AND THE MUSLIM BROTHERHOOD II

In recent decades, this rather unique relationship between the Jordanian state and the Muslim Brotherhood has come under severe strain. The previous cooperation in shaping a modern Islamic order has gradually given way to more open contestation. The reasons for this are manifold, but two transformative trajectories stand out. First, the organizational nature of the Brotherhood itself has changed. From being primarily concerned with religious, social, and cultural activities, the movement has developed into a much more political organization. Setting up a functionally differentiated organizational structure, the Muslim Brotherhood has not only strengthened its organizational interests and profile, but also entered more directly into political affairs. This applies in particular to the period of timid liberalization that has taken place since 1989, when martial law was lifted and more pluralist politics were initiated with the general elections to the new Lower House. In these elections, Islamist candidates performed extraordinarily well. Of the 80 seats in parliament, 34 went to Islamist representatives, among whom the Muslim Brotherhood represented the strongest group with 20 elected candidates (Robins 2004, 171).

With the legalization of political parties in 1992, the Muslim Brotherhood formally established its own political arm, the Islamic Action Front (IAF), now clearly opting for more organized participation in the political system. The IAF quickly developed into Jordan's only mass party, as witnessed by a comparatively high degree of recognition in the population. Consequently, the power monopoly of the king increasingly became an obstacle to the political aspirations of the Brotherhood. In addition to engaging in parliamentarian politics, the movement began to challenge official policies through their participation in professional associations and student unions. Since the end of the 1980s, the Brotherhood has enhanced its influence in professional associations and among students through electoral processes (Kassim 2006, 90).[13] To be sure, this was not directed against the very nature of Jordan's Islamic modern, but the way in which this established system of order should be developed. The strong political performance of the Muslim Brotherhood has triggered a number of administrative and coercive attempts by the regime to restrict the influence of the IAF, such as the introduction of new electoral laws, manipulating constituencies, reducing the autonomy of professional associations and student councils, or suppressing various forms of popular protest (cf. Clark 2012; Abu Rumman 2007).

The second transformative path in the relationship between the regime and the Muslim Brotherhood is related to a series of events in regional and international politics, aggravating the inbuilt contradictions in the royal representation of Islam. Among these events, the kingdom's problematic positioning in the three Gulf Wars, its peace treaty with Israel (1994), and the regime's response to Islamist militancy after the terrorist attacks of 9/11 are crucial cases in point. In particular, the peace agreement with Israel and the government's "normalization" policy met the open resistance of the Brotherhood. The peace treaty and the failure of the related economic peace dividend did not only deepen the gap between state and Brotherhood, but also brought together previous ideological enemies in a resistance committee, which the IAF formed with seven leftist parties (Kornbluth 2002).[14]

From its foundational phase, the Palestinian question has been a core issue in the ideology of the Muslim Brotherhood. In line with the general Islamist worldview, the organization considered the whole of Palestine to be Islamic lands. Moreover, Jordanian citizens of Palestinian origin make up the main constituency of the Muslim Brotherhood in Jordan. In the Brotherhood's eyes, recognizing the state of Israel, therefore, meant compromising Islam, a position that seems to be widely shared among Jordanians. Consequently, the Brotherhood and the IAF agitated fiercely against the treaty in mosques and other public arenas, with the result that many of their members were detained and brought to trial (Brand 1998, 59).

Through this chain of political events and the parallel decline of Arab nationalist and socialist ideologies, a new antagonism has been on the rise in their relationship with the West, separating the Islamic modern of the palace from the Islamic social imaginary of the Muslim Brotherhood. While Islam long represented the ideological glue between the regime and the Brotherhood, now the replacement of secular nationalism by the West in the identification of the excluded Other of Jordan's Islamic modern has developed into a major point of contention between the previous allies. Thus, beginning in the late 1980s, the very nature of Jordan's Islamic modernity has been increasingly contested.

Since Abdullah II assumed the throne in 1999, these tensions have grown into open conflict. The regime has taken various steps to curb and restrain the influence of the Muslim Brotherhood, whereas the Brotherhood has sought to retain the important role it has played in shaping the religious field in Jordanian society. In this struggle, the interpretation of Islamic traditions has become one of the major battlefields. Although previously the regime seemed to be comfortable with the Brotherhood's management of public religion according to its vision of an organized Islamic modern, the state is now apparently trying to regain this terrain. In particular, since 9/11 and the 2005 bombings of three hotels in Amman, the king and the royal family have more intensively promoted their so-called moderate understanding of Islam, perhaps most clearly expressed in the Amman Message.[15] Through inter-Islamic and interfaith initiatives, international conferences on dialogue, coexistence, and moderation, as well as support of political parties and organizations promoting these interpretations of Islam, the royal family has actively engaged in shaping the image of the Islamic modern inside Jordan, putting forward the image of "a religion of tolerance, wisdom and charity,"[16] in contradistinction to the Brotherhood's imaginary of an Islamic social system.

The struggles over Jordan's modern representation of Islam, however, are not restricted to the field of formal politics and official statements. In particular, the field of our study, Islamic charity and social welfare associations, has become a major scene for the struggle about the very nature of Jordan's Islamic modern. Through his public support to the governmental Zakat Fund, the king underlines the importance of Islamic charity, nursing his own image of being a good Muslim who lives up to religious duties by paying *zakat*. In addition, the regime challenges the relative hegemonic interpretations of Islamic traditions by the Muslim Brotherhood through the so-called royal nongovernment organizations (NGOs). Established by members of the royal family and including organizations such as Tkiyet um Ali, they are actively engaged in promoting and disseminating the regime's version of Islam in the provision of nongovernmental social welfare.

Besides their active engagement in promoting particular interpretations of a modern Islamic society, the king and the regime have also employed more coercive means, increasing the bureaucratic supervision and direct state control over the religious field, in particular, the mosques as popular centers for social, religious, and cultural activities. This control is based on a law that then Prime Minister Zeid al-Rifai pushed through parliament in the late 1980s. The law assigns state authorities the right to select and dismiss preachers and to supervise and control religious sermons, thus enabling the regime to prevent Muslim Brotherhood members from preaching if necessary (Harmsen 2008, 144). The implementation of this law is the responsibility of the ministry of religious foundations, more specifically the department of preaching and guidance. The ministry uses a range of different tools to ensure control over the imams and the mosques. First, it can dictate the subject of the *khutba*, the Friday speech of the imam, if it finds that there are important topics that need to be addressed. Secondly, when selecting imams to speak in the mosques, the ministry makes sure to choose people who are not critical of the government. In recent years, there has been a shortage of government-educated imams, compelling the ministry to employ personnel from outside the state system. Thirdly, the ministry applies a system of rotating imams from mosque to mosque, therewith limiting the possibility of individual imams generating a loyal following among local communities. Finally, the state can simply ban imams from preaching. Every week before the Friday *khutba*, government officials receive a list of preachers, and they can without further explanation deny them—temporarily or permanently—official permission to speak (Wiktorowicz 2001, 59).

ISLAMIC CHARITIES AND THE MANAGEMENT OF COLLECTIVE ACTION IN JORDANIAN CIVIL SOCIETY

The Jordanian regime's control and monitoring of Islamic activism is not restricted to the religious field alone. As a part of authoritarian politics, state authorities try to organize and manage civil society at large. The regime's Islam policies are, therefore, part and parcel of controlling society in a more comprehensive way. To maintain its control over collective action, the state has developed a number of administrative and repressive means of observing, recording, controlling, and monitoring civil society organizations of all kinds. The key to this state monitoring of civil society is the systematic classification of collective action according to different categories. Political parties, for instance, fall under the surveillance of the ministry of interior, cultural associations under the ministry of culture, sports clubs and youth centers under the ministry of youth and sports, and charities and social welfare organizations are subject to the control of the ministry of social development. In this way, the state fragments society, putting civil society organization under the supervision of different ministries and laws, thereby facilitating an effective and manageable system of control by various state agencies. Through detailed and cumbersome application procedures, constant reporting requirements, intensive monitoring, unannounced inspections, and a multiplicity of other measures, each ministry registers, supervises, and controls the respective organizations, their members, and their social activities.

In comparison to political parties, student unions, and professional associations, charities and social welfare organizations, however, have traditionally been allowed much more room to maneuver. Under martial law, for instance, all political organizations and parties were banned, while most charities and social welfare organizations could continue their work relatively undisturbed as long as they stayed clear of any kind of open political activity. This relative freedom of action reflects the regime's ambiguous relationship with welfare and charity organizations: On the one hand, they are effective and popular providers of social care and relief for the country's poor, offering the regime much needed assistance. Given the economic problems of the country, the poverty rate in Jordan has been on the rise and the state itself is not capable of ameliorating the situation of the needy.[17] On the other hand, it is precisely this efficiency and visibility with respect to poverty relief that makes these organizations so popular. With their social commitment and popular appeal, they almost automatically assume a political role, in particular, in a country in which formal politics has been so strongly constrained. Consequently, social welfare organizations became relevant actors in societal negotiations about Jordan's political identity and as such potential sites for the rise of popular resistance against the regime.

In light of this potential threat, the regime implemented different measures to legally control social welfare organizations. In Law no. 33, or Law on Societies and Social Organizations, we can discern one of the most important instruments of this form of governmental control. This law has been described as one of the oldest and most arbitrary NGO laws in the Middle East (Elbayar 2005, 14).[18] Enforced in 1966, it was aimed at discouraging the formation of welfare organizations based on family, ethnic, or religious ties, as Princess Basma Bint Talal described it in her book *Rethinking an NGO* (2004, 53). Furthermore, the law stresses the distinction between social and political forms of collective action, explicitly restricting the purpose of associations to the social and cultural realms. Article two of the law states that no organization under this law is allowed to engage in "fulfilling any political objectives."[19] Political activities are strictly reserved to formal political parties, regulated by the Political Party Law no. 32 from 1992. According to this law, political parties are not allowed to cooperate with nonpolitical organizations: "The use of premises, instrumentalities, and assets of associations, charitable organizations and clubs for the benefit of any partisan organization shall be prohibited" (Wiktorowicz 2001, 29).

These legal arrangements grant the ministries in charge wide and rather arbitrary powers to reject applications, leaving the rejected organizations with no right of appeal. The cumbersome application procedures often take several months and in some cases even years, raising suspicions among applicants that they may be subject to detailed investigations and surveillance by the *mukhabarat* (intelligence service) and the ministry of the interior. Once formally acknowledged, all organizations are subject to constant and thorough control and monitoring. They have to submit annual reports to the ministry in charge, including information on activities, finances, correspondence, board meetings, and members (Wiktorowicz 2001, 26). Likewise, ministerial agencies are free to send representatives to observe any meeting or election or to simply control the implementation of activities. Organizations are not free to engage in any kind of activities, but may only carry out activities listed in their original application. Thus, an organization involved in educational activities for orphans cannot expand its realm to include disabled children without prior permission from the ministry. If the ministry is dissatisfied with the activities or the behavior of the members of an organization, it can dissolve it, replace individual members, or replace entire boards by governmentally appointed substitutes, all without judicial oversight or the possibility of appeal (Elbayar 2005, 15).

In this system of state surveillance, the General Union of Voluntary Societies (GUVS) has historically played an important role as an institutionalized linkage between state and civil society. Established by the state in 1959, GUVS is the official coordinating body of all charities and social welfare organizations for which the membership in GUVS is obligatory. Among other things, GUVS is responsible for setting general policies, ensuring coordination and cooperation among member organizations, and providing its members with financial support, technical advice, and training. The Union is financed by the national lottery, and as such financially independent from the government. However, in reality, connections between the GUVS and the ministry of social development are close, and the Union plays a crucial role in the disciplinary oversight of nongovernmental charities and social welfare organizations in Jordan. Having access to all reports and budgets of their member organizations, GUVS can provide the ministry with a variety of information about its member organizations, and the ministry reportedly consults with GUVS on decisions about the registration of new organizations or the closure of existing ones (Wiktorowicz 2002, 116–118).[20]

Under martial law, the state closed down many secular and left-wing organizations, while Islamic organizations enjoyed much more freedom of action. During this period of time, the regime considered these organizations to be instruments in the construction of Jordan's Islamic modern according to a state-centered top-down model of organized first modernity. Today, the Muslim Brotherhood and other Islamic organizations constitute the most serious challengers to the regime and its vision of an Islamic modern. Consequently, these organizations have become major targets of the punitive actions under Law no. 33.[21] In July 2006, for instance, the ICCS was charged with corruption and board members replaced with a government-appointed committee (Clark 2012). Another organization, Al-Farouq, faced investigations on the grounds that it supported only Palestinians, thus violating Law no. 33's provision not to engage in sectarian activities. In our fieldwork, a number of our interlocutors told us about the extremely long application procedures to which Islamic organizations were exposed in comparison to non-Islamic organizations. Moreover, many of them complained about frequent control visits by government representatives.

This situation has been aggravated further with the introduction of new antiterror laws since 2001. Like many regimes in the region, the Jordanian state has used this new form of legislation as an effective tool of control and intimidation regarding the activities of Islamic civil society organizations. Moreover, economically oriented laws have been put into place to restrict the international transfers of money to terrorist networks and individuals. This has severely hampered the flows of donation to many Jordanian charities, in particular, Islamic ones. All major donations from international organizations or institutions have to be approved by state agencies, and even petty international transactions are strictly controlled and investigated. Individual donors have to provide their name, address, and identification number to the organization, which should then send a copy of the receipt to the ministry. By preventing the donor from remaining anonymous, these procedures decisively curtailed an income source for Islamic charities in which anonymous donations have a strong tradition. In addition, the increased governmental control of international transfers has strongly impacted on institutional and individual donors from the Gulf countries. Their submission of donations has been severely encumbered, leaving many Islamic organizations under financial strain.[22] As the director of one organization said, explaining why he preferred not to receive any funds from abroad:

> It's too complicated. Anyone who wants to give us money has to provide his name, address, identification number, a long list of information, and we have to send a copy of the receipt to the ministry. Even for one JD. It's too much.

CONCLUSIONS

Focusing on the relationship between the Jordanian rulers and the Muslim Brotherhood, we suggested interpreting the changing nature of this relationship within the broader context of the social and cultural construction of modern Jordanian society. From the beginning, Jordanian state makers framed their state- and nation-building efforts according to the model of an Islamic modern. They presented the newly formed state as a "morally authentic sovereign" in close reference to Islamic traditions, which served as a central source for gaining national authenticity and political legitimacy (cf. Duara 2004, 3). At the same time, the Hashemite rulers built their state in close collaboration with, and with economic and political assistance from,

Western powers, in particular, Great Britain and later the United States. In combining Western support with religious symbolism, they were able to consolidate their rule against regional and domestic competitors, challenging their claim to power and the mere legitimacy of the Jordanian state as a "construct of colonialism." Yet in doing so, the rulers established a double discourse with respect to religion: While in the international arena, the state elite would present their vision of Islam as a modern religion, functionally restricted to the domain of a transcendental anchor for individual and public morals, domestically they would follow the path of Islamic reform by justifying modern social institutions in reference to Islamic traditions, thereby "Islamizing" the Jordanian discourse on modernity. Sharing the Hashemite's general vision of the Islamic nature of modern Jordan, the Muslim Brotherhood allied itself with the crown, playing an essential role in shaping the religious character of first modernity in Jordan. In delegating the symbolic control of Islam in society to the Brotherhood, the regime fostered an interpretation of Jordan's Islamic modernity at home that was different from the more individualistic image, basically representing Islam as a moral code alone, which it has promoted internationally.

This inbuilt rift became apparent with the political and social changes that have characterized the region since the 1980s. While both state and Brotherhood previously stood united against regional and local opponents in defending the vision of an Islamic modern, the regime's cooperation with the West and Israel alienated the Brotherhood from the regime. In particular, since the introduction of the regime's policy of normalization with Israel in 1994, the West increasingly assumed the role of the prime antagonist in the social imaginary of the Muslim Brotherhood. The competition between an Islamic and non-Islamic Jordan has been replaced by contestations about the very nature of this Islamic modern—a topic on which the Brotherhood and the regime no longer agree. Moreover, given its organizational diversity and engagement in participatory politics, parts of the Brotherhood began to question the authority structures of Jordan's first modernity, which has prevented the organization from assuming more power in the field of formal politics. Concomitantly, the regime itself has increasingly linked its external representation of Islam to discourses on democracy and human rights that resemble the discursive patterns of second modernity, a discourse that, in turn, empowers the internal opposition against the king's autocratic rule. Apparently both the form of Islam and the organized nature of modernity as such have come under question. This erosion of Jordan's authoritarian Islamic modern has generated complex societal negotiations in which formerly fixed social and political positions have come into flux. The following pages will examine these negotiations about Islam and modernity in one specific social arena, focusing on the organizational and individual levels of social welfare and Islamic charity organizations.

CHAPTER 5

Charities and Social Welfare Organizations in Jordan: Negotiating the Islamic Modern

Jordanian charities and social welfare organizations have—as previously indicated—a long history, even preceding the foundation of the modern Jordanian state. While most of the earliest charities limited their activities to serving specific ethnic or religious communities, the first organizations with a broader reach emerged during the interwar period. The Jordanian Youth League, for instance, was established in 1937 and the Women's Social Solidarity Society in 1944 (Harmsen 2008, 155). Following the first Arab–Israeli war in 1948 and the influx of hundreds of thousands of Palestinian refugees, the country witnessed a pronounced increase in voluntary activism and the foundation of numerous new social welfare organizations, among others the Jordanian Red Crescent, which was established in 1951. Since then the number of charities has grown steadily, reaching an estimated figure of more than 800 organizations in 2006 (Kassim 2006).

Many of the newly established organizations adopted the officially sanctioned framework of Jordan's Islamic modern, claiming an Islamic identity and promoting Islamic concepts in their work. In this sense, they also represent organizational manifestations of the social imaginary promoted by the state. The emergence of social welfare organizations closely interlaced with the discursive structures of opportunities and constraints given by the official discourse on Islamic authenticity. The most prominent of these Islamic organizations is the already mentioned ICCS, established by Muslim Brothers in 1963, but many others followed in the years to come. Some are related to or supported by the Muslim Brotherhood, such as the Islamic Bani Hassan Welfare Association and Urwa al-Wuthqa Welfare Association; others are independent, such as the Al-Fayhah Association and Anwar al-Huda Islamic Society (AHIS). In 1978, the ministry of religious foundations founded the national Zakat Fund as a governmental counterpart to these popular nongovernmental Islamic charities. Since the end of martial law in 1989, the majority of new organizations have been founded on nonreligious grounds, for example, the Arab Organization for Human Rights (1990) and the Jordan Hashemite Fund for Human Development (JOHUD; under this name in 1999). However, there have still been new organizations that claim to have an Islamic identity, such as the Al-Farouq Society established in Irbid in 1991. Rather than focusing entirely on traditional forms of charity, many of the new organizations introduced concepts into their organizational communication such as sustainable development, human rights, capacity building, and empowerment. This discursive shift was also reflected at state level, perhaps most clearly in the change of name of the ministry of social affairs to the ministry of social development (Harmsen 2008, 161).

In the following, we will take a closer look at four organizations in the field of welfare activities: the JOHUD, the national Zakat Fund, the Muslim Brotherhood's ICCS, and the AHIS. These four organizations position themselves differently in relation to the king, the state, and the Muslim Brotherhood, just as they represent different interpretations of Jordan's Islamic modern. While JOHUD is a nonreligious royal organization chaired by Princess Basma, the Zakat Fund is part of the official state structures, whose religious discourse is somehow in competition with the ICCS of the Muslim Brotherhood.[1] AHIS is a local organization that represents the independent Islamic organizations with no or weak institutional ties. We take these four organizations as kinds of ideal types in the Jordanian social welfare sector, representing the royal NGOs, state institutions, organizations framed by the Muslim Brotherhood ideology, and independent organizations.[2] In examining their discourses and practices, we will explore the organizational rationale of these four types and link them to the different forms of successive modernities. Predominantly engaged in social welfare, these organizations have established more or less formalized ways of communication that cross-cut the self-referential communications of function systems. They pursue their objectives by applying elements of political, economic, religious, and other semantics in idiosyncratic ways. In our analysis, we will specifically focus on the ways in which they employ religious language in their institutionalized communication and the role that Islam plays in framing their collective actions. More precisely, we are interested in the various discursive representations of Islamic traditions that these organizations have constructed, expressed, and disseminated in Jordanian society.

In our analysis, we approach these four organizations as important sites for contemporary negotiations about the authentic form of Jordan's Islamic modern. Moreover, we treat them as social sites for the construction of meaningful selfhoods among its members. Each of the following sections starts with a short description of the respective organization and its history, moving on to an analysis of the ways in which the organization portrays itself and its work with reference to Islamic traditions. In particular, we look at the various forms through which the organizations construct their identities with respect to their members and volunteers, as well as in addressing their two main target groups, namely, donors and beneficiaries. Against this background, we then ask whether these organizations can be understood as religious, measuring this according to the religious communication they employ in both their self-reference and in their self-representation vis-à-vis external addressees.

In claiming a religious identity, the traditional Islamic institution of *zakat* appears to be a central reference point. In Islam, as in many other religions, there exists a close relationship between religion and charity. The prophetic traditions offer a host of stories and sayings of the Prophet and his companions in which charity is narrated as a religious duty. From the perspective of religious social action, activities in the field of social welfare grant *thawab*, divine rewards with respect to individual salvation. Visiting the sick, giving alms, helping the poor, and persuading others to charity are forms of action that generate most rewards on the final Day of Judgment. *Zakat* refers to the religious obligation for all sincere Muslims whose annual wealth exceeds a certain minimum level to pay 2.5 percent of it for morally good purposes (Benthall 1999, 28).[3] While the nature and extent of *zakat* has been interpreted differently throughout Islamic history, the principle and its central role in the Islamic belief system are unanimously acknowledged (Dean and Khan 1997, 196). *Zakat* is one of the five pillars of Islam and is often described as "the companion of prayer" (Zysow 2008).[4] To pay *zakat* is a way to praise God who in return blesses the wealth from which it was given (Davis 2003, 315); as such, it is an economic transaction that belongs to the field of religious communication. In claiming an Islamic identity, charities have made *zakat* an important part of their organizational rationales and societal actions. However, as we will see, they do so in different ways, not always phrasing the payment of *zakat* in terms of religious action alone and relating it to different forms of modernity.

Jordan Hashemite Fund for Human Development: The Humanist Approach

Originally named the Queen Alia Fund for Social Development, JOHUD was first founded in 1977. Today, it is one of the country's largest NGOs, with an estimated annual budget of about four million JD and community centers spread over the whole country.[5] Chaired by Princess Basma bint Talal, JOHUD is a so-called royal NGO, a popular term for the various organizations established and chaired by members of the royal family. The first royal NGO, the Young Muslim Women's Association, was founded by Princess Thermat in 1974 and has since been followed by dozens of others.[6] The royal NGOs are all highly professional organizations, typically engaged in developmental activities of various kinds, including community development, women's empowerment, children's rights, and micro-finance programs. While most of them are formally nonreligious, basing their work on values such as universal human rights and sustainable development, they also engage in activities with religious traits such as JOHUD's annual Goodwill Campaign, "based on Islamic values of solidarity and support," as a PR brochure of the organization states.

The royal NGOs are registered with the state as private societies and as such not subject to the same laws as the other charities and social welfare organizations, giving them a privileged position among Jordanian civil society organizations. Royal NGOs are to a large degree exempted from state control and therefore free to cooperate with and receive funding from international donors without applying for ministerial permission. JOHUD's activities are primarily financed by institutional donors, including various ministries such as the ministry of planning and international cooperation, the ministry of social development, and the ministry of health, as well as international aid agencies and transnational NGOs such as USAID, DANIDA, CARE, and Save the Children. Coupled with general preferences for royal NGOs by international donors, this gives them an enormous economic advantage in comparison to regular NGOs, clearly reflected in the fact that they receive an absolute majority of foreign funds (Clark and Michuki 2009, 332). International donors prefer to fund royal NGOs for several reasons: as a way of maintaining good relations with the regime; because of their comparatively professional nature; and, last but not the least, because their approach to social welfare closely mirrors the outlook of Western organizations (Hawthorne 2004, 97f). Thus, while organizations such as the ICCS receive the bulk of their funding from private and domestic donors, JOHUD's economy is grounded in international and public funding. In addition to public and international funding, the organization enjoys extensive support from private businesses, such as PepsiCo, Phosphate Company, or Intel, the latter sponsoring JOHUD's Intel Computer Clubhouse for after-school activities. Finally, through its Goodwill Campaign, the organization also collects funds from private donors, in 2007 amounting to about 1.5 million JD. JOHUD's economic wealth is clearly displayed in both its headquarter facilities, located in one of Amman's fashionable neighborhoods, and its many community centers, which are all well kept and fitted with modern IT equipment. Likewise, the organization's 450 employees allegedly enjoy much higher salaries than those of many other social welfare organizations, including the ICCS.[7] As a JOHUD representative told us, "We don't have any problems getting funding."

That the royal NGOs do not receive the main bulk of their funding from individuals does not mean that they do not enjoy popular support. Because of the close connection between them and the royal family, their work is often perceived as a direct expression of the royal family's good-heartedness. This image is nurtured and reinforced by members of the royal family through frequent visits to the organizations, often ostentatiously presented in national newspapers and television. "We all have to work together to spread the good," as Princess Basma said at the launch of one of JOHUD's Goodwill Campaigns.[8] Our interlocutors from JOHUD frequently referred to the royal connection and emphasized the passionate and hands-on involvement of the royal family. The director of the Jordan River Foundation, for instance, explained, "Nobody could have survived the struggles we had at the beginning if not for Her Majesty backing up these programs. She does it because she has the passion for it."[9] Despite this apparent dependence on the royal family, royal NGOs nevertheless seek to depict themselves as independent from the political establishment and like to appear as critical watchdogs with regard to the regime. Consequently, the royal NGOs are among the few Jordanian organizations that engage in advocacy work and, at least on the surface, question the authoritarian policies of the regime.[10] Yet even they do not enjoy unlimited freedom of expression. As a Jordanian researcher noted, royal NGOs essentially remain royal. While they are able to criticize the government and parts of the state apparatus, this criticism does not include any questioning of the legitimacy of the absolute powers of the Jordanian King.[11]

Like most of the royal NGOs, the organizational rationale of JOHUD does not build on religious communication, but mainstream development and human rights discourses. On its website, for instance, JOHUD declares poverty to be a denial of basic human rights.[12] The organization portrays itself as rooted in humanist universalism following developmental strategies in its work. The core concept in these strategies is empowerment. JOHUD states, "Over the years JOHUD has come to realize that all the focus of its work should be to empower the poor, so that they themselves have access to, and control over, the resources that are necessary to create a viable and sustainable livelihood."[13] Rather than providing traditional social welfare, the royal organizations seek to empower people through activities such as "awareness-raising," "community mobilization," and "capacity building." The beneficiaries of these activities are not defined by any religious or ethnic boundaries, and JOHUD follows a strategy of inclusion with regard to both beneficiaries and members. Generally speaking, JOHUD's self-understanding resembles that of mainstream international organizations in the fields of humanitarian aid, relief, and development work as expressed by the principles of the Red Cross: humanity, impartiality, neutrality, independence, voluntary service, unity, and universality.

In line with its universalistic and humanist outlook, references to Islamic traditions are not an essential part of the organizational rationale of JOHUD. From its pluralist perspective, the organization may consider religion as a potentially important motivational factor for some of its members, but membership as such is not linked to generalized forms of religious motivations. In organizational terms, religion is a means to differentiate the "modern" developmental approach of JOHUD from the "traditional" approach of its Islamic competitors. In the discourse of JOHUD and its staff members, Islam is closely associated with traditional charity, pictured as a kind of short-term relief with no long-term developmental value. The distinction between charity- and development-oriented approaches is common among development and human rights organizations. Here charity refers to "traditional" forms of short-term almsgiving and service provision in the form of material or financial aid, health services, and care taking. Development, by contrast, emphasizes participation and empowerment of the poor in achieving self-sustainable goals and invokes social and economic rights. With regard to Islamic organizations, a member of JOHUD told us, "Their work is really important, but still, it's only charity, it doesn't really change things." According to representatives from JOHUD and other royal organizations, religiously based aid is almost per definition traditional charity and alms-giving.

While Islam is irrelevant for the organizational identity of JOHUD, the organization nevertheless uses religious communication if considered to be useful. This applies in relation to both donors and beneficiaries. By applying a religious language, holding annual Ramadan *iftars* for potential donors, and offering to collect *zakat* from believers, the royal organizations successfully try to tap into religious constituencies.[14] JOHUD's annual Goodwill Campaign during the month of Ramadan, for instance, is launched as an Islamic initiative, "drawing on Islamic values of solidarity and bringing together the entire Jordanian community."[15] Furthermore, Islamic symbols function as a communicative tool in JOHUD's efforts to reach out to its beneficiaries, as a representative of JOHUD confessed in one of our interviews: "If we want a message disseminated, we will talk to the preachers." To a certain extent, the organizational rationale based on global discourses of development and human rights seems to be not mutually intelligible in Jordanian society. In order to reach people and convey its message, JOHUD has to translate concepts such as children's rights and women's empowerment into popularly recognizable and morally acceptable terms. This vernacular of Jordanian society is closely linked to the religious language of Islamic traditions. A representative from the Jordan River Foundation, for instance, told us that the organization's awareness-raising campaigns to promote children's rights include several verses from the Koran phrasing children's rights in an Islamic idiom. Likewise, JOHUD and other royal organizations regularly consult with religious leaders in order to get their views before they launch campaigns or programs on gender issues, family planning, and other potentially controversial topics. Thus, Islamic traditions seem to serve as useful tools in JOHUD's communication with donors and beneficiaries. In order to make a social impact, JOHUD has to respect the discursive imperatives Jordan's Islamic modern has shaped.

In this process of translation, JOHUD cooperated primarily with the so-called moderate Islamic organizations. An example is the Al-Aqsa Association, lead by the famous women's activist Nawal al-Faouri. Al-Faouri left the Muslim Brotherhood in disagreement over the movement's "conservative" views on women, and has, at least in some circles, become a known representative of liberal Islam and women's rights in Jordan. Another, more recent, partner is Sunaa al-Hayah, an organization established by young activists inspired by the Egyptian TV preacher Amr Khaled.[16] When we visited JOHUD, it was together with Sunaa al-Hayah planning to introduce what an employee called "productive projects," offering financial aid and training to poor families in order to help them in establishing small businesses. This acknowledgment of the importance of Islamic discourse in Jordanian society is even more obvious in Tkiyet um Ali. Established in 2004 by Princess Haya, this royal organization specifically relates to the traditional Islamic concept of *tkiyet*, going back to a Sufi-inspired provision of food for the poor in the eleventh century.[17] The Islamic character of this royal NGO is further stressed by campaigns strongly relating to *zakat*. During Ramadan, Tkiyet um Ali runs campaigns to encourage Jordanians to pay their *zakat* through Tkiyet um Ali under the slogan: "Pay your *zakat* by a telephone call which allows you to perform your duties in the spirit of the age." Thus, building explicitly on Islamic traditions of charity, Tkiyet um Ali makes religion a central part of its organizational rationale, deviating from the largely nonreligious identity of most royal NGOs.

Generally speaking, then, JOHUD and other royal NGOs construct their identities with respect to the global discourses of development and human rights. They represent organizations with a pluralist rationale appealing to members and volunteers who more or less relate themselves to the individualized, postmodern forms of second modernity. This does not exclude individual or collective references to Islam. However, in mirroring the royal representation of Islam as a functionally separated source of morality, religion is not a core element of their organizational communications. In terms of membership, Islam does not play a necessary role. While royal NGOs' self-representation is nonreligious, they nevertheless apply religious communication when addressing donors and beneficiaries, using religion instrumentally as a means to translate internal developmental discourses into a mutually intelligible idiom in Jordanian society. Recently, however, royal NGOs have become more directly engaged in the conflict between the regime and the Muslim Brotherhood, and they are increasingly playing a part in confrontations about the interpretation of Jordan's Islamic modern. This is apparent in the search for cooperation partners among the so-called moderate Islamic organizations, as well as in the foundation of Tkiyet Um Ali, which seems to be a direct attempt to challenge the dominance of the Muslim Brotherhood ideology in Jordan's Islamic civil society, a function that was previously exerted by the national Zakat Fund.

THE ZAKAT FUND AND THE ZAKAT COMMITTEES: ISLAMIC CHARITY BY THE STATE

The royal NGOs are not the only institutional forms through which the monarchy and state authorities engage in the field of charity. The national Zakat Fund was established in 1978 under the ministry of religious foundations. Explicitly based on the Islamic principle of *zakat*, the institution's task is to collect alms and distribute them among the poor and needy. Through local *zakat* committees, the Fund grants financial and in-kind assistance and carries out a number of other activities benefitting the poor, including the celebration of religious holidays, provision of health care, and administration of orphan sponsorships. While it is difficult to present concrete figures, the local committees seem to be popular institutions to which an increasing number of Jordanians pay their *zakat*, especially during the holy month of Ramadan (Benthall and Bellion-Jourdan 2003, 14). As a member of a local *zakat* committee told the *Jordan Times*, "I recollect 30 to 40 years ago these forms of financial worship were almost non-existent, except by a few merchants and people with deep religious conviction."[18]

The Zakat Fund is the second largest governmental provider of welfare assistance in the country, only exceeded by the nonreligiously framed National Aid Fund. Besides a minor decrease in 1988–1990, it has grown consistently in terms of both the amount of *zakat* distributed and the number of its beneficiaries. When founded in 1978, the Fund distributed less than ten thousand JDs, benefitting only a few thousand families. Thirty years later, it disposed over an annual budget of about JD five million and provided assistance to more than 100,000 people.[19] The Fund's work is supported by approximately 170 local *zakat* committees spread throughout the country, primarily in lower-income areas, staffed by volunteers who are responsible for collecting alms, assessing community needs, and providing services to the poor. The committees enjoy a very good reputation in society, and the mostly pious volunteers are well-respected and trusted community members. Each committee consists of between seven and fifteen members, elected for a period of two years. All members have been approved by the ministry of religious foundations, which also supervises the work of the committees.[20] The ministry requests detailed records of the committee's weekly meetings and their financial records, as well as annual reporting. Through these bureaucratic measures and surprise inspections of the committees, the ministry closely monitors them and controls their loyalty to the crown and the regime. In some cases, Muslim Brotherhood members have, often successfully, tried to infiltrate and coopt the *zakat* committees, which then resulted in their immediate dissolution and the establishment of new committees by the state. Thus, while the *zakat* committees may be formally independent from the state, in practice they are heavily controlled by the state, functioning as its civil society branches (Wiktorowicz 2001, 65). Their apparent task is to counterbalance the Islamist activities of the Muslim Brotherhood with a state-controlled discourse and practice of Islamic charity that partly resembles the Brotherhood's approach.

Even the name of the Fund signals its very close relationship to Islamic traditions. The religious rationale of the Zakat Fund is further demonstrated by slogans such as "paying *zakat* will give you happiness and blessings," "*zakat* is a reward," and "*zakat* will purify your soul and money," which are displayed on its posters and in brochures. Emphasizing the individual benefits of paying *zakat* with respect to a religious system of benevolent deeds and rewards, the Zakat Fund clearly addresses the public in religious terms, calling individuals to religious forms of action. Yet parallel to its appeal to religious action, the Fund also applies a rather different discourse of social ordering. In one of its brochures, we read: "*Zakat* is a community service and charity performed in an Islamic way. It prevents poverty and gives the poor a good life. And most importantly, it unites the classes with love and compassion."[21] In this social understanding of *zakat*, the religious discourse of duty is often replaced by a more legalist discourse of rights. Arguing against a view of the poor as beggars, the director of the Fund told us, "The poor people should know that this is their right—they have the right to this money." In a similar vein, information material from the Zakat

Fund explains *zakat* as a form of social order given by God, combining religious discourses about duties with legal discourses about rights.[22] Giving *zakat* is a religious duty for the wealthy, and it is a right of the poor. Thus, this governmental institution frames social assistance in fusing religious and legal discourses in the construction of its organizational rationale. In this way, the Fund aims at the stabilization of a socially increasingly fragmented society:

> Islam encourages the rich people to give and the poor to receive. The purpose of *zakat* is for the rich to give to the poor, not because they have to, but because they love the poor. When the rich people give, they feel better because they help people. And when the poor get money, they will not hate the rich. This will contribute to the creation of a more secure community, there will be no hatred between the classes [...]. We believe that when a person is hungry, this will cause problems in the community. We want to balance class differences. We focus on education as well as financial support to take away the envy of the poor.[23]

According to this statement by the Zakat Fund's director, poverty and unequal socioeconomic relations lead to social conflict and instability. In collecting and distributing *zakat*, the Fund wants to contribute to easing economic inequalities, therewith reducing tensions and creating social stability in the population. The goal is not a different kind of social order, but a stabilization of the existing one. This promotion of *zakat* as social stabilizer reflects the Fund's function as an integral part of the institutional structure of the state. As a governmental institution, the organizational rationale of the Fund is to support the existing power structures. This function is clearly visible in the Zakat Fund's close relationship with the king. The king pays regular visits to local *zakat* committees, donates large sums of money to the Fund, and often expresses his support of it in national media, encouraging Jordanians to pay their *zakat* to this governmental organization.[24] As the director of the Fund puts it, "The king is an idol for charity work, just like the queen. He visits the Fund every Ramadan, he's the model for all people, he pays *zakat* to this Fund every year."

The particular role of the Zakat Fund is also apparent in the discursive framing of the relationship to its beneficiaries. While the majority of the Zakat Fund's aid goes to Muslim beneficiaries, the Fund—like JOHUD— argues for an inclusive approach to beneficiaries, targeting non-Muslims through a specifically designated account and juxtaposing itself with Islamic organizations such as ICCS, characterized as discriminatory, exclusivist, and particularistic in their focus on fellow Muslims and prospective converts. However, rather than legitimizing this approach by reference to principles of humanitarian universalism, as we know from JOHUD and other royal NGOs, the director explains the practices of the Fund as a way of promoting interfaith dialogue and peaceful coexistence: "This is to contribute to peace and compassion between Muslims and non-Muslims."[25] This approach is further stressed in the Fund's educational activities with the poor: "We teach people about love, security, child rearing, Islam in general, how you treat non-Muslims and Muslims equally," the director explained to us. In this way, he clearly echoes the royal family's discourse on interfaith dialogue and moderation, and the Fund can be seen as an important part of the regime's strategy to challenge the relative hegemony of Islamist discourses in Jordan and beyond.

Even more than the royal NGOs, the Zakat Fund must be seen as a direct competitor with the ICCS, which represents the Muslim Brotherhood movement and its vision of an Islamic modern in the arena of Islamic charity and social welfare activities in Jordan. In terms of members, donors, and beneficiaries, the Fund addresses the same audience as the Muslim Brotherhood; however, it does so with a message that largely affirms the public order. In its organizational representation, the Fund fuses religious communication with the political intentions of state authorities to enhance their legitimacy and to stabilize the system of rule in the existing social order. The official communication of the Zakat Fund clearly contains elements of both the political and religious systems; however, measured by its inner rationale, it is a part of state politics rather than representing a religious institution. The Fund's rationale fits best into an institutional setting of first modernity, in an organized Islamic society in which religion serves to maintain the status quo of an Islamic modern organized from top to bottom by an authoritarian state. While the character of JOHUD resembles the monarchy's external representation of Islam, as a source for the moral autonomy of individuals, the institutional logic of the Zakat Fund is perhaps better conceptualized as part of its domestic discourses, aimed at shaping a national collective loyal to the autocratic political system.

THE ISLAMIC CENTER CHARITY SOCIETY: THE CHARITABLE WING OF THE MUSLIM BROTHERHOOD

In one of Amman's Palestinian refugee camps, we visited the Nasr Area Community Center. The center is located in a run-down three-floor building situated at the corner of two unnamed dirt roads. It offers health services, education, and in-kind assistance to some of the many destitute families that inhabit the camp. In the sparsely equipped health clinic on the first floor, a doctor and a nurse provide free treatment and distribute medicine that has been donated to the clinic. On the ground floor, teachers offer courses in English for teenagers, provide job training to young men, and give lectures on issues such as marriage, women's rights, and health. In the basement, volunteers bake bread to be distributed among the elderly and disabled people in the camp.

The community center belongs to the Islamic Center Charity Society. The ICCS is one of Jordan's biggest NGOs, with a budget of six million JD[26] almost entirely collected from individual donors. The organization employs about 4,000 employees and 700 volunteers, and runs community centers, health clinics, hospitals, universities, schools, and kindergartens in most parts of the country.[27] Due to its urban middle-class character and the relationship to the Muslim Brotherhood, the ICCS is dominated by Jordanians with a Palestinian background with regard to both members and beneficiaries.[28] However, in our interviews and participant observations, this ethnic bias was never articulated. ICCS provides social welfare services, including health services, education, and job training, as well as financial and in-kind aid, to more than 100,000 people.[29] While activities of the community centers and health clinics are primarily directed at poor people, the hospitals, schools, and universities cater to a large degree to the middle classes. We were told that most of the Dar al-Ahram School's 3,500 students, for instance, come from wealthy families—their fathers are politicians, doctors, or business-men.[30] Likewise, the Islamic Hospital is certainly not the most expensive in Amman, but its fees are still far too high for people from the refugee camps. Thus, the ICCS seemingly addresses two different constituencies, the country's poor and the pious sections of Jordan's middle class, something that is also noted by Clark (2004). While different parts of the organization are clearly directed toward different target groups, there is a certain level of cooperation and interchange between them. For example, the Dar al-Ahram School offers 50 scholarships every year to the most gifted children related to the ICCS' community centers, all paid by the school's orphans fund. Moreover, students from the Islamic Community College go to the centers to volunteer, and medical students from the university do their internship at the hospital.

The ICCS is a good example of the internal organizational development of the Muslim Brotherhood. The ICCS was established in 1963 in order to functionally separate the Brotherhood's charitable activities from its more politically oriented ones (Clark 2004, 86).[31] Relations between the ICCS and the Muslim Brotherhood have remained close, in later years also including links to its party organization, the IAF. However, it is difficult for the observer to judge precisely in which ways these three organizations relate to each other and what kind of cooperation takes place between them. While high-profile members of the Muslim Brotherhood publicly acknowledge the connections, stating that the ICCS is formally part of the Brotherhood, ICCS representatives seem much more reluctant to do so. Most ICCS members we met either avoided the topic or denied that there was any connection. Only one of our informants spoke openly about it, bluntly stating that "in reality, the ICCS, the Muslim Brotherhood and the IAF have the same thoughts. (. . .) We have the same goals." Other interviewees acknowledged connections but did not want to talk in public about them. They often stated the secret nature of these relations: "They have a consultancy board consisting of people from the Islamic Action Front, the Muslim Brotherhood and the ICCS–it's hidden, but they make the decisions," we were once told. This attitude on the side of ICCS most likely reflects the tension between regime and Brotherhood and the fact that in 2006, the ICCS was put under control of a government appointed committee, due to accusations of corruption (cf. Clark 2012).

This reluctance among representatives of the ICCS to talk about their relationship with the Muslim Brotherhood clearly reflects the change in the regime's attitude toward the Islamic movement, now a target for harassment by the police and the secret service. During our fieldwork, we heard countless stories about people who had been interrogated or even arrested, whose telephones were tapped, or who had lost their jobs without any explanation. Thus, it is only understandable that most ICCS representatives would choose to downplay their relations with the Brotherhood, at least in public. Behind the scene, however, nothing seems to suggest that relations have weakened in recent years; in fact, they have probably strengthened. The two organizations share office buildings, several Muslim Brotherhood leaders and board members have filled positions in the ICCS and vice versa, and there is a great degree of overlap, if not complete similarity, in the two organizations' constituencies. As one ICCS representative put it: "Before, we used to be separate, every organization working on its own, but now it all goes together, it all goes according to the Islamic movement."

In general, the ICCS seems to enjoy strong support among Jordanians. Many consider it to be one of the most reliable and efficient providers of social welfare services in the country. The community centers reach poor people almost everywhere, strongly contributing to the image of the ICCS as an omnipresent and reliable organization.[32] At the same time, the Islamic Hospital and the prestigious schools are proof of the organization's professional qualities. With the majority of Jordanians being practicing Muslims, the ICCS' Islamic identity further enhances its popularity. As a Jordanian researcher noted in an interview:

> The fact that they are Islamic makes people think that they are good and nice. Even if you are not religious, you are programmed to think that they are good and nice. The label is important. It gives them acceptance and credibility— sometimes over-credibility.

Although skeptical of the links between the ICCS, the Islamic Action Front, and the Muslim Brotherhood, even non-Muslims and staunch secularists seem to acknowledge the quality of the ICCS' services and its position as one of Jordan's most influential social welfare organizations. Here, professionalism and the hegemonic role of Jordan's Islamic modern apparently go hand in hand.

Given its affiliation with the Muslim Brotherhood, the organizational rationale of ICCS is, not surprisingly, firmly anchored in a religious discourse. This means that the institution of *zakat* plays a central role. However, the interpretation of this Islamic principle visibly deviates from mere religious communication. Similar to the governmental Zakat Fund, ICCS does not solely view the payment of *zakat* as an individual means of collecting *thawab*, divine credits for the final Day of Judgment, but stresses its societal function. Yet, while the Zakat Fund aims at the stabilization of the political status quo, for ICCS *zakat* should be used to change society according to Islamist ideals of an Islamic order. Moreover, poverty is not fate but a result of societal deficiencies. In the words of one of our informants from ICCS, "If the proper Islamic approach was applied, there would be no poverty." This seems to be a general position among ICCS members who perceive *zakat* as an instrument of social change rather than a patronizing institution for giving alms to the poor. For them, *zakat* can and ought to be used to implement social reforms leading toward the ideal Islamic order. Consequently, ICCS members criticize the official social welfare institutions, the Zakat Fund, and the National Aid Fund, as inefficient and corrupt: "The people in government are not interested in serving the people; whatever they do, they do for their own benefit."

Many of ICCS' community centers display a relatively comprehensive developmental approach, based on concepts such as empowerment, sustainability, and rights. As a director of an ICCS community centre told us:

> In the beginning, the poor and the widows would just come here for money. We try to convince them to work, to change their lives. And I can see how they have changed. They have better morals, their aims in life have changed. The women now guide their children to education.

Like royal NGOs, the ICCS contrasts its own work with more charity-oriented approaches. Yet, while the royal organizations accuse the Islamic organizations of relying on these "outdated approaches," ICCS members point to the governmental Zakat Fund and its local committees as examples of traditional charity and hand-outs: "The role of the *zakat* committees as it is now is just to give money to the poor—they will buy food and eat it and that's it." This statement made by a representative of ICCS clearly shows that the organization competes with the Zakat Fund about the right Islamic approach to social welfare. In this case, the competition between the state and the Brotherhood about Jordan's organized Islamic modern becomes a competition about the right interpretation of *zakat*. In this competition, representatives of the ICCS clearly apply the distinction between tradition and modernity in a normative way, turning it into a measurement for "true Islam." In closely relating concepts such as "empowerment" and "sustainability" to an Islamic institution, ICCS grants them modern authenticity, following the tradition of the Islamic reform movement more generally. Portraying activities such as courses on women's rights, micro-finance projects, and job training in an Islamic idiom, the ICCS Islamizes the contemporary discourses on development and human rights, making them an authentic part of their vision of an Islamic modern. On our question about the specific Islamic nature of their activities, ICCS members laughed and answered: "Everything we do is Islamic. Islam is empowerment, Islam is participation, Islam is human rights."

From this holistic perspective, the work of ICCS is carried out within an Islamic framework, making references to Islamic traditions an integral part of both its self-identification and its external representation in Jordanian society. Narrating current tropes of developmental discourses in an Islamic vernacular, however, does not exclude differences to the liberal mainstream of these globalized discourses. With respect to women rights, for instance, many ICCS members would focus on equity rather than equality. Several times we were told that women and men are equal but not the same: "There are things that men do best and there are things that women do best. We should not try to be the same. God created us differently." In this way, ICCS acknowledges the beneficial nature of non-Islamic institutions and ideas, but does not advocate their uncritical adoption. "We benefit from the Western development approach—but we only take the good things," we were told by one of our informants. Many community centers have started to enter into cooperation projects with organizations such as Save the Children, UNICEF, or the royal Jordan River Foundation, blurring previously demarcated areas in Jordan's field of social welfare activities. However, this cooperative and inclusive trend has also met resistance from inside. Some ICCS members at the headquarters and at local centers articulate criticism of this cooperation with organizations "hostile" to Islamic values. For instance, headquarters turned down a proposal from one of the community centers to enter into cooperation with an American NGO on a project to provide services to Iraqi refugees in Jordan. Similarly, some people criticize activities such as women's rights education and empowerment training as essentially un-Islamic attempts to please the West, seeking to counter this intrusion of characteristic elements of second modernity into the Brotherhood's established discourse of an organized first modernity by more rigid interpretations in juxtaposing Islamic modernity with the West.

This battle about Jordan's Islamic modern, however, is not only fought out from within. In 2005, the Jordanian regime put pressure on UNICEF to end its cooperation with ICCS, accusing the organization of being corrupt and undemocratic. Through its cooperation with UNICEF, ICCS got access to international funding opportunities as well as to important new professional relationships and international networks, strengthening the organization and at least indirectly also the Muslim Brotherhood in their struggle with the regime about the very nature of Jordan's social and political order. Furthermore, the fact that ICCS was working together with UNICEF made it more difficult for the state to maintain its system of surveillance and control imposed on Islamic organizations. In this perspective, the regime arguably felt compelled to do what it took to end the cooperation, seeking to weaken the position of the ICCS and the Brotherhood. Although deeply anchored in religious discourse, in its action, ICCS' religious rationale seems to be a hostage of the Brotherhood's political aims. Pursuing social welfare activities in order to change society and the existing political institutions of the country, the organization definitely followed the logics of the modern political system. In the context of the Muslim Brotherhood's political aim to get influence on collectively binding decision making, the religious communication of ICCS seems to be also increasingly dominated by politics.

ANWAR AL-HUDA ISLAMIC SOCIETY: AN INDEPENDENT ORGANIZATION

While the previously described organizations are all affiliated with political institutions relating to either the state or the Muslim Brotherhood, there are a number of organizations whose roots are more tangled and whose affiliations are less discernible with respect to Jordan's internal power structures. Some of them might prefer the regime over the Muslim Brotherhood, others might not. Some might pay their *zakat* to the Zakat Fund, others to ICCS and yet others to none of them. In numbers, these independent organizations make up a relatively large part of Jordanian charities and social welfare organizations. However, the fact that the independent organizations are per definition not part of a larger network often means that they are small, with no or only a few paid employees and with weak financial means. Some have their headquarters in the basement underneath a mosque, others rent a small room in an office building, and yet others use their own homes. They depend on the support of their friends, families, colleagues, and other people in the local community. Often they do not have regular financial contributions, meaning that their help to the poor might have a random and unstable character. The typical activities of such small, independent organizations include minor financial and in-kind assistance, training courses for women on topics such as flower decorations, kitchen hygiene, or marriage preparations, the celebration of religious events such as the *iftar* during Ramadan, and support to orphans. Their general aim is to offer immediate relief for the needy rather than long-term activities such as education and economic empowerment.

The AHIS is one of these independent organizations. AHIS is a women's organization, established in 1982 by 15 women of a mixed ethnic background, most of them retired school teachers. The organization is located in Wadi Sir, a wealthy area on the outskirts of Amman. At the time of our visit, it was run by nine elderly housewives, all working as volunteers. They had established a bakery and employed six poor women to work in their kitchen, producing healthy food to be sold to wealthy families in the neighborhood. Together with donations, the money earned from the bakery was used to pay the salaries to the women who worked in the kitchen, as well as to provide a number of poor families with financial and in-kind assistance on a more regular basis. Apart from this, the organization offered courses in cooking, computer skills, and other topics of interest to the, primarily wealthy, women in the area. Like most other small, independent organizations, AHIS predominantly caters for Muslim beneficiaries, although they claim that they are in principle open to non-Muslims. However, as one woman said: "There are no Christians in our neighborhood."

Through its local activities for women, the organization has established a strong base of support in the local community, achieving a steady level of donations. "People know about our work. They trust us—that's why they give us money," the director of the organization confidently told us. AHIS does not receive any support from the ministry of social development, nor from any international organization. As in many other Islamic organizations, members of AHIS feel restrained by the fact that cooperation with other organizations has to be approved by the ministry of social development, and they therefore prefer to focus on local donors rather than going through the difficulty of getting such approval. The organization nurtures an explicitly nonpolitical image, denouncing any connections to the Muslim Brotherhood. When asked about their relations to other Islamic organizations, including the ICCS, the director of AHIS replied, "They are different from us," dismissing any further questions on the nature of these differences. Likewise, other members expressed a carefully balanced position when asked about AHIS' relations with the regime, pointing to the frustrations of bureaucratic regulations while simultaneously adding those benefits in preventing fraud.

This detachment from politics is deeply rooted in AHIS' organizational rationale, which the director explained to us as follows: "We think that this job pleases Allah. You have to do something for your next life. You have to do good things. This is the first motivation [for establishing this organization]." According to her and her fellow volunteers, doing good things such as helping poor women to find a job and paying *zakat* pleases Allah and contributes to ensuring one's place in paradise. As noted above, this understanding of good deeds is firmly embedded in Islamic traditions. The members of AHIS perceive their engagement within the religious coordinates of *thawab* and *ithim*. On the Day of Judgment, God will make an account of one's deeds. With a plus on the side of *thawab*, you will go to heaven, but if you collect more *ithim*, you go to hell.

This understanding of charity work as an individual religious duty, carried out with the purpose of ensuring one's place in paradise and the purification of one's wealth, is widespread among independent organizations. However, the language of religious awards and duties also applies to the Zakat Fund and to organizations associated with the Muslim Brotherhood movement. Apparently, the Islamic discourses of all three kinds of organizations draw on similar forms of religious communication as defined by Weber, addressing issues of inner- and outer-worldly salvation by referring to a transcendental actor. These forms of communication may define the organizations as Islamic, at least in contradistinction to an NGO like JOHUD. Yet in our interviews, most of the independent organizations applied Islamic discourse with a strong emphasis on personal piety and individual religious morality, seemingly distinguishing themselves from the collective social and political demands by the Muslim Brotherhood. They are driven by a wish to help the poor in the name of God and do not aim to establish a just social order through collective social action or by consciously maintaining the status quo. Social change, in their view, comes through individual improvement and not through collective political action. Through "a positive moral approach," encouraging people to perform good deeds and reminding them of the rewards awaiting them, one might contribute to a changing society, a former director of Anwar al-Huda said in an interview with Egbert Harmsen.[33]

In principle, it is the religious duty of every believer to give alms, and organizations such as AHIS do not link the concept of *zakat* to any authoritative and organized mechanism for the collection and distribution of alms. In fact, some might even argue that the individual solution is better, insofar as it avoids tedious organizational procedures and administration. But as long as not everybody pays *zakat*, there is a need for religiously inspired organizations such as Anwar al Huda. In short, the organizational rationale of these independent associations is firmly rooted in religious communication and religious social action as defined by Weber. At least in their official representations, they address donors and beneficiaries through charity issues of inner- and outer-worldly salvation with reference to transcendental actors. The fact that they hold on to a traditionalist and nonpolitical kind of social welfare, emphasizing piety and individual religious morality over social change and downplaying the potential of collective action, makes them the favorite grass-roots organizations of the regime and the royal family who arguably consider them harmless promoters of a locally anchored social Islam that does not threaten the legitimacy of the regime and the political order at large. Thus, Queen Rania has visited AHIS several times, commending the organization on its work with women in the community.[34] Similarly, governmental representatives have only good things to say about these organizations.

CONCLUSIONS

Our analysis of four different welfare organizations in Jordan reflects the heterogeneous nature of Jordanian society. Applying our conceptual tools, we can discern elements of first and second modernity, as well as features of all three types of modern subject formation behind this heterogeneity. In terms of the concepts of successive modernities, JOHUD fits most closely to the model of second modernity, while the other governmental institution, the Zakat Fund, seems to be a typical representative of first modernity. Apparently, these two organizations are an institutional expression of the inbuilt contradiction with regard to the regime's employment of Islamic traditions. While it represents Islam to an international audience as a religious source of individual morality and private piety, it has used the religious field domestically as a source in legitimizing authoritarian rule. ICCS displays an increasing hybridity in which elements of second modernity challenge its more general and still dominant vision of an organized Islamic modern from within. Thus, while the regime seems to handle this general cultural conflict between first and second modernity through two types of organization with different rationales, the ICCS and the Muslim Brotherhood experiences it as an internal conflict. On closer inspection, all four organizations reveal themselves to be relatively hybrid social forms that only the observer can frame in accordance with analytically defined ideal types. However, we can also observe some more fundamental patterns that serve as central references in this complex mesh of discourses and practices.

First of all, in the context of Islam as a key symbolic resource for Jordan's modern state and nation building processes, Islamic traditions are almost indispensible reference points for all four institutions. This applies especially with respect to communication with donors and beneficiaries. Thus, perhaps with the exception of AHIS, a certain instrumental approach to religious language is discernible in all organizations, although to different degrees. Religious communication is not necessarily dominant in organizational rationales, but it serves as the primary vernacular of social welfare activities in the Jordanian public at large. Secondly, conducting social welfare activities is a means of shaping collective identities with respect to religion and based on a dichotomy between charity and development. This dichotomy, easily translated into the classical sociological distinction between tradition and modernity, structures the field in a normative way. At least three out of four organizations advocate their modern-cum-advanced status, expressed in the developmental character of their work. Thirdly, although formally independent from the state, the organizational rationales of all four organizations show clear traces of the authoritarian political power structure of Jordan. Their status is not guaranteed by the rule of law but in direct reference to state institutions and the internal power struggle between the regime and the Muslim Brotherhood. Consequently, there is a tendency for the language of politics to colonize religious communication. To what extent then are we dealing with "religious organizations" according to our definition of modern religion?

The first type of organization, epitomized by the royal NGO JOHUD, certainly does not present itself as a religious organization at all. Basing its organizational rationale on global discourses of human rights and development, JOHUD most closely represents an issue-oriented civil society organization, although as a royal institution it is dependent on the royal family. As such, membership results from an engagement with respect to specific issues and is not based on religious motivation. From the perspective of JOHUD's organizational rationale, religion is a private matter that might play a role in the motivation of its members but that is not a membership requisite as such. JOHUD is definitely not an Islamic organization. When applying religious language, JOHUD does so in a mere instrumental way in order to facilitate communication with donors and beneficiaries it would otherwise have difficulties reaching. In JOHUD's communication, religion links humanist values to Islamic traditions adjusting them to its basically "secular" rationale. However, this does not mean that JOHUD does not take part in the struggle about the very nature of Jordan's Islamic modern. The organization's approach to Islam closely reflects the external discourse of the royal family, portraying Islam as a modern religion and focusing on individual values and morality, as a form of religion often described as "moderate Islam."

As a domestic instrument for the religious policies of the regime, the Zakat Fund has made Islamic traditions a core reference of its organizational rational. The Zakat Fund emphasizes the public relevance of Islam in the provision of social welfare, shaping the rationales, strategies, and target groups of the institution. In so doing, the Fund, at least to a certain extent, combines the regime's external and internal discourses on Islam. While its emphasis on the dialogical nature of Islam resembles the royal family's external representation, internally religion plays the role of granting legitimacy to existing state institutions and therewith to stabilizing the structures of Jordan's organized Islamic modernity. According to this perspective, Islamic social welfare is not only a way for the individual to fulfill his or her religious obligations, but it is also a tool for generating political loyalty and moderating social conflict. In short, the Zakat Fund plays a key role in the state's religious technologies of domination. Therefore, the religious communication of the Zakat Fund is not directed toward transcendent actors but addresses utterly inner-worldly forces. As an integral part of the state apparatus, the organizational rationale of the Fund appears to be primarily political and its task is to help maintain the existing power structures of the country.

Being a part of the organizational structure of the Muslim Brotherhood, ICCS seems to be the nonstate twin of the Zakat Fund. This position is also expressed by the mutual competition and relative hostility between these two organizations, both driven by a desire to shape an Islamic version of an organized modern society. Viewed independently, the ICCS might build on a religious rationale. Indeed, Islamic traditions play an eminent role in its self-representation, societal strategies, and with regard to its target groups. Relating to global developmental discourses, the ICCS also incorporates a number of elements linked to second modernity, making them parts of its Islamic discourse and practice. Similar to the Islamic reform movement in the nineteenth century, the organization seeks to Islamize them as tools in striving for social change. However, as part of the Muslim Brotherhood movement, its blueprint of an Islamic society is mainly oriented toward an organized form of modernity in which the ideal Muslim subject is constructed according to a generalized model of an average type of peer. While the ICCS might have been founded on religious grounds, the political struggle of the Muslim Brotherhood in general has superimposed a stronger political rationale on its activities. Nonetheless, to a certain extent, this imposition seems to be not as strong as we can observe it in the Zakat Fund. In comparison to this state agency, the ICCS shows more internal competition. This internal conflict about appropriate Islamic approaches to social welfare can be interpreted as being due to discursive interlacements with both competing religious and political logics. Moreover, the internal strife in the Muslim Brotherhood seems to be characterized by the fact that the organized model of an Islamic first modernity of the conservative wing has been challenged by reformist forces orienting themselves toward elements of second modernity.

Finally there are independent Islamic organizations such as the AHIS. In this type, the rationale is clearly religiously defined. According to AHIS, involvement in social welfare is a religious duty. By carrying out activities of social welfare, one pleases God, collects points for one's afterlife, and purifies one's wealth. Likewise, Islam shapes the strategies and the target groups of the organizations, outlining the guidelines for how and whom to help. In Weberian terms, the organization clearly follows the model of religious social action. As such, this kind of Islamic charity stays within the boundaries of the religious social sphere, as demarcated by governmental laws and regulations, which reflect the principles of functional differentiation in modern society. Yet it would be wrong to see in them remnants of traditional social forms alone. On the one hand, AHIS apparently respects most closely of all organizations the separated domains of modern society. At organizational level, it does not claim Islam to have a holistic nature but interprets Islamic traditions according to the model of a modern religion relating to the transcendent realm. In this sense, AHIS proves that there is nothing traditional per se in restricting an organization to religious communication alone.

On the other hand, independent organizations with a religious rationale might also be open to new forms of action going beyond the merely charity-oriented model. An example is Khawla bint al-Azwar, a small, independent organization working with prostitutes in an industrial town outside of Amman. The organization was established by a group of women who met in a mosque where they participated in weekly religious lessons. Their teacher, an enthusiastic older woman, encouraged them to fulfill their religious obligations by helping other women in need rather than just sitting and praying. Starting out from a pious desire to fulfill general religious obligations, the organization has developed in a direction that no longer reflects traditionalist attitudes. In its core a religious organization, Khawla bint al-Azwar resembles royal organizations in their focus on empowerment. Offering vocational training and health information to approximately 20 women, Khawla bint al-Azwar seeks to empower them to take responsibility for their own lives. The director told us that she is often asked why she does not just focus on getting these girls married. With a determined expression she replied: "No, I want these women to be able to take care of themselves." Demonstrating the success of the organization, a former prostitute who was at the time of our fieldwork working as a voluntary health advisor in Khawla bint al-Azwar told us, "Before I came here, I was lost. I didn't know what I was capable of. Here, I learned about my rights, I learnt what I was capable of, and I learned to stand up for myself." Thus, apparently religious rationales and modern empowerment concepts are not mutually exclusive. On the contrary, the statement of our informant points to the fact that she was able to acquire modern technologies of the self while being engaged in an Islamic charity. The next chapter will look more closely at the individual level and the ways in which our interlocutors use these welfare organizations as social sites to construct meaningful forms of modern Muslim selfhoods.

CHAPTER 6

Charity and the Construction of Modern Muslim Subjectivities in Jordan

The activists, volunteers, and employees we met in Jordanian charities and social welfare organizations make up a very diverse group of people. Some organizations are run entirely by volunteers, others by paid staff, and yet others by a mixture of volunteers and staff. In a few organizations, the members are young, while in most, they are older. Some come from the lower middle class, a few may even have experienced poverty themselves, and others have very wealthy backgrounds. Most of our interlocutors had a formal education, whether as electricians or doctors. A number of them had studied at expensive universities abroad, but most had received their qualifications from local schools and universities. The majority of social welfare activists in Jordan are men, in particular at the management level, but there is an increasing number of female activists especially in the royal NGOs. In the following chapter, we treat our four social welfare organizations as institutional sites for individual processes of modern subjectivity formation, asking the question of how employees and volunteers construct specific forms of meaningful selfhoods as modern Muslims through their engagement in Islamic charities and social welfare organizations in Jordan.

In order to answer this question, we observe the everyday practices of our informants from the theoretical perspective as working subjects who apply certain technologies of the self in constructing modern Muslim subjectivities. We put specific emphasis on the role that references to Islamic traditions play in this process. In doing so, we conceptualize religion in modern terms as a functionally differentiated social system whose self-referential communication is based on a code of blessed/cursed. Religion serves as a moral and cognitive order of knowledge providing not only practices as technologies of the self but also normative guidance for religious social action. However, at individual level, religious discourses and practices are not independent sources for shaping modern selves. On the contrary, religious knowledge is woven into other orders of knowledge and subject to constant reinterpretations. These interpretations are closely linked to more general orientations that evolve from the organizing power of the successive models of modernity to which individuals refer. We will characterize this reference by modeling three different types: the postmodern professional and volunteer who frames individual selfhood with strong references to pluralist elements of second modernity; the peer-group-oriented religiously devoted staff member guided by ideas of a form of first modernity based on Islamic principles; and the piously committed citizen who resembles more the classical bourgeois subject.

These three types are, of course, highly aggregated ideal types and none of our interlocutors corresponded to them entirely. Identity constructions remain idiosyncratic and ideal types simply represent abstract heuristic instruments to make sense of these idiosyncrasies. Consequently, subordinating our observations under these types is an exercise in finding approximations and deviations, not congruence. Moreover, our analysis only builds on small fractures of reality, focusing on a very limited field of work. Given the enormous problems of the labor market in Jordan, it makes sense to treat both employees and volunteers of welfare organizations as working subjects. Unemployment rates are very high; according to official statistics, about 15 percent of the labor force is without a job, while unofficial numbers range around 30 percent. Among young people in their early twenties unemployment numbers reach a staggering 41 percent (Guégnard et al. 2005).[1] In this perspective, our four welfare organizations seem to be good sites for examining the ways in which Jordanians build successful forms of modern selfhoods through work, whether voluntary or paid. However, they have clear limitations. They are very specific working places, attracting a certain kind of people and as such they are clearly not representative of Jordanian society at large. Moreover, working places are just one of many fields shaping modern subjectivities. For example, we largely exclude the important field of private and intimate relationships, including it only in discussions of the networks and friendships that have been built up in the organizations. In addition, we could only observe technologies of the self directly linked to this particular field of work defined by Islamic charity and social welfare. In other words, what we present is merely a picture of a very small segment of contemporary modern Muslim subjectivity formation in Jordan.

In asking questions as to the ways in which religious convictions play part in making modern Muslim subjects, we also marginalize a host of other motivations with respect to individual engagement in social welfare activities. This becomes particularly clear when looking at the reasons given by staff members of ICCS. Despite the overarching religious rationale of the organization, our informants told us about a multiplicity of different motivational factors behind their engagement in social welfare. For a few of them, for example, their work was—not surprisingly—simply a way to earn money:

> I applied for a job in the ministry of education, but my husband thought it was too far away. This here is closer to my home. I heard about the place from friends, I applied and I passed the test. It doesn't matter to me whether it is an Islamic place or not, I just wanted to work.

While this social worker from ICCS spoke frankly about her instrumental reasoning, many staff members and in particular volunteers might be motivated to engage in social welfare activities by a mixture of instrumental and ideational factors, such as a wish to contribute to the relief of suffering and poverty, to achieve personal redemption and salvation or economic gain, to find friendships, or to gain political power and social status (cf. Bonner, Ener, and Singer 2003, 2). In addition, Islamic organizations must also be understood as important providers of social networks. Here religious frames serve as a means of getting access to relevant resources, of connecting people, and of facilitating the exchange of favors and services.[2] Many of our interviewees among the ICCS staff got into the organization through a neighbor or relative who was part of the Islamic movement. Once working for ICCS, they became part of a larger network through which they could get access to business partners and new employers, as well as new friendships and even marriage opportunities (see also Clark 2004, 106; Wickham 2004, 234). Here, religion works as a facilitator rather than a motivator. In short, when zooming into the individual level, even the relatively narrow field of Islamic social welfare organizations becomes an enormously complex and blurred social arena. At this level, we can only make sense of individual subjectivities through a theoretically informed, but nevertheless very reductionist approach.

In distinguishing between paid and unpaid work, we organize our observations with the help of four types of individuals engaged in social welfare in Jordan. Among employees we find the development professional and the religiously devoted staff member, reminding us again of the two types of second and first modernity, respectively. The development professional is typically found at JOHUD. She (because it is often a woman) is from the upper middle class, well-educated, and might have studied abroad. She was employed because of her professional qualities and skills, not because of her religious or political conviction. The religiously devoted staff members are found at the ICCS and partly at the Zakat Fund. They usually come from the middle class or lower middle class, hold a college degree or perhaps even a university degree, but from a public university in Jordan, rarely from abroad. They might also have an education in Islamic sciences or some other form of religious training. Their employment is not only predicated on professional skills, but just as much—and perhaps even more—on their appearance as dedicated Muslims and/or supporters of the Muslim Brotherhood ideology in the case of ICCS.

Similarly, we might detect two different kinds of volunteers in the organizations of our sample: the young activist and the committed citizen. The young activist most closely displays ideals of the postmodern self and is primarily found at JOHUD. However, there are signs that they have also made inroads to ICCS, where some managers seem eager to recruit this type of volunteer. The young activists come from the upper middle class, they are university students or recent graduates, and many of them have traveled and studied abroad. Even as volunteers, they have been employed through relatively formal procedures, focusing on their professional skills, and they work with projects or activities that match their professional backgrounds. The other type of volunteer, the committed citizen, is found in independent organizations such as AHIS, in the local *zakat* committees of the Zakat Fund and in local branches of the ICCS. As such, this type covers a broad range of volunteers, including both seasonal and regular volunteers, volunteers with different educational backgrounds, and volunteers from different economic classes. Likewise, these volunteers might relate to elements of all three forms of successive modernities, without showing a clear affinity to one particular model. The committed citizens used to be older people who had retired or housewives with grown-up children, but there is also a growing number of younger activists who fall under this rubric. They have not been employed as volunteers through formal procedures, but heard about the organization through friends or family, and their work as volunteers does not necessarily have anything to do with their professional qualities.

JOHUD: Royal Organizations and Postmodern Muslims

At the time of our fieldwork, JOHUD employed about 450 professionals and more than 4,000 volunteers. The majority worked in local community development centers, spread all over the country, while some worked in the Queen Zein al-Sharaf Institute for Development (ZENID), in the Small Business Development Center or in Princess Basma Youth Resource Center (PBYRC), all located in the headquarters in Amman where we visited the organization. The offices were spacious and light and some were colorfully painted—one was green and another blue. The walls were all adorned with human rights posters and children's drawings. A group of women with tight white headscarves and trendy clothes had gathered in the tea kitchen and a young man walked by, saying something that made them all laugh. A girl in jeans ran by with a concentrated look on her face, carrying a pile of papers and crayons. A man and a woman sat on the couch in a corner, discussing the afternoon's activities with the children in the Intel Computer House.

The majority of people working at JOHUD, both volunteers and employees, are young and resourceful people with a (upper) middle class background. Almost all have a university degree, many from a foreign university. In their studies, JOHUD's members represent a variety of disciplines, including law, business, economics, development studies, and general social sciences. Not many have any particular knowledge of Islamic sciences. According to a recent study of women in Jordanian advocacy NGOs, including five royal organizations,[3] education levels are higher in these organizations than in others. About 85 percent have a BA degree, and 31 percent an MA degree, while only five percent have no other education than high school. Almost 40 percent of those with a degree have studied abroad, primarily in Europe and the United States (Clark and Michuki 2009, 334).

Application procedures at JOHUD reflect this strong focus on professionalism, higher education, and internationalism. Job announcements, always posted in English, underline the importance of relevant skills, experience, and capacities in development, project management, and capacity-building, and in the same way the organization's website repeatedly underlines the strong "technical skills," "human resource capacities," and "in-house expertise" of its staff. Thus, JOHUD's official employment discourse contains all the relevant buzzwords related to the social imaginary of the creative, dynamic, and self-reliant worker, characteristic of the postmodern type of modern selfhood. Even potential volunteers and interns have to live up to these standards and must apply formally for a position. Once accepted as volunteers, the successful applicants undergo training at ZENID. Here, they participate in courses such as "Management and Leadership Skills," "Training of Trainers," and "Community Development," learning different techniques to use in their work, including learner-led presentations, simulation games, field visits, role-play, and teamwork.[4] Such application procedures clearly demonstrate that the organization attracts and wants to attract people who are well educated, internationally oriented, and experts in the field of development. At least formally, JOHUD hires staff because of their professional skills—not because they know somebody or because of their religious or political leanings.

Another characteristic of members at JOHUD has to do with gender. Walking through the organization's premises, we saw many women. We asked one of our interviewees—a woman—and were told that among regular staff the majority is female. However, unlike many other organizations, women were found not only at the level of regular employees. At JOHUD, many midlevel and top managers were female, including, for instance, the directors of ZENID and of JOHUD's external relations department. This reflects trends in other royal organizations—at the time of our visit, the general director of the Jordan River Foundation was a woman, as was the director of the Young Muslim Women's Association.[5] The aforementioned survey of women in advocacy NGOs confirms this observation, revealing that 15 out of 19 advocacy NGOs have more female than male staff members (Clark and Michuki 2009, 335). This predominance of women distinguishes royal NGOs from other Jordanian organizations, Islamic as well as non-Islamic, which are generally male dominated. We can only speculate about the reasons for this difference. One possible explanation is that the predominance of female staff in royal NGOs is a result of conscious gender policies of the organizational management and boards. Furthermore, the royal chair persons of JOHUD, Jordan River Foundation, YMWA, and Tkiyet um Ali are all women (Princess Basma, Queen Rania, Princess Sarvath, and Princess Haya, respectively). This royal female leadership might send positive signals, encouraging women to apply to royal NGOs rather than to other organizations. Finally, general issues of gender discrimination in the private sector may also play a part. It is easier for educated women to get a job in an NGO focusing on women's rights than in a private business where she has to compete against men in a traditionally male-dominated environment (Clark and Michuki 2009, 337).

The majority of the members of JOHUD and other royal organizations are relatively young, most of them in their twenties. This is particularly true in relation to the volunteers, another aspect that distinguishes the royal organizations from most other Jordanian organizations. In many organizations, volunteers are older, often elderly women who have retired from their work. For them, volunteering is not some sort of training for a job. However, the volunteers at JOHUD are of a different kind—they are young and resourceful university graduates. This type of volunteer seems to be a relatively new species in a Middle Eastern context. In Jordan, they are primarily found not only in the royal organizations and other advocacy groups concerned with issues such as human rights but also in some new Islamic organizations such as Sunaa al-Hayah ("Life Makers"), a newly established youth organization, inspired by Amr Khaled's movement of social entrepreneurs, and its offspring, an organization like Zedny.[6] Like JOHUD, they attract young, well-educated people, many of whom have worked or studied abroad. Here, the oldest participant is 35, and people proudly told us anecdotes about how government officials in the NGO registration office thought they had put down the wrong age in their application. "Young people just don't do this kind of work," one informant told us. In Jordan, this phenomenon was in its inception and numbers were still relatively low, whereas in Egypt, some of the new Islamic youth organizations already counted several thousand volunteers. In 2007, Sunaa al-Hayah in Jordan had approximately 100 members, but it has grown rapidly since then.

In sum, JOHUD gives us the impression of being an organization that fits into the institutional setting of second modernity. It combines relative institutional autonomy with issue-oriented professionalism and an international outlook. The members of JOHUD are well-educated young people, many of them women, who have been employed on the basis of their professional skills and competencies. With its organizational rationale firmly anchored in global discourses on development and human rights, JOHUD attracts employees and volunteers whose education reflects the organization's self-representation and who want to further their professional careers. This constituency, whether religiously minded or not, largely displays the characteristics of postmodern forms of subjectivity with their preferences for creative, nonbureaucratic styles of work. Apparently these forms of subjectivity mirror a certain social class background, as staff and volunteers at JOHUD primarily come from the (upper) middle classes. We now will look more closely at the ways in which these people construct their subjectivities within JOHUD and in relation to their religious attitudes.

During our fieldwork, we met with Mariana and Hala, two young women in their late twenties. Mariana wore jeans and a t-shirt, and Hala a more formal suit. Neither of them wore a headscarf. They were working in management positions in royal organizations, Mariana at JOHUD and Hala at the Jordan River Foundation. They were very well educated and spoke perfect English. Hala had lived in Canada and held an MBA from a prestigious Canadian university. They had probably traveled a lot and their current jobs took them to conferences and workshops all over the globe. As such, they represented two typical development professionals. Apart from a belief in humanitarian ideals, their choice to work in social welfare was a professional decision, motivated by the desire to have a challenging and satisfying career in a creative working environment. As Ateka, another young development professional working at JOHUD, told us: "Working at JOHUD was a chance for me to get an exciting job. This is not routine work as in many other places." Thus, the typical development professional is motivated by career aspirations and the possibility of contributing to the goals of the organization in which they work in an individualized and creative way (cf. Clark and Michuki 2009, 337).

When talking about their motivations for volunteering at JOHUD, many young activists echoed the development professionals, emphasizing aspects such as professional experience and individual responsibilities, seeing their voluntary work as a way to strengthen their CV and prepare themselves for the job market. Nancy and Diana, two young Christian women, are good examples of this. Like most other young activists at JOHUD, they were both from the upper middle class, had university degrees, and spoke English very well. Nancy had lived in Florida for several years, where she studied music. Diana was a mechanical engineer. They both started working as volunteers immediately after graduating from university as a way of getting work experience. Nancy had taught the children in the Intel Computer House to make small films, while Diana had spent most of her time in the robotics workshop, teaching children about mechanics. Diana now had a full-time job, but she continued to volunteer one day a week. Nancy had not yet managed to find a full-time job as a music teacher, so she gave private piano lessons and volunteered full time at JOHUD. In her view, working as a volunteer was a way of building experience and strengthening her competences while searching for a real job:

> I get more professional experience working here. It's good for your CV, better than having two years where you didn't do anything. When I was in the USA, I got used to doing something all the time, I can't just sit at home and do nothing, just waste time.

As a volunteer, she not only learned how to deal with children, but also enhanced her knowledge of digital technologies, becoming an experienced user of Flash, PhotoShop, and other computer programs. This understanding of volunteer work as a way of preparing oneself for the job market was common among people at JOHUD. As Hanin, a former volunteer-turned paid staff member, said, "They [JOHUD] asked for volunteers to teach elderly people about computers. I was studying computer science, so it was a perfect way for me to start my career." Volunteers also mentioned the wish to contribute to community development by helping people and giving them a chance: "When I was younger, nobody helped me think about my future, develop dreams and make my own decisions. I love to give young people that possibility. You can see the appreciation in their eyes," a male volunteer said.[7] Young activists often perceived members of the royal family somehow as idols or role models who had helped them on their way, and many talked enthusiastically about Queen Rania and Princess Basma, seeing them as strong and modern women and praising their engagement in the organization.

Among the young activists and development professionals we met from the royal organizations, many did not consider religion to be a relevant factor in their motivation. Instead, they focused on more general values such as development, human rights, and humanitarian aid, as well as on instrumental gains through professional challenges and experiences. However, as a pluralist organization, JOHUD also has staff members for whom Islam plays an important role in their self-representation and identification as modern working subjects. Like most Muslims, they emphasize the duty to help the poor as a basic Islamic principle. But while they may agree on some of the fundamentals in Islamic traditions, their religious worldviews are in many respects very different from the kind of Islam we find in the Muslim Brotherhood and the ICCS. The religiously minded young volunteers and professionals at JOHUD tended to focus on individual values and morality rather than on the publicly observable application of rules and obligatory practices. Similar to their working attitudes, we could observe an individualistic fashioning of their religiosity. In this perspective, being a good Muslim does not necessarily mean praying or dressing the right way, but thinking, acting, and working as a morally sovereign Muslim subject; for this, a social welfare organization provides you with an ideal working environment.

A paradigmatic example of this postmodern view on being a Muslim is Hanin, the volunteer-turned staff member mentioned above. Hanin, a tall and confident woman in her mid-twenties, wore a long turquoise dress and a matching headscarf.

> I don't know how many people here are practicing Muslims. I can't judge. Wearing *hijab* or praying is not necessarily the same as being a practicing Muslim. Religion is a personal issue, it's between you and your God. No one is allowed to judge, even the Koran says that. Someone with a *hijab* can be a terrible person and someone without a *hijab* can be the best person.

Hanin had a degree in computer science, and could have gotten a job in a private company but preferred to work as a community trainer at JOHUD. Not only was this job highly interesting and challenging, but also it also gave her an opportunity to fulfill her Islamic obligations. In our conversation, Hanin explained to us her Islamic approach to social welfare activities:

> To be honest, for the first two or maybe one year, I didn't really know what the Princess Basma Youth Resource Center was about, I didn't understand all these big words—human development, sustainability, how to reach people, all that. I worked in many different projects, and maybe after one year, I suddenly realized that human development actually matches my own goals and ideas. I don't know how to explain this to you—but we Muslims believe that Allah has

said to us that we were created to pray, to get people into Islam and to improve
things, to make things better. This is the mission of every Muslim. But that is
also the mission of human development. It's about creating better lives, better
opportunities for people.

Hanin interpreted her work within an Islamic framework, seeing the human
development approach of JOHUD as consistent with Islamic values. In this,
she applied translation strategies similar to those of the Islamic reform movement more than 100 years ago. Yet in contrast to the nineteenth-century
movement, she did so in a very individualized way. Hanin was, in other
words, self-fashioning the Islamic character of her work. For her, it did not
matter whether she was employed by an explicitly Islamic organization or
not: "I haven't thought about working in an Islamic organization. It doesn't
matter to me." It is not the peer-group-oriented approach of being part of a
collectively defined Islamic working place, but her individual religious interpretation of her work that makes her a successively religious modern subject.
Consequently, she told us, "Even though JOHUD is not an Islamic organization, and we don't go to the people and tell them about Islam, the work
is still Islamic." Thus, the important thing is not whether you work in an
Islamic organization, but whether the work you do is Islamic. In fact, according to Hanin, it is better that the organization is not explicitly Islamic. In
her eyes, the existence of both Islamic and non-Islamic organizations in society contributed to diversity, variety, and pluralism, which was an important
ideal in her vision of true Islam. Without a doubt, Hanin interpreted Islamic
traditions in close reference to social imaginaries more generally associated
with second modernity. In the same vein, she appreciated the fact that people
working at JOHUD were from different religious backgrounds: "People that
work here are a mixture. There are Christians, Muslims, Muslims that don't
act like Muslims, all kinds of people. I think that diversity is what makes this
place great." Furthermore, Hanin perceived the non-Islamic character of the
organization a benefit rather than a disadvantage for her work: "For example
in the village of Fayhez, there are no Muslims, only Christians, and we are
able to deal with them, we include them. If we were an Islamic organization,
they wouldn't have accepted us."

The kind of Islam that Hanin and other young activists formulate is an
individualistic interpretation of Islamic traditions that focuses on internal
values and principles rather than on externalized rules and rituals. For these
young people, Islamization of society is not about reforming the political
system, introducing a *sharia*-based rule, but about promoting Islamic values
of diversity, justice, and social welfare. They are pious Muslims who reject
the state-centered model of an organized Islamic modern with its preference
for the collectively regulated coordination of social action. Instead, their
ideal religious community emanates from individual forms of pious behavior.
Considering the background of these young people, this may come as no
surprise. Many of them come from homes where Islamic traditions were not
practiced in a very active way. In comparison to many Jordanians, their own

religiosity has been a matter of personal choice, rather than something that was handed down by their parents. As Halima, a volunteer at Sunaa al-Hayah explained, "Many volunteers have become religious even though their parents were not particularly religious. My own childhood, it wasn't true religion. It was more about don't do this, don't do that, they never explained to me why. So I didn't know it very well. But when I got married, I started to read." Often our informants couched religious motivation in a very emotional language: "When I help others, I feel I can fly," a young woman told us, looking like a loved-up teenager. Another woman said: "Everyone should do charity—not just because of religion but because you help others and because it makes you feel good."

Emphasizing emotions and personal choice, this postmodern type of an Islamic subjectivity refutes the model of a rigid social order based on a binding Islamic system. As at JOHUD and the Jordan River Foundation, the volunteers at Sunaa al-Hayah are well-educated young people from the middle class, all university graduates or students. Before becoming members of JOHUD, Hanin and Mariana both volunteered at Sunaa al-Hayah, which provided them with free training in developmental issues. Underlining an understanding of Islam as something other than prayer and rituals, another volunteer told us that social welfare work is a way of expressing Islamic dedication: "Other people think that if you become a Muslim that cares for her religion, you are supposed to stay in the mosque, stay in your house and pray all the time, but that's not the aim of Islam." The young activists at Sunaa al-Hayah also shared JOHUD volunteers' views on diversity and pluralism:

> We have Christians here. How can we deal with Christians? We don't talk about these things together. We say we are brothers and sisters in humanity. We accept people as they are. We don't say, no you are not a Lifemaker, go away. Many of our volunteers do not wear a scarf, we are not judgmental. We don't ask where people are from.

This acceptance of diversity both within and among religions was something that the development professional and young activists at JOHUD constantly underlined. Mariana, for instance, compared young religious activists to the Muslim Brotherhood as follows: "People at Sunaa al Hayah are very different from the Muslim Brotherhood, they are very modern, they work in mixed groups, they respect diversity—for instance, I don't wear the *hijab* and they respect that." Apparently these religious activists combine their Islamic identities with the acceptance of the explicitly humanist position in which Charles Taylor sees the specific trait of Western modernity as a secular age (Taylor 2007). To be sure, they do not necessarily accept this position with respect to themselves. On the contrary, for religious professionals and activists, Islamic traditions essentially frame their lives. However, they increasingly accept exclusive humanism as a legitimate alternative for others; a position that certainly does not reflect the current societal mainstream in Middle East societies. Moreover, they distinguish their postmodern interpretation of Islamic traditions from the managerial, peer-group-oriented approach of the Muslim Brotherhood in a normative way. In applying the dichotomy between tradition and modernity, Marianna and other members of JOHUD claimed that their approach represents authentic Islamic modernity alone. They consider as backward the ideals of an organized Islamic modernity as represented by the social imaginary of the Muslim Brotherhood, something that still played a central role in the worldviews of many people we met at the governmental Zakat Fund and the ICCS.

THE ZAKAT FUND AND ICCS: ORGANIZED MODERNITY AND ISLAMIC PEER-GROUP ORIENTATION

The members of the Zakat Fund and ICCS consist of both paid employees and volunteers. In the Zakat Fund, however, only the headquarters is run by paid staff, while all local committees are run by volunteers. The majority of these volunteers are middle-aged men with a middle-class background and a university degree. In general, the Zakat Fund recruits its members through formal procedures and all potential volunteers are subject to security control by the ministry of religious foundations. The volunteers in its local committees are not selected because of professional expertise and only a few of these people have experience in the field of welfare assistance. The qualifications of the successful applicants are often more intangible, related to criteria such as familiarity with the local community, respectability, and religiosity. The director of the Zakat Fund underlined that members of the local committees should be practicing Muslims who pay *zakat* and go to the mosque, thus setting a good example for their local communities. Furthermore, volunteers have to be familiar with the neighborhood—who is sick, who is unemployed, and whose children are not going to school—thus being able to determine who deserves aid and who does not. Likewise, being anchored in the local community ensures maximum success in fundraising. Local connectedness and personal credibility, often based on religious reputation, are the most important qualities of a volunteer.

In comparison to the Zakat Fund, the ICCS relies much more on paid staff. When conducting our fieldwork, the organization employed about 3,400 staff members and approximately 700 regular volunteers. During Ramadan and other special occasions, however, the number of volunteers would increase. Working at an ICCS center is definitely not something that will make you rich. At the time of our visit, the average salary for a regular employee was about 250 JD per month, which, compared to salaries offered in private health clinics and international NGOs, was not much. "It is not even enough to buy gas for your car," an employee of ICCS told us. Although ICCS staff structures may resemble those of JOHUD, salaries, facilities, and working conditions are very different. A closer look at its members also reveals that the kinds of volunteers and staff working at ICCS differ markedly from people working at JOHUD, guided predominantly by a worldview that we described as an Islamic version of the organized modern.

When we asked the taxi driver to take us to one of the ICCS centers, located in East Amman, he looked worried and asked if we really wanted to go. For most people living in West Amman, East Amman is a dangerous no-go area, ripe with crime, poverty, and desperation. In fact, most city maps do not include East Amman, although more than half of the city's population lives there. Yet many of ICCS' community centers were located in East Amman, just as the people working at them were born and lived there. Our destination was a center close to the Palestinian refugee camp Al-Wihdat, which has grown into a suburb of East Amman; most of the center's services were directed toward the people living there.

At the center, we were greeted by two young women in headscarves and long dresses, one brown and the other dark blue. Their appearance was modest and far from the latest fashion of girls in Amman's fancy shopping malls and cafes—or at JOHUD, for that matter. Staff members at ICCS were relatively young, as at JOHUD, but the leadership was generally much older. As at JOHUD, the majority of staff at ICCS were educated professionals with university or college degrees. In contrast to JOHUD, however, most people had obtained their degrees from public universities in Jordan, and only a few had studied abroad or at private universities. Common degrees among ICCS participants included teaching, social work, accounting, computer science, and engineering. Many had combined their studies with a degree in Islamic sciences or another kind of religious education or training. Some staff members actively used their religious education after graduation—such as the director of one of the ICCS schools, who also preached regularly at a local mosque.

Religious rules and practices visibly shaped staff relations at the ICCS centers, framing the extroverted peer-group character of the organization in Islamic terms. All women working at ICCS wore headscarves and long dresses, just as most men had at least a short beard, thus displaying a much more homogenous dress code than what was the case at JOHUD. In some centers, activities were gender segregated, and women put on a full-face veil before entering the men's domains. At other centers, activities were mixed and some women wore face veils, while others were content with the headscarf alone. All of the centers had rooms for prayer and most staff members would take time to pray during their workday, unless they had a valid excuse. This focus on religious practices by staff was reflected in employment procedures, pointing toward substantial differences between JOHUD and ICCS. When employing people, the ICCS put emphasis not only on capacities and technical skills, but also on religious dedication and behavior: "People work at the centre because of their religion. Everybody is a practicing Muslim. You have to wear the veil and the proper Islamic dress," an employee told us. Thus, the choice to be made is rarely between religious and nonreligious candidates—instead, it is a choice between different religious candidates. Here, people who are in one way or another connected to the Muslim Brotherhood are often chosen over other qualified candidates (Clark 2004, 106; Roald 1994, 173). According to Wiktorowicz' estimates, as many as 90 percent are members of the Muslim Brotherhood (2001, 107).

Apart from paid staff, ICCS is also supported by volunteers. The majority do not volunteer on a regular basis, but offer their help during Ramadan, the busiest month of the year for Jordanian social welfare organizations. Some help distribute gifts and clothes, others prepare the food for the daily *iftar* meals breaking the fast, and yet others provide snacks—a cup of water, three dates, and a biscuit—to hungry people driving home from work. In a newspaper article describing these activities, one of the volunteers, a young boy, said, "I distribute dates and water for the sake of God's satisfaction."[8] At thirteen years, this boy certainly stands out from the crowd of ICCS volunteers—normally, they are older people who are retired workers from one of the various institutions attached to the Muslim Brotherhood. Young activists were comparatively rare among ICCS volunteers. There were signs, however, that this is slowly changing. The director of one community center was actively working to introduce a new kind of volunteer. He had traveled and studied abroad and was very impressed with American and European volunteering: "Voluntary work [among the young people] is still something new in Jordan. But I would like to change that [...]. Volunteer work is actually part of Islam, but you don't see it much. You can find it in Europe and the States, and we have to find a way to activate it here."

A specific kind of ICCS member was the former beneficiary who now worked in the organization. A staff member explained:

> Some of the volunteers used to be beneficiaries. All volunteers come from the area. Most of them are girls, they are housewives or other people who don't work. They work during the day. The male volunteers mostly work at night. They cover a big part of the work at the center.

These were all people from the local area who had no education and no job and who were therefore unable to provide means for themselves or their family. By offering them a low-paid job at one of the centers, the ICCS was trying to help them out of this deadlock. Often, these jobs were manual, including kitchen work, construction, or cleaning. The ICCS paid the beneficiary-turned employees a low salary for their efforts (between 50 and 100 JD), thus maintaining the distinction between them and "real" employees. Helping some beneficiaries out of poverty through low-paid jobs seemed to be a common practice not only at the ICCS, but also at many independent organizations.

At the time of our fieldwork, women made up a large part of employees at the ICCS, in many cases even at midlevel management, working as deputy directors, team leaders, teachers, PR people, social workers, and so on. As the assistant director of one of the ICCS schools jokingly put it: "Apart from maintenance, all educational staff and directors are women. The dean is a man—but we would like to change this to a woman also." Likewise, a large proportion of volunteers were women. However, all leading positions were without exception filled by men, including the directors of all community centers and of the departments in the headquarters, as well as the current and all former general directors of the organization. This applied also to the boards at headquarter level and of the community centers. The reasons for the lack of female leadership at ICCS are at least twofold. First, the Jordanian Islamic movement as such has been male dominated since its establishment. Unlike the Muslim Brotherhood in Egypt, the Jordanian Brotherhood never established a Muslim Sisterhood. Women did not make an inroad in the movement until the establishment of the Islamic Action Front (Hanieh 2008, 92). Despite lofty rhetoric and promises to work for "broadening the role of women's leadership in political life" (cf. Robinson 1997, 378), even in IAF women—so far—have not played very significant roles. Only 11 of the party's 353 founding members were female, and historically, very few female candidates have run for the party in elections. More recent increases of women's participation in the IAF seemingly has not yet resulted in giving women a more vocal role in the party (Clark and Schwedler 2003, 309). Second, the male dominance of ICCS simply reflects Jordanian gender roles more generally. Although often perceived by European and North American scholars and media to be more liberal than other Muslim countries, Jordan is in fact highly conservative with regard to gender issues. For instance, only 57 percent of the population advocate equal rights for men and women, compared to 90 percent in Bangladesh and Indonesia, 85 percent in Iran, and 77 percent in Pakistan (Esposito and Mogahed 2007, 51). Ranging from 12 to 26 percent, the rate of employment among women is also relatively low in comparison to other Middle Eastern countries (Rabo 1996, 162).

While development professionals and young activists are predominantly found at JOHUD, most of ICCS staff fall under the category of religiously dedicated staff. They certainly expressed a varied range of different reasons for working in social welfare, but unlike JOHUD's religious professionals and young activists, who primarily saw Islam as a part of personal motivation and self-identification, the ICCS members tended to understand all aspects of their engagement within an Islamic framework. A good example is a female ICCS member who described her personal motivations and emotions as emanating from her faith. While emphasizing that her work was an essential part of Islam she told us:

> I love to help people out of poverty, help them to a better life. The best moments are when an orphan graduates or when we are able to provide people with immediate help in an emergency. That is what I love about my work.

Unlike the young activists we met at JOHUD, most of the religiously dedicated staff at ICCS strongly underlined the connection between Islam and social welfare while applying a specifically religious discourse. Although the young activists at JOHUD talked about "inner peace," "human development," and "individual motivation," stressing their individualist approach, our interlocutors at ICCS often quoted verses from the Koran and traditions of the Prophet Muhammad, framing their own activities with strong reference to the collectively authoritative traditions of Islam.

We found a general tendency among ICCS employees to downplay economic interests as part of their motivation, something that might be due to the fact that the salaries provided were often very low, as mentioned above.[9] Instead, people pointed to less tangible aspects of their work such as the atmosphere of the workplace and the interaction with their colleagues. Our interview with Rula, Alaa, and Sylvia illustrates this dimension of their involvement at ICCS very well. The three young women worked at an ICCS center in East Amman. Rula served as a PR manager, Sylvia was employed as a Koran teacher, and Alaa worked as a project manager for women's and children's activities. Their jobs reflected general ICCS patterns of assigning women responsibilities in the areas of child care, women's activities, and teaching, all considered to be "appropriate" female activities. Like all other women working at ICCS, the three women wore headscarves and the typical long, traditional dresses. Rula wore a bit of make-up, but the other two did not. They were young and giggly, impatiently interrupting each other from time to time and clearly eager to tell us about their work. "We are so proud of our work," Rula said, "many organizations come to us and ask for advice." Alaa had worked at the center for three years. Previously, she used to work at a manufacturer's shop, but had to quit when her mother died and she had to take care of her father. Frustrated and bored with being a housekeeper in her father's house, she asked her friends about possibilities of volunteering at the ICCS and soon after started working as a volunteer. During her time as a volunteer, she received training in women's rights and child care, and now she is a paid staff member. Rula had worked here for five years, but as she added with a smile: "I wish that I had known about this place many years ago so I could have worked here even longer." The three women all agreed that one of the main reasons for working at the ICCS was the good atmosphere and the relations with colleagues, in this sense also relating the role of the organization as a social site for constructing forms of intimacy and personal relationships. As Alaa put it, "The salary is quite low—but money doesn't buy happiness. We don't work here because of the money, we work here because of the atmosphere, the relationships." In this comfortable working atmosphere, Sylvia explained, Islam plays an important role:

> It means a lot to me that this is an Islamic place. Perhaps in other places I would feel a gap of belief. I am not sure I would get along with my colleagues. The fact that it's an Islamic place means that you get support of your own beliefs. You already have the beliefs, but you want to work in a place that supports these beliefs, and makes it easier for you to practice your beliefs.

This understanding of Islamic traditions as shaping communality was supported not only by Rula and Alaa, but by almost all staff members we met: "There's a special atmosphere among the staff here. We love each other, we are like brothers. If there is a problem we help each other," we were told by one of our interviewees. The use of the terms "brother" and "sister" further nurtured this feeling of community and collective intimacy. In organizational terms, this feeling of religious community based on the ideal of collectively shared religious regulations not only strengthened horizontal bonds among colleagues, but was also a part of the ICCS leadership strategy, as the assistant director of an ICCS center frankly admitted:

> If someone asks me if they can take a day off, I always allow them, because I know that I can trust them. They would never leave without finishing their work. Our religion gives us guidelines. They wouldn't cheat or do bad work. They know that God is watching them, they have an internal check.

Through the lenses of our typology of modern subjectivity formation, the members of ICCS strongly identify with the imaginary of the peer-group-oriented salaried masses. To be sure, given the low salaries and generally modest economic background of ICCS' employees, this does not apply so much to the consumptive patterns that play an essential part in the Western forms of this type of subjectivity formation. Yet, they share the features of an embraced mass collectivity, following ideals of collective regulation and coordination of action. They do not share the ideal of the performing individual of second modernity, but resemble the extraverted group or average type of a mass society in which individuality is meaningfully expressed through the similarity of norms, values, and appearances with their peers. Thus, the reference to Islamic traditions does not serve the self-fashioning of the modern autonomy as a morally sovereign and creative subject, but religion plays a role in the collectively binding construction of individual selfhood.

When talking about their motivation for working at the ICCS, however, Rula, Alaa, and Sylvia not only mention this collective atmosphere of their work place but they also pointed to other dimensions of their work, characterizing it as fun, challenging, and exciting. As Sylvia said, "When you work at other places, for instance in government, you get stuck in the same routines every day. This is different." Rula added, emphasizing her point, "During Ramadan, we sometimes work here until ten or eleven at night, in the Qader night we stayed up until dawn and fed people who were praying at the mosque. Even though we were tired, we were happy. It was so much fun." They were proud of the work they did, emphasizing its creative aspects, and were very ambitious on behalf of the center. In Rula's words, "We would like to be the best center of them all. Just like I like to make myself pretty, I like to do a good job." In particular for Alaa, working at the ICCS also contributed to her personal growth: "When I started, I was so shy, I didn't know how to do speeches and lectures. They taught me at the center and I am still learning." Apparently, the work at ICCS provided her with successful means in the sense of technologies of the self. As such, the more individualized set of postmodern values also seems to influence the self-imagination of some of our interlocutors at ICCS. At least in terms of working subjects, our three female interviewees here present hybrid combinations of peer-group-oriented and postmodern forms of subjectivity.

In their focus on work experience, personal growth, and professionalism, the young women resembled the development professionals and young activists at JOHUD, although they used a different language to express themselves. In contrast to our young interviewees at JOHUD, these members of ICCS framed their participation within a discourse of Islamic community, referring to Islamic concepts, traditions of the Prophet, and verses from the Koran. Like many of the religiously minded young activists we met at JOHUD, they were motivated by a wish to fulfill religious obligations. Yet they interpreted Islamic traditions not through the lenses of individual values and principle, but applied a framework of collectively shared norms. Phrasing it in terms of family atmosphere and a sense of solidarity, many of our interviewees connected their reasons for working at ICCS to the religious identity of the organization as such, as well as its promotion of Islamic community. Yet others also emphasized tangible benefits such as the facilitation of jobs, favors, and personal relations as their prime motivation, underlining the network character of the Islamic movement.

Staff members—consciously or unconsciously—sought to transfer and extend their ideal of an organized Islamic community to the beneficiaries, in talking about them in terms of "friendship," "family," and "sisterhood" (Harmsen 2008, 335). A female beneficiary at one of the centers told us about her experiences with staff: "It's really nice talking to the employees here, they are so nice, it feels like talking to a sister, they are so helpful. It's a very comfortable atmosphere, we feel like we are surrounded by family." We could observe this inclusion of beneficiaries by ICCS while attending the anniversary of the Islamic Hospital where hospital staff, ICCS volunteers, and beneficiaries celebrated the anniversary together. Likewise, Ramadan parties, Koran reading competitions, and other festivities served to strengthen bonds and create community among different kinds of participants in the organization. Yet these activities also serve ideological purposes, indicating the ongoing struggle about the very character of the Islamic modern in Jordan. During the entertainment program at the anniversary of the Islamic Hospital, for instance, an old man entered the scene. "This is an important man," the woman next to us whispered. The man started talking in a loud, angry voice, referring in his speech to the people in government, "Why do you think we are the enemy? We build hospitals, we help people. We are the ones who can unite Jordan," he said, clenching his fists and emphasizing the main antagonism of the Muslim Brotherhood's ideal of Jordan's Islamic modern. "Look at Bush and Olmert, they are the enemy, do you want the country to end up like Lebanon or Iraq?"

The idea of an organized Islamic community is combined with individual strategies to find the good life: Working in an Islamic organization makes you happy, safe, and comfortable, feeling part of something bigger. This feeling of community and group solidarity seemingly contributes to the creation of a normative ideal of Islam as an alternative social order—a vision of an Islamic society as opposed to the existing social reality (cf. Wickham 2004, 238). In other words, working at ICCS partly gives the experience of living the ideal of a modern Islamic society; or, as many of our informants put it, "Here, we are honest and hard-working, not like the corrupt government" and "we do this out of love and charity, not for the money, like the secular organizations do." Through the community centers, schools, hospitals, and clinics, the ICCS provides a social space where this vision of Islam as an alternative society can grow. In turn, these centers and institutions become proof of the validity of the vision, showing the outside world that an alternative Islamic society is in fact possible (Clark 2004). This dimension of ICCS, to provide a training ground for living the collective ideal of an Islamic modern subjectivity, is almost absent in independent organizations, where religion and social engineering are not as closely connected as in the case of the Muslim Brotherhood movement.

INDEPENDENT ORGANIZATIONS: THE ISLAMIC BOURGEOIS SUBJECT

Detached from larger political and economic networks, the independent welfare organizations often rely primarily on donations from individuals and small businesses in their local community, meaning that funds are often limited and their budgets correspondingly small. This is reflected in the employment structures and the variety of individual motivations of engagement, making it more difficult to associate members to one of our types. Thus, while some may hire a few paid employees to take care of administrative matters, most of them choose to rely solely on volunteer work. In AHIS, for instance, the organization's fifteen participants all worked as volunteers. Some were in the organization every day, others spent no more than a few hours per week. We met the women in their office, located in a wealthy neighborhood in Amman. They were all relatively well-to-do women, all of them living in the neighborhood or its immediate vicinity. Our assistant described them with a smile as "nice old women with too much time on their hands."[10]

While belonging to the same economic class as JOHUD's participants, in almost all other aspects they were very different. First of all, ranging from 45 to 70 years, the women of AHIS were comparatively much older than JOHUD's employees and volunteers. This age group is typical of most independent organizations, although some of them do attract younger people. Many members of independent organizations have retired from their jobs or, in the case of the women we met, are housewives with children in school or grown-up children. Quite a few women have an education, the majority as teachers. In AIHS, for instance, the director worked for several years as an English teacher in Kuwait. Likewise, most male volunteers in independent organizations have some sort of college education. However, in the context of the organization, their professional background is rarely of relevance. People are not employed because they are skilled social workers or economists—in fact, they are not employed at all. Instead, most of them join the organization as volunteers because a friend or a family member told them about it, thus reflecting the local character of most independent organizations. Often, they are established as a consequence of meetings in the local mosque.

There is an increasing number of independent associations based exclusively on female participation, AHIS being only one example. Other examples are That al-Netaqueen, Khawla bint al-Azwar, Umm al-Qura, and Al-Rabi. However, the majority of independent organizations are still male dominated. An example is the Islamic Science League Society, run by two 70-year-old brothers whose father established the organization in 1952. Another example is the Al-Farouq Society, which distributes financial aid to families and orphans and runs a mosque. In both cases, the organizations rely almost exclusively on male volunteers. Thus, while women are increasingly active in independent organizations, they are primarily so in women-only associations such as AHIS, while most other organizations are still the domain of male volunteers.

In these independent organizations, the typical member resembles most closely the type we have called the committed citizen, sharing elements with the classical form of a bourgeois subject.[11] Like the dedicated staff members we met at ICCS, most of these volunteers were motivated by an overall desire to fulfill their religious obligations. As the founder of AHIS expressed it in an interview with Egbert Harmsen, "I am just doing my duty, in obedience to God" (Harmsen 2008, 184). Likewise, the ladies from Khawla bint al-Azwar kept telling us, "We do this *fi sabilillah*, for the sake of God." But apart from this pious desire to fulfill general religious obligations, the volunteer's work also seemed to be driven by a number of other factors, some of which we shall explore in the following, taking a closer look at a few of the women working in AHIS, Khawla bint al-Azwar, and That al-Netaqueen.

The director of AHIS was Buthaina, a 65-year-old woman. She was tall, wearing a grey headscarf and a long purple dress. Her handshake was strong and her eyes looked at us with mild skepticism. We started telling her about our research, but before she had heard us through, she interrupted us: "I assume that you are going to ask about women and Islam. You always ask about that, you all assume that women are so oppressed." For her statement she received a few approving nods from her eight fellow volunteers, all sitting around us in big leather chairs in the organization's meeting room. Listening to her, one quickly realized that she was far from oppressed. Like her predecessor, Noor, who established the association in the 1980s, Buthaina had been a teacher. Like many other Jordanians, she had worked in Kuwait for several years, but she was retired now and lived around the corner from the organizational headquarters. She spent her retirement working as the director of AHIS and visiting her children and grandchildren abroad—a son living in the United States and a daughter in Britain. In fluent English, Buthaina told us why she had started working as a volunteer in the organization. When she resigned from her job after working as a teacher for more than 35 years, she was afraid that she would feel useless if she just stayed at home doing nothing. Instead, she started volunteering at AHIS: "I came here to learn how to sew, and the other women said: 'You are active, you can help.' Now, I work here every day, whenever they need me," she said, adding in her characteristically firm voice, "I am not useless!"

This desire to be active and to play a useful role in society is reflected in statements made by many other representatives of independent organizations, in particular by women. For these women, volunteering is not something that is taken lightly, in fact many volunteers talk about their duties with more seriousness than any paid employee would do. In our interviews, people would emphasize over and over again how much time and energy they spend on their work as a way of demonstrating their dedication and commitment: "I spend a lot of time here," one woman said. "It's only supposed to be two hours a week, but I'm here a minimum of six hours, sometimes more. And I also work from home." Another told us, "I work here every day, whenever they need me."

To most of these women, their social commitment is closely linked to their faith. In practical terms, many got involved in volunteer work through the mosque where preachers taught them about social responsibilities in Islam and encouraged them to help people in need. Inspired by this, some women decided to form an organization, offering support to poor women in the local community. Many of our interlocutors invoked Islamic discourses of social responsibility when justifying or explaining their involvement in volunteer work: "Islam is not about just sitting at home doing nothing. You have to engage in society, you have to accomplish something," one woman explained to us, reflecting a commonly expressed attitude. Talking about *takaful ijtimai*, or mutual social responsibility (cf. Deeb 2006, 86), and referring to famous Muslim women such as That al-Netaqueen and Khawla bint al-Azwar,[12] the volunteers locate their activities in a long-standing Islamic moral discourse, connecting their own contemporary activities to the historical and religious past of the community (cf. Deeb 2006, 97). In this way, Islam becomes a tool for empowerment, a means of achieving the modern autonomy of a morally sovereign subject, confirming these women in their conviction that their participation in society is legitimate and needed.

In many interviews, we learnt from these committed female citizens that religion might also serve as a means of convincing skeptical parents and husbands of the appropriateness of their active participation in social organizations. The leader of Khawla bint al-Azwar, for example, told us that, in the beginning, her husband did not want her to work with prostitutes at all. The argument that eventually convinced her husband was of a religious nature: "You have to think of the prostituted woman as someone in trouble," she told him. "How can I as a Muslim abandon her?" This strategy seemed to be widely used among the women we met. Presenting their volunteer work as a kind of "female jihad," as their way of exerting themselves toward the furthering of Islam and their community, the women succeed in establishing for themselves a relatively free space for active participation in society. Volunteering in an Islamic organization becomes a morally acceptable way for women to get out of the house, escaping social pressures reinforced by their husbands (cf. Deeb 2006, 97–9). Wickham also points to the liberating power of Islamic discourses with respect to traditional gender relations:

> By adopting "correct" Islamic behaviour, young women gained an aura of respectability that enabled them to move more freely in public spaces without fear of social sanction. In addition, they were able to invoke their "rights in Islam" as a means to mobilize social pressure against parents or spouses who mistreated them (2004, 244).

This female liberation is far from unrestricted, but takes place within the limits of social norms and traditions, underlining a wife's subordination to her husband: "Most husbands support this work. If he doesn't, you can't work here," one of our interviewees said and continued, "You have to have extra time on your hands and you have to have the support of your husband." Likewise, many women emphasized the primacy of their role as caretakers, stating that their volunteer involvement is contingent on their children having grown up, thus leaving them with more spare time. Thus, rather than breaking the limits for female agency in a conservative religious society, introducing radically new social norms, the volunteer women are gently stretching these limits by reinterpreting old norms.

In sum, it appears as if the committed citizens we met in the independent organizations—like the dedicated staff members at the ICCS—were to a large degree driven by a value-rational motivation to fulfill religious obligations, traditionally understood as pleasing God. At the same time, however, these women apply the concept of social activism as an equally important religious obligation. In doing so, they emulate nineteenth-century Islamic reformers' appeal to perceive religion as a means of social engagement, although these reformers did not necessarily apply it to women. Pleasing God is not about staying at home and praying—it is about being active and participating in society. This ideational motivation is closely linked to instrumental and emotional factors: By fulfilling the religious obligation to social engagement, the women can also satisfy their desire to feel useful and accomplish something in their lives. To a certain extent, the older women we met in the independent organization display a form of classical bourgeois subjectivity. Firmly anchored in a society based on conservative values, they construct their moral sovereignties through voluntary work in an Islamic framework. They combine this reflexive process with the moral regulation that references to Islamic traditions provide. At the same time, their interpretation of these traditions is a means of mediating the conservative, patriarchal norms and values within the largely imperative context of Jordanian society as an Islamic modern.

Conclusions

Our inquiry into the ways in which Islamic charities and social welfare organizations in Jordan serve as social sites for the construction of modern

Muslim subjectivities generally confirms the findings of the previous two chapters. At the micro level, we can also observe social negotiations about the legitimate interpretation of Jordan's Islamic modern with respect to different models of successive modernities. We can understand different ways to be a modern Muslim as idiosyncratic combinations of these different models of modern orders with elements of the three general types of modern subjectivity formation, as described in the first chapter. In treating Islamic charities as social sites for the self-realization of modern individuals as working subjects, we can support the conclusion of Janine Clark that these organizations predominantly cater to the interests of a religiously minded, educated middle class. The engagement of our interlocutors is intimately linked to their educational backgrounds, career aspirations, and social status in a society that only provides limited opportunities for the younger educated middle class to construct meaningful selfhoods through work. However, stratifications among Jordan's middle class seemingly make a difference according to which model of an Islamic modern society these activists pursue in their aspirations. While the more affluent upper middle classes tend to combine Islamic traditions with the pluralistic and individualized set of postmodern values of second modernity, such as at JOHUD, the lower middle classes rather identify with the peer-group-oriented model of first modernity represented by the Muslim Brotherhood and ICCS.

PART III

Politics of Muslim
Subjectivities in Egypt

Until recently, the relationship between youth, religion, and social activism in Egypt was closely associated with the images of bearded young men in violent clashes with Egyptian security forces at which they were shouting "Islam is the solution!" Yet the Egyptian scene has decisively changed since the 1980s and 1990s. The Mubarak regime managed to contain the militant Islamist groups through utmost state repression and most of the country's Islamist activism has transformed. The Muslim Brotherhood seems to have moderated its ideological approach and appeared in formal politics as the strongest political force in the first Egyptian parliament after the fall of Mubarak. In June 2012, Muhammad Mursi, the previous chairman of the Freedom and Justice Party, the political arm of the Brotherhood, became Egypt's first president elected by a free popular vote. Even the Muslim Brotherhood movement's militant offspring, Al-Jamaat al-Islamiyya, joined formal politics and participated in the 2011–2012 elections in an alliance with other Salafist political parties. It remains to be seen whether this moderation of the Islamist camp will come to an end in the future political development of Egypt, after the Egyptian military has toppled President Mursi and turned against the Muslim Brotherhood in July 2013.

Parallel to the gradual demise of militant Islamism, we have witnessed the emergence of new phenomena such as popular television preachers, *daiyat* movements,[1] and the religiously motivated engagement of young people in a new kind of Islamic charity. With respect to the latter, a new group of youth organizations has made its imprint on this change in Islamic activism. Beginning around 2000, a steadily growing number of youth organizations working within the field of social welfare have emerged. They have been founded and led by well-educated young representatives of the middle and upper middle classes.[2] Emphasizing religious norms and values as their primary motivation, the members of these organizations engage in Islamic charity by using vocabulary and tools known from the international development industry and modern management sciences. To a certain extent, they represent a new Islamic movement, challenging the dominant role that the organized form of an Islamic modern of the Muslim Brotherhood has played so far in Egyptian history.

In the following, we will explore this movement by selectively putting our focus on a sample of nine of Egypt's new religious youth organizations and their members. To be sure, Egypt has known a broad range of youth and welfare organizations without a religious character. Yet we want to understand the specific nature of this new Islamic movement. We try to detect its modern Islamic imaginary and how this imaginary relates to the ways in which a particular segment of young Egyptians construct individual forms of modern selfhood through their engagement in social welfare activities. Although Islamic groups were not prime movers in the events of the Arab Spring, we have learnt that many of our interlocutors emphatically joined the demonstrations against the Mubarak regime. The religiously minded young Egyptians in our study share many of the grievances of Egypt's youth in general. Thus, the analysis of their aims, motivations, and worldviews will also tell us something with regard to the social unrest in the Arab world. In our interpretation, the rapid growth of these youth organizations in number and size is an integral part of the overall social transformation that was epitomized in the Arab Spring.

We will argue that this new form of Islamic activism, in particular its specific perception of social change with reference to Islamic traditions, is both a continuation of and a break with Egypt's long tradition of Islamic social movements. While it bears many similarities with both the nineteenth-century Islamic reform movement and the well-established tradition of Islamic charitable associations in Egypt, it is also characterized by remarkable innovations regarding the public manifestation of youth, religion, and activism in Egyptian society. By applying our theoretical frame of successive modernities, we will interpret this transformation of Islamic activism in Egypt and the emergence of these youth organizations, in particular, in the context of our analytical devices of first and second modernity. We suggest understanding current social change in Egyptian society as a conflict between ideas of second modernity and visions of an organized modernity to which both the Egyptian state elite and the Muslim Brotherhood have subscribed, although in very different versions. This conflict, according to our analysis, is also visible in Egypt's contemporary politics of modern Muslim subjectivities, however, in a complex configuration in which individuals refer in idiosyncratic ways to various elements of all three of our types of modern subjectivity formation. While the trend toward more individual interpretations of Islamic traditions in creative ways suggests perceiving this new Islamic movement as resembling a postmodern version of the Islamic modern, we can also detect a revival of some elements of the classical bourgeois type and its restricted liberalism, as well as tendencies to shape individual subjectivities according to a model of peers. In particular, ordinary followers of the movement and many volunteers of our youth organizations adhere to a new peer-group-oriented model of modernity, which is expressed by the movement's leaders. Serving as models of "Muslim professionals," however, these leaders themselves construct modern identities that incorporate many elements of the postmodern type of selfhood. Evidently the contemporary politics of Muslim subjectivities in Egypt are characterized by a high degree of hybridity.

Once again, we organize the third part of our book in three steps, each of which represents a distinct level of analysis. Chapter 7 will position the new Islamic movement within the structural coordinates that have been given by Egypt's official state-controlled Islam and the Islamist imaginary of the Egyptian modern by the Muslim Brotherhood. In sharp contrast to Jordan, Egypt looks back on two centuries of modern state formation. In this long process of state building, however, ideas of an Islamic modern have never dominated the social imaginary of Egypt's various ruling elites. In Egypt, the Islamic modern has rather been an antagonistic vision of the, in principle, secular rationale of the state. We analyze the ways in which the Egyptian state has exerted control over the religious field while being confronted with this alternative model of an organized society by the Muslim Brotherhood. In putting the rise of the new youth organizations in the power context of this contestation about Egypt's authentic modern, we try to understand the role of religion in this new form of Islamic activism that has partly separated itself from the mainstream of Egyptian Islamist politics. Revolving around notions of morality, individual empowerment, and social responsibility, these organizations are part of a larger movement that distinguishes itself from both the official Islam propagated by the state and the political Islam of the Muslim Brotherhood. The key messengers in this movement and its new imaginary of an Islamic modern are lay preachers like Amr Khaled, and its primary adherents are recruited from the urban middle-class youth. The youth organizations under scrutiny in this chapter represent institutionalized forms of this movement whose ideological positions strongly impact on the construction of individual selves among its followers.

Chapter 8, then, takes a closer look at the specific organizations that we have selected for our investigation. We describe and analyze their activities, dominant discourses, and organizational structures. In particular, the role and manifestation of religious discourses and practices will be examined and discussed. To what extent do they represent religious organizations? To what kind of modern imaginary do their organizational rationales refer? Following a short introduction to the field of new youth organizations, we first try to answer these questions by exploring the ways in which these organizations identify societal problems, propose solutions, and develop strategies for carrying out their plans of social reform. Secondly, we investigate the means of recruitment and mobilization applied by them and their leadership, as well as the discursive mechanisms that link these organizations to the subjectivity formation of their members. In particular, we introduce the normative ideal type of a Muslim professional to which they refer in their individual identity constructions.

Finally, we move to the individual level and try to understand the ways in which these new youth organizations serve young Egyptians as social sites for the construction of meaningful modern Muslim subjectivities. We do so with respect to three characteristic types of personalities: the leader, the female organizer, and the regular volunteer. On this level, we try to understand the specific meanings that members and volunteers associate with their engagement. We argue that engaging in charity often appears as a means rather than an end for many activists in our fieldwork. From a micro perspective, all three types of activist use the organizations as social fields for the construction of meaningful selfhoods in teaching, learning, and applying specific technologies of the self. Again, particular attention will be paid to the role and place of religious discourse and practice in this context. In addition, we will touch upon the significance of gender in relation to patterns of involvement and participation. We conclude with a brief examination of the ways in which these organizations work as social networks, whose ideals, values, and bodily practices deliver relevant technologies for the construction of contemporary forms of modern Muslim subjectivity. In theoretical terms, the common thread running throughout this case study is the contention that these organizations play a central role in transforming references to Islamic traditions from being a means of the technologies of domination to a means of establishing technologies of the self.

CHAPTER 7

State and Islam in Egypt: Competing Models of Organized Modernity

MODERN EGYPT: SECULAR RULE AND RELIGIOUS CONTROL

The beginning of the history of the modern Egyptian state might best be dated with the massacre of the remaining Mamluk princes in the Cairo Citadel in 1811. From this time onward, Muhammad Ali consolidated his power, built up a set of state institutions, and made Egypt factually independent from the Ottoman Sultan. The Viceroy of Egypt[1] embarked on a top-down reform program that focused on the centralization of state power, transforming the Ottoman province into a kind of absolutist state. In modernizing the military, state administration, education, and the economy, Muhammad Ali largely by-passed the Islamic establishment of the country and increasingly subordinated the *ulama* to his absolutist rule (Vatikiotis 1985, 58). In initiating modern state formation in Egypt, he did not, however, follow a clear vision of a modern order beyond his mere claim to power. Throughout the reign of Muhammad Ali (1805–1849), modernization was a means of consolidating the autonomy of the Egyptian state, which was represented by its despotic ruler alone. This situation changed under the rule of his grandson Ismail. During his regency (1863–1879), the Khedive Ismail tried to develop Egypt according to a model of modernity that could be labeled a European modern. While in principle remaining absolutist in its political institutions, Ismail's European modern aimed at emulating European models in architecture, transportation, education, and appearance. The khedive embarked on constructing a modern Cairo, building railway connections, establishing secular schools, and implementing new dress codes for public servants. The epitome of Ismail's project of establishing an Egyptian version of a European modern and the source of its ultimate financial downfall was the construction of the Suez Canal, which was opened in 1869 (Osman 2011, 26–7).

The modernization process under Ismail generated a new stratum of national elite consisting of state officials, military officers, and intellectuals who increasingly questioned the absolutist nature of his aristocratic rule. From the late nineteenth century onward, this elite demanded constitutional

reforms and the independence of Egypt from both formal Ottoman supremacy and colonial domination, which began with the British occupation of
Egypt in 1882. The rise of Egypt's new nationalist elite was paralleled by
the formation of the Islamic reform movement, which also left its imprint
on Egyptian nationalism. In particular, nationalist figures such as Mustafa
Kamil and Ali Yusuf demanded an "Islamic liberation" of Egypt from colonial rule. However, the mainstream of Egypt's nationalist movement prior to
the First World War eventually turned to a secular bourgeois interpretation
of the Egyptian modern somehow in continuation of Ismail's attempts of
Europeanization (Vatikiotis 1985, 213). The eventual failure of bourgeois
political liberalism and Egyptianism as its nationalist ideology in the 1920s
and 1930s, epitomized in the political decline of the Wafd Party, did not
change this direction of the Egyptian state. While the revolution in 1952
replaced the constitutional monarchy with a republican regime, Egypt's subsequent autocratic presidents continued to govern according to an essentially
secular imaginary of organized society.

Although formally basing their rule on the secular modern concept of popular sovereignty, Nasser, Sadat, and Mubarak ruled Egypt through personal
social networks in which power emanated from "personality and proximity
to the 'boss'" rather than being derived from modern political institutions
(Waterbury 1983, xiii). The backbone of the three subsequent presidential
periods of rule was, however, Egypt's military establishment, which included
the armed forces and the country's intelligence services. While Nasser furnished this military pillar with an ideological stance combining anticolonial
rhetoric with populist socialism, Sadat replaced Nasserism with his *infi-
tah* policies of opening the country to the West, implementing a moderate
Islamization of society and introducing a selective and still state-controlled
liberalization of the economy. In principle, Mubarak continued this course,
yet transforming Sadat's *munfatihun,* the profiteers of his commercial open-
door policies (Waterbury 1983, 172–5), into a new power group of crony
capitalists as the second pillar to his rule (Osman 2011, 243). Until the fall of
Hosni Mubarak in February 2011, however, the concept of an Islamic modern, represented in its most influential form by the Muslim Brotherhood,
remained a counter-model to the ways in which Egyptian state makers have
envisaged the country's modern social order.

This subordination of the model of an Islamic modern in Egyptian state
formation does not mean, however, that its various forms have not left visible traces in Egyptian politics. On the contrary, since the foundation of
the Muslim Brotherhood in 1928, the antagonism between a secular state
and an oppositional Islamic modern has left its mark on the legal and social
practices of the Egyptian state. A case in point is Article 2 of the Egyptian
constitution of 1971, which declares Islam the official state religion and ele-
vates the principles of the Islamic *sharia* to the principal source of legislation
(Lombardi 2006, 125).[2] Furthermore, according to constitutional law, the
Egyptian President must be a Muslim. Hence, Islam is not just the majority
religion of Egypt but holds an exceptional position among other religions,

making it a fundamental part of Egypt's proper social order as such (cf. Beyer 2006, 290). In 1992, in the mid of the violent struggle between the state and militant Islamists, Egypt's minister of the interior even went so far as to publicly denounce the secular nature of the Egyptian state, claiming that all laws were based on the *sharia*.[3] However, despite such bold statements, the Mubarak regime also never aspired to establish a social order that would correspond to an Islamic state.

In Egyptian politics, references to Islamic traditions have primarily been used to complement the technologies of domination of essentially secular regimes. Both President Hosni Mubarak and in particular his predecessor Anwar Sadat tended to portray themselves as dedicated Muslims as a means of gaining popular support and distancing themselves from the secular Arab socialist image of Gamal Abdel Nasser (Sullivan and Abed-Kotob 1999, 72). Since Sadat, a renewed commitment to Islamic symbols has become part of state policies, and the regimes of Mubarak and Sadat have increasingly used references to Islam to bolster their autocratic rule. Even more important, Islam has been a matter of vital government interest in its confrontation with the Muslim Brotherhood and its alternative model of Egypt as an Islamic organized society. In light of this alternative, state authorities have been "compelled to adopt a religious discourse in order to regain moral mastery over society and secure political legitimacy" (Bayat 2007, 173). Recent decades have thus witnessed a strong politicization of the religious field and continuous efforts by the Egyptian state to collectively enforce a specific official understanding of Islamic precepts and practices when using legislative, legal, administrative, and military means. The formation of the Egyptian state has, therefore, been accompanied by various regime strategies to control religious communication by either coopting or suppressing religious institutions, organizations, and movements.

The educated class of Islamic legal scholars, the *ulama*, has been a prime target of these attempts to control the religious field by the state. Muhammad Ali already incorporated the *ulama* in and subordinated them to the state apparatus by making them paid employees under the supervision of the Grand Sheikh of Al-Azhar (Ibrahim 1988, 636). From the late nineteenth century onward, the reform of the Al-Azhar was a central issue of state policies to control religion. Prior to independence, Egyptian governments imposed a state-controlled reorganization of curricula and undermined the independence of the Al-Azhar in terms of administrative and financial reforms (Vatikiotis 1985, 300). Later, President Nasser strengthened the dependence of the *ulama* on the state further. He abolished *sharia* courts, put all religious endowments under state control, and made with the Reorganization Law of 1961 the Al-Azhar and Islamic education entirely subject to state supervision (Lapidus 2002, 523, 529). The enactment of two new legal provisions in 1996 is another and more recent example of these continuing moves to control religious institutions by the Egyptian state. While the first law aimed at the nationalization of 30,000 mosques within five years, the second required all imams to undergo a two-year training program administrated by the ministry of religious endowments (Mahmood 2005, 75). In this way, the Mubarak regime attempted to control the content of Friday prayers and to better monitor the activities of Islamic organizations in general (Sullivan and Abed-Kotob 1999, 128). Under Mubarak, the Grand Sheikh of Al-Azhar even showed a previously unknown "readiness to pronounce his views on political issues," basically endorsing major regime policies (Amin 2011, 122).

Religious education in public schools marks another field of action for the state in order to control religious communication and making it a part of its own technologies of domination. Of course, the sources for religious socialization in Egypt are varied. Egypt's children and youth are influenced not only by school but also by their parents and relatives, the local mosque, a multiplicity of television and radio programs, public and private youth organizations, and various forms of religious publications. However, since the mid-1970s, the state-designed introduction of new forms of religious education has represented one of the most powerful tools of the regime to influence religious socialization through primary and secondary education in public schools. Based on moral indoctrination rather than the recitation of sacred texts, this educational program has been a state attempt to shape the religious attitudes and worldviews of Egypt's children and youth. Inspired by colonial administrators' programs of mass public instruction, educators since Sadat have insisted that religious education should serve moral and not merely ritual ends. Through examples such as standing in straight lines of prayer, students are taught that "Islam is a religion of order and discipline," and sacred texts are at the same time linked to their observation and comprehension of everyday life (Starrett 1998, 151).

The consequences of this teaching method are that children learn "to interpret aspects of social reality as having meanings beyond those that they proclaim or manifest directly" (Starrett 1998, 151). The students learn to articulate their own daily experiences in terms of religious communication. In direct contrast to the intention of the regime, the reform of religious education in public schools generated among young Egyptians an increasing need for religious information and a tendency to answer social and individual questions with reference to Islamic traditions. While intended to be a technology of domination, religious education in public schools also facilitated the recourse to Islamic traditions as a means of technologies of the self that tend to escape state control.[4] The new Islamic movement propagates Islamic morals as technologies of the self and therefore partly represents an unintended result of these state policies.

We can observe similar developments with regard to the mass media. The government's intensive use of the media to propagate its own version of official Islam has unintentionally contributed to the creation of a market for religious cultural goods. On this market, however, the religious commodities offered by the state may not be the most attractive products. Indeed, the young interlocutors of our fieldwork clearly indicated that they consider the religious goods provided by the official Islam of the Egyptian regime as the least attractive ones. Thus, an increasing number of young people turned in their search for religious inspiration toward the private sector. In its attempt to control religion, the state apparently also enhanced the significance of religious communication in Egyptian society. While opposing the model of an Islamic modern of the Muslim Brotherhood, the Egyptian state unwillingly contributed to making Islamic traditions a more important part in the formation of contemporary Muslim subjectivities in Egypt. In this way, state authorities, in fact, helped the Muslim Brotherhood promote the Islamic modern as an alternative to the secular top-down modernization of Egyptian society by the state. Yet as the following section will show, a growing number of religiously minded young Egyptians, and among them especially the more privileged representatives of the middle class, do not consider the organized form of an Islamic modern promoted by the Muslim Brotherhood or any of its more radical offsprings as an alternative to the official Islam of the state. In their search for religious and social engagement in society, they look for other organizational and ideological forms than the political Islam of the Brotherhood provides.

The Organized Modern of the Muslim Brotherhood

The growing significance of religious communication in Egyptian society since the 1980s, in which the youth's interest in alternatives to the official Islam of the state plays a part, is thus to a certain extent a result of larger institutional transformations such as the reform of religious education in public schools and the government's utilization of Islamic traditions in its attempt to control religious communication via the mass media. State attempts to manage religious communication have worked paradoxically to fragment religious authority structures and to inspire competing interpretations of Islamic traditions. In direct contrast to the regime's intentions, many young Egyptians began to articulate their discontent in religious language. In this way, the secular state participated in the promotion and consolidation of the rising hegemony of Islamic discourse. But why does this younger generation of Egyptians tend to engage in social welfare organizations instead of joining political Islamic organizations or parties such as the Muslim Brotherhood? Why is formal political organization not the preferred option? An important part of the answer to this question is found in the relationship between the state and the Islamist opposition in Egypt.

As mentioned before, the movement, organization, and party of the Muslim Brothers, founded by Hasan al-Banna in 1928, have been the central opposition force to Egypt's changing but altogether secular-oriented regimes. As noted by Ibrahim (1988), contemporary Islamic activism in Egypt has its roots in the Brotherhood. Yet unlike in Jordan, where the Muslim Brotherhood both joined with and contested the state in its attempt to construct an Islamic modern, the Muslim Brotherhood in Egypt was made an illegal organization that was not recognized as a political party before Mubarak's fall. However, members of the Muslim Brotherhood have been known to express their views in public, although they normally did not explicitly identify themselves as members of the organization. In parliamentary elections, they typically competed as independent candidates or as members on the lists of other parties. Furthermore, the Muslim Brotherhood has dominated the councils of the five most active professional syndicates, namely, doctors, engineers, pharmacists, scientists, and lawyers (Abdel-Rahman 2004, 115; El-Daly 2006).

Initially, Hasan al-Banna founded the Muslim Brothers in reaction to British colonial rule, the influence of Christian missionaries, and a society in which the people had "departed from the goals of their faith" (Banna, cited in Mitchell 1969, 6). The Brotherhood called for opposition to what Banna saw as the illegitimate rulers and for a mass mobilization of Muslims to return to the faith. The movement grew rapidly and by 1949 it covered most of Egypt with more than 2,000 branches and with a membership estimated to comprise between one and two million people (Bayat 2007, 37). The years from 1945 to 1965 saw the most violent period in its history; the Brotherhood was involved in numerous riots, protests, and assassinations of political opponents, and in 1952, the Muslim Brothers joined the Free Officers under Nasser in overthrowing King Faruq (Mitchell 1969, 101–104). However, in the competition for power and after an alleged assassination attempt on Nasser by a Brotherhood member in 1954, the new regime ordered the Brotherhood to be dissolved. Hundreds of its members were imprisoned and six leading Muslim Brothers were executed (1969, 151–62). Furthermore, the ministry of social affairs took administrative control over the Brotherhood's many welfare centers, arguing that they were sites of illegal activities (Abdel-Rahman 2004, 126–9).

In the following 15 years, the Brotherhood kept a low profile while slowly recovering from the state's crackdown. After Nasser's defeat in the Arab–Israeli War in 1967, it carefully started to reorganize, and the remaining leaders made the strategic decision to discard violence (Ibrahim 1988). This decision by the older leadership, however, was not accepted by all members of the younger generation. The consequence of this strategic disagreement was a split of the organization into two wings: a "gradualist" mainstream led by Hasan al-Hudaybi and a "revolutionary" wing inspired by the writings of Sayyid Qutb (Bayat 2007, 38–9).[5] While Hasan al-Hudaybi, the successor of Hasan al-Banna, pursued a reformist agenda and a policy of moderation with regard to the regime (cf. Zollner 2009), Sayyid Qutb developed an ideological fundament for Islamist revolution that inspired subsequent militant groups. In particular, two conceptual innovations by Qutb were instrumental in justifying an Islamist revolution. First, he developed a concept of divine authority (*hakimiyya*) in fusing the Koranic concept of rule (*hukm*) with the modern notion of sovereignty. Accordingly, he defined the legitimate authority of the modern state as emanating from the divine sovereignty of God. Secondly, Qutb revised the meaning of the Koranic term *jahiliyya*. Often translated as the "epoch of ignorance," *jahiliyya* refers to the times before the revelation of the Koran. In radicalizing the interpretation of *jahi-liyya* as a form of modern barbarism as first defined by the Indian Islamist Mawdudi, Qutb extended its meaning to all kinds of worldly rule, branding existing forms of political institutions, and in particular the rule of Nasser in Egypt as heretic and a violation of the sovereignty of God. Having been imprisoned several times by the Nasser regime, Qutb was eventually publicly executed in August 1966.[6]

To be sure, on the basis of ideological concepts rooted in Hasan al-Ban-na's ideas, both wings of the Brotherhood strove for the transformation of Egypt into a society oriented toward the model of an organized Islamic modern. They aspired to the establishment of an Islamic social order epito-mized in the creation of an Islamic state. Thus, agreeing on the ends of their political struggle, the two wings were separated by their means. The revolutionary wing advocated political action, by violent means if necessary, while the gradualist wing called for the transformation of Egyptian society through religious mission (Bayat 2007, 38). In terms of popular support, the Muslim Brotherhood found most adherents to its political vision among middle-class students, university graduates, and professionals in cities and provincial towns. Initially, this group was similar to the supporters of the radical wing, but the militant Islamist groups of the 1980s and early 1990s increasingly recruited their followers further down the socioeconomic scale (Ibrahim 1996). Among the most influential of these militant organizations were Al-Takfir wa al-Hijra, Al-Jihad, and Al-Jamaa al-Islamiyya. It was these organizations that carried out the terrorist attacks among which the most infamous were the assassination of President Sadat in 1981 and the Luxor massacre in 1997.

To a certain extent, President Sadat became a victim of his own political strategy to employ religion in order to foster his personal rule, to support the selective liberalization of the Egyptian economy, and to balance domestically his pro-Western shift in Egyptian foreign policy. Undermining the two pil-lars of the Nasserist state, preemptive corporatism, and its monopolistic state capitalism (Waterbury 1983, 429), Sadat initially tried to counter the leftist and Nasserist trends in Egyptian society by religious means. He released imprisoned Muslim Brothers and facilitated the activities of Islamic student associations, such as Al-Jamaa al-Islamiyya, in universities. Later realizing that the growing number of Islamist organizations posed an increasing threat to his own regime, Sadat changed this strategy. Subsidies to student associations were withheld, Islamic organizations and summer camps were shut down, and finally a few months before his assassination on October 6, 1981, wide-scale arrests among the leadership of the militant organizations were carried out (Ibrahim 1988; Sullivan and Abed-Kotob 1999, 72–5).

When Mubarak succeeded Sadat in 1981, he soon continued to repress militant Islamist organizations. Apart from police raids, arrests, and impris-onments, he embarked on a public relations battle with the militants through posters, films, television, and government spokesmen (Sullivan and Abed-Kotob 1999, 89). At the same time, Mubarak's regime balanced this state repression by showing a continuing openness toward the Muslim Brotherhood. In its efforts to accommodate the nonviolent mainstream of the Islamist movement, this openness was a means of defusing tension and consolidating the regime's own position with regard to Egypt's religious constituency. As a result of these ambivalent policies of the regime, the influence of the Brotherhood grew, and by the early 1990s, it controlled numerous mosques, syndicates, unions, schools, and associations. Furthermore, representatives of the Muslim Brotherhood constituted the most pronounced opposition in Parliament (El-Ghobashy 2005; Bayat 2007, 143). Following an alleged assassination attempt on Mubarak while participating at a conference of the African Union in Addis Ababa in June 1995, the regime decided to change previous policies and launched a comprehensive crackdown on the Islamist movement by its security forces. The state encroached on the Muslim Brotherhood's hold on universities, manipulated the election procedures of professional syndicates, arrested prominent Muslim Brothers prior to national elections, and incarcerated leaders of Islamist syndicates. In the late 1990s, the Brotherhood was thus forced to limit its activities to Koran recitations, Ramadan feasts, and religious funerals, shifting its language of agitation from politics to public morality, Islamic virtues, and international issues (Bayat 2007, 143–5). Although being a politically banned organization, the Brotherhood nevertheless was able to gain 88 seats, equivalent to almost 20 percent of the votes, in the 2005 parliamentary elections by participating with independent candidates (Bayat 2007, 185). In order to limit the Muslim Brotherhood's ability to compete on equal terms for parliamentary seats, the government amended the Egyptian constitution in April 2006, adding a complete prohibition on the formation of political parties based on religion.[7]

Since Sadat the Muslim Brotherhood appears to have transformed itself into an organization in which political aspirations increasingly dominated its activities in the realms of religion and social service provision. In curtailing its political ambitions, the repressive move of the Mubarak regime tried to push the Brotherhood as an organization back into the religious realm. From a perspective of social structures, the struggle between the state and the Brotherhood might be interpreted as a process of boundary drawing between the social domains of religion and politics. Once evolved from a religious movement, as a religious organization the Muslim Brotherhood transgressed the boundaries of religious communication at several points in time of Egyptian history. In pursuing its ideal of an Egyptian Islamic modern, its political rationale has tended to supersede its religious identity in its organizational nature. Witnessing the killing of innocent people by militant Islamist groups in the 1980s and 1990s and the state's subsequent crackdowns and containment of the Muslim Brotherhood, many Egyptians have most likely become disillusioned with a political Islam engaged in a fierce struggle about the nature of Egypt's organized modernity. This contestation of the boundaries between state and religion has taken place in an authoritarian environment in which the regime laid claim to the domination and control of all other realms of society. It propagated an extremely state-centered version of a type of first modernity against which the Brotherhood placed an Islamic modern no less state centered in its nature. It looks as if the nonintended outcomes of this struggle not only strengthened the communicational boundaries among social domains in Egyptian society, but also resulted in more pluralist attitudes among the Egyptian population. The emergence of a new Islamic movement—religious believers distrusting political Islam (Bayat 2007, 164)—could be interpreted in this direction.

"THE AMR KHALED PHENOMENON": EGYPT'S NEW ISLAMIC MOVEMENT

I heard about him [Amr Khaled] and I started to attend his lessons. They were still at Masjid al-Husary here in Agouza. This is more than four or five years ago. I found him really, really interesting, and I couldn't imagine that number of people. I have never seen anything like that in Egypt. (...) It was not only during Ramadan. It was every Thursday. It was really amazing...amazing. Can you imagine that the whole street was full of people everywhere? (...) And the atmosphere...all the people were sitting together and listening to good things. Also he speaks "*ammiyya* [colloquial Egyptian Arabic]. (...) He can reach all the people, all the classes of people. For example, many girls were not wearing the *hijab* at the beginning, and they were really on another trip. But when they heard his tapes or when they attended his lessons, they started to be good, and they wore the *hijab*, and they became much better than any other girls. And I think this is good.

This is how a 26-year-old volunteer at Resala described to us her encounter with Amr Khaled. Her enthusiastic description and the charismatic experience through which she apparently went are characteristic of the way in which many among Egypt's youth refer to a new Islamic movement. The followers of this movement take the interpretations of Islamic traditions by new lay preachers such as Amr Khaled as their inspiration and motivation for engaging in various kinds of social activism. The adherents of this religious awakening are more concerned with personal morality, individual improvement, and community development than with issues of political reform by means of formal politics. Moreover, while the social backbone of the Muslim Brotherhood and its aim of an organized Islamic modern predominantly targeted the lower middle class, this new movement has been characterized by the engagement of young Egyptians first representing the country's upper middle class, but in more recent years also increasingly spreading among lower middle class youth. Manifested in various youth organizations, this new Islamic movement combines social awareness with faith and ethics packaged in "compelling and contemporary ways to young middle-class consumers" (Peterson 2011, 124). It allows its followers to assert their individuality by adherence to active piety (Bayat 2002). In addition, the movement appeals to the creative and artistic values of second modernity by bringing "art, leisure and entertainment in accordance with religious commitments" (van

Nieuwkerk 2008). Amr Khaled, for instance, invited his audience to send in their own lyrics in the preparation of one of his forthcoming Ramadan shows (Otterbeck 2008, 221). When looking more closely at Amr Khaled, we do not consider him to be the "great founder of a movement," but the epitome of a religious movement generated by structural transformations understandable as a move from organized first to second modernity.

Amr Khaled was born in 1967 and grew up in an upper middle-class family in Cairo. After graduation from the faculty of commerce of Cairo University, he entered the private sector as an accountant. While still working as an accountant, Amr Khaled started preaching in mosques and private clubs in the early 1990s. His audience grew rapidly and his public speeches soon attracted thousands of people. In 2001, he entered television with the religious Ramadan show "Words from the Heart." It was a great success, and he signed a contract with the Saudi-owned religious satellite channel Iqra. From this followed a number of other programs, which all focused on how contemporary Muslims could improve themselves by looking at examples from the time of the Prophet. In 2002, Amr Khaled left Egypt, "reportedly after he was informed by the Mubarak regime that his presence was no longer welcome." Khaled continued his programs from Great Britain until his return to Egypt in 2007 (Rock 2010, 16). His main audience in Egypt initially was "Westernized" and "globalized" young people from the upper class, in particular young women (Wise 2003). Yet soon his appeal extended well into the broader middle class. His shows have been broadcast widely on a number of satellite channels, including Iqra, Dream TV, and Orbit, and his speeches and programs are available on audio- and videotape, as well as being disseminated through his extensive website.[8] His messages reach millions of young Muslims all over the Middle East, as well as in Europe and North America.

Rather than representing an isolated phenomenon, it seems that Amr Khaled has become the catalyst for a much broader trend facilitated by new media such as the Internet and satellite TV. The growing number of preachers with a similar style and message, such as Mustafa Hosni, Khaled el-Guindy, Moez Masoud, and Mona Abdel-Ghani, must therefore be seen as an element of modern religious reorganization in the context of the technological revolution by digital media closely associated with second modernity. This movement is spearheaded by spokespersons who are religious lay people, transmitting their messages in an easily understandable colloquial Arabic rather than employing the classical high-standard Arabic spoken by traditional sheikhs. These lay preachers are young, come from comparatively privileged social backgrounds, and have acquired their religious knowledge by themselves. Consequently, representatives of the religious establishment such as Sheikh Qaradawi lament that these self-declared Islamic messengers do not hold the necessary qualification to preach (Wise 2006). In comparison to the strict and disciplining voices of classical *ulama*, their style is soft and compassionate. In Amr Khaled's words, "My main concern is to make young people love religion instead of fearing it."[9]

In form and content, Amr Khaled's sermons and TV shows differ markedly from the preaching of traditional Al-Azhar sheikhs such as Sheikh Shaarawi and he makes no secret of not being trained in the Islamic sciences. On the contrary, he insists on the fact that he is "just an average Muslim performing *da'wa*, not a scholar practicing *fiqh*" (Wise 2003, 58). These lay preachers do not have religious authority because they are hierarchically different from their audience, representing the religiously educated Islamic establishment, but because they closely resemble those lay people who listen to their message (Moll 2010, 13). Amr Khaled describes his work in terms of a *nahda*, the "revival" of society through religion, apparently linking himself to the modern Islamic reform movement of the nineteenth century. Khaled is close shaven and often wears a suit and a tie, and his style is similar to that of American televangelists. He does not dwell on rigorously detailed rituals and regulations, which for many young Muslims are irrelevant and incomprehensible. Weaving together stories from the Koran with issues of contemporary society, his sermons focus on reconciling Islamic faith and practices with modern lifestyles. His usual themes are love, forgiveness, morality, and social responsibility, and he reassures his listeners in their desire to have fun, money, and success as long as they respect certain boundaries of moral behavior and act as good role models for their fellow Muslims. Khaled combines religious observance with the enjoyment of life (Amin 2011, 130). For example, he declares making money and being wealthy as something that is encouraged in Islam. Being visibly wealthy and sincerely religious at the same time, according to Khaled, will encourage other people to be better Muslims. Thus, for him religious observance does not mean sacrifice but certain moral adjustments to the lifestyle of the middle class. In Asef Bayat's eyes, Amr Khaled articulates "a marriage of faith and fun," and he conveys "simple ethical messages about the morality of everyday life" (Bayat 2007, 152–53).

Clearly in continuation of the ideas of modern Islamic reform, this new religious movement stresses that Muslims have to go back to the "normative" sources of the Koran and the Prophet Muhammad. The new lay preachers offer a religious product that is fully compatible with the modern expectations of the young urban middle classes. While nineteenth-century reformers such as Muhammad Abduh combined their interpretation of Islamic traditions with patterns of classical bourgeois subjectivities, this new movement alludes in its understanding of Islamic traditions predominantly to the postmodern imaginary of the creative, consumption-oriented, and self-reliant entrepreneur, which dominates the subjectivity formation of second modernity. However, both Abduh and Khaled stand for more liberal forms of an Islamic modern in comparison to the social imaginary of Islamist ideologies that dominated visions of an Islamic modern throughout the twentieth century. Contrary to the coercive implementation of an organized Islamic order by the state, they appeal to the idea of a morally autonomous individual (although with very different lifestyles) and promote societal change through the slow individual transformation of Muslim subjects by education and persuasion. In his messages, Amr Khaled has deliberately avoided both addressing domestic

politics and issuing *fatwas*. For him, the connection between religious messages and the sociopolitical order is primarily of an ethical and moral nature.
In this way, he has tried to avoid entering the dangerous turfs of the regime
and the religious establishment. Indirectly, however, he has fully engaged
in the competitive politics of Muslim subjectivities in Egypt and challenged
both Egypt's official Islam represented by many orthodox *ulama* and the
country's so far dominant model of an Islamic modern advocated by the
Muslim Brotherhood.

The major social carrier of this new Islamic movement, the educated and
internationally oriented youth from the upper middle classes, has not been
religiously socialized by the imams of conventional state-controlled mosques.
Given their social background, orthodox sheiks preaching with a raised
index finger on damnation and hell are a deterrent for them rather than calling them to religion. In the social contexts of this urban middle class, the
moral binary of good and bad, therefore, offers a suitable backup code for
the religious distinction between blessed and cursed (Beyer 2006, 88). Amr
Khaled continuously differentiates between the morally acceptable and the
morally wrong, and between what is "good" and what is "bad." He argues,
for instance, that hard work, career ambitions, and good manners are signs
of respect for God and the community, while apathy and immodest behavior
are the exact opposite (Wise 2003, 55, 78). Yet the distinct religious code of
blessed versus cursed is not entirely absent from the preaching of Khaled. In
Wise's analysis, Khaled treats the issues of sin and damnation indirectly by
inviting his audience or guests to describe life-changing events that caused
them to turn toward religion. Often these accounts center on threats of death
and hell, and sometimes he even talks directly about Satan and the threat he
poses to young Muslims (2003, 68–9,78). This more classical religious communication goes along with Khaled's use of scripture in which he remains
relatively literal and does not advocate critical approaches to the traditions.
For Asef Bayat, Amr Khaled is therefore an innovator in style rather than in
overcoming orthodox approaches to Islamic traditions (cf. Bayat 2002). The
conservative religious flavor of his message also comes to the fore regarding
gender. He discourages dating among young people and perceives the role
of women predominantly in raising children. Pursuing a career is legitimate,
however, secondary to the role of a caretaking mother (Rock 2010, 32).

Given this ambiguous nature of his preaching, Amr Khaled has been
attacked by Egypt's religious establishment, as well as by secularist and
Islamist sides. While secular intellectuals accused him of being too conservative, traditional sheikhs, Muslim Brothers and Salafist groups found him
too moderate (Atia 2005). Among the Islamists, and the Muslim Brothers
in particular, Amr Khaled's preaching is often referred to as "Islam light"
or "air-conditioned Islam," and he has been criticized for failing to address
current political issues such as the lack of government accountability, the war
in Iraq, and the Israel–Palestine conflict (Haenni and Tammam 2003). As
to the Egyptian state, his exile in 2002 speaks for itself; although Al-Azhar
has officially remained silent, a number of its sheikhs and professors have

described Khaled as "a dangerous, unlicensed and untrained imposter: a Muslim Brother, false prophet, or extremist in disguise" (Wise 2003, 9). Clearly, the representatives of Egypt's official Islam have repeatedly tried to portray the religious communication of the movement as being outside the confines of recognized religion (cf. Beyer 2006, 8). Nevertheless, Amr Khaled has managed to establish an alternative religious discourse that "not only threatens to be more popular and better marketed than the Azhar's official version, but also wrecked havoc with the state's attempt to categorize Islamists as poor, uncouth, fringe extremists" (Wise 2003, 10).

Similar to the state and Egypt's religious establishment, many secular-minded observers lament the influence that Amr Khaled exerts on a significant part of Egyptian youth. The following statement is from an interview with an Egyptian researcher about Amr Khaled and his primary target group, the country's upper middle-class youth:

> He is the symbol of a young Muslim from the upper middle class, who can still do everything—go abroad, wear fashionable clothes and have a relationship with girls. He has thousands of young followers who can't find other leaders. He plays under the umbrella of religious culture, which is horrible. And he made a very good business. (...) It is suitable for the upper middle-class youth. It gives them peace inside. It is like a policeman giving a person a license to drive. And he is intelligent and smart looking.

According to this Egyptian researcher, Amr Khaled's messages might give this particular group of young people "peace inside,", but they also pacify them. This is without doubt an important aspect of the discussion about Amr Khaled and other lay preachers like him. Many scholars and journalists dismiss the idea that Amr Khaled is a "liberal Muslim thinker." According to Bayat, some of Amr Khaled's ideas are highly conservative and his methods manipulative, for example, his insistence on a "complete, head to toe *hijab* as an obligation in Islam" (Bayat 2007, 153). In emphasizing the movement's inherent conservative traits and the quietism it has promoted with regard to formal politics, however, these critics play down the socially mobilizing power that Amr Khaled and others simultaneously convey. Inspired by Amr Khaled's TV program, *Sunaa al-Hayah*, as a part of Egypt's new Islamic movement an ever growing number of activist youth organizations have recently emerged.

THE NEW RELIGIOUS YOUTH ORGANIZATIONS: MAKING THE MOVEMENT WORK

Since 2004, Amr Khaled has focused more explicitly on issues of community development, social change, and dialogue between Islam and the West. For example, in his TV program *Sunaa al-Hayah* from 2004–2005, he shifted focus from predominantly religious issues to projects of social engagement. Promoting social responsibility, Amr Khaled encouraged young people especially to develop themselves and their fellow citizens by actively participating in their communities. As he puts it, "Guys, do not wait for something to happen. Let's do it ourselves!" According to him, Islam is not only about praying five times a day and wearing the *hijab* the correct way. Likewise he portrays *daawa* not simply as a call to live by religious rules. In the message of the new lay preachers, Islam is about improving yourself and your community, and *daawa* is a call for engagement and social reform. In Amr Khaled's own words, he wants "to encourage our men and women, both young and old, to have effective and beneficial roles in serving our country."[10] Awareness campaigns on drugs and smoking, as well as the collection and distribution of food and second-hand clothes in poor areas, are some of the projects suggested by Amr Khaled and carried out by young people.

Amr Khaled's *Sunaa al-Hayah* program has inspired young people all over Egypt and beyond. Religiously motivated activists have established their own organizations and the program impacted on the self-understanding of already existing ones. By 2008, 1.5 million people globally were supposedly engaged in Sunaa al-Hayah-inspired organizations, some 500,000 of them in Egypt (Mandaville 2008). Thus, what was primarily the concern of a social movement, namely, a reinterpretation of the concepts of individual improvement and social responsibility in an Islamic framework, has now also been "reconfigured" in the structure of a specific form of civil society organization. The new youth organizations lend this religious movement form and mark its relative success (cf. Beyer 2006, 52–3, 110). Amr Khaled has opened up a space where religion is articulated to achieve social change in new ways (Mandaville 2008). Following the call of Amr Khaled and similar lay preachers, the young activists in these organizations aim at making Islam a natural part of their own daily lives and those of their target groups. Moreover, for them, religious engagement goes hand in hand with an involvement in developing their society. In the spirit of the movement, these young Egyptians make religion an integral part of their modern Muslim selfhoods.

Taking their point of departure in a religious movement, the new youth organizations represent a peculiar combination of conventional social welfare activities, concepts, and tools of the international development industry and patterns from modern management and business studies. In the eyes of many of the young activists, however, Amr Khaled was only a catalyst for a form of social engagement already growing among Egypt's youth: "Amr Khaled has a great influence on all youth in Egypt as to charity work. But if he had not come and talked about it, it would have happened anyway, maybe just a few years later." The opinion of one of our interlocutors indicates the broader structural context in which these youth organizations have emerged. At best, Amr Khaled and similar lay preachers promulgated a vague normative model to which this otherwise decentralized and rather diffuse group of organizations refers. They delivered a number of specific religiously inspired themes around which new organizational forms have emerged. The more general religious messages of the movement have inspired students, businessmen, and professionals to establish and join various new organizations that reflect the vision and norms of the movement, however, without being under the leadership of Amr Khaled or other ideological spokespeople of the movement.

The new religious youth organizations represent a minor but growing part of Egyptian civil society. They are established and led by young people who aim to assist in solving the country's many poverty-related problems and who wish to improve what they see as a general lack of religious ethics and morals in society. Apparently, these organizations are a form of organized politics through other means. For religiously minded young people who are disillusioned with political Islam and do not want to risk a confrontation with state authorities, activism within the sphere of social welfare was a welcomed opportunity. Yet it was not entirely without personal risk. Due to the state's ambiguous relationship with many religious civil society organizations, participants have had to be very careful not to cross the red lines drawn by the regime. On the one hand, there was the fear held by state authorities that these organizations would in one way or another join the political opposition of the Muslim Brotherhood or other Islamist groups against the state. Even if this political support does not eventuate, these organizations still "offer concrete, visible examples of what Islam can provide, in contradistinction to the state's secular modernization failures" (Wiktorovicz 2004, 11). On the other hand, and similar to the situation in Jordan, the regime was well aware of the fact that such organizations provide good and much needed services to the poor. Thus, letting them operate was a handy remedy for the strained social situation caused by the chronic underperformance of the welfare system of the Egyptian state. This ambivalent relationship was very much reflected in the regime's stance vis-à-vis the different kinds of Egyptian civil society organizations. According to Abdel-Rahman, "the regime wished to neutralize the power of Islamic NGOs by attempting to co-opt those with no strong political inclinations, while subjecting the more politically active Islamic NGOs, for example Al-Gamaiaa al-Sharaia, to its most extreme measure of scrutiny" (2004, 114).

Not surprisingly, the new youth organizations—like other so-called voluntary civic associations—have been subject to a number of very extensive rules and regulations made by the Egyptian state, which closely resemble the regulatory regime of the Jordanian monarchy. As outlined in NGO Law 84 of 2002,[11] civil society organizations must register with the ministry of social solidarity, where they are classified according to their activities. They are restricted to working within this field of activities and cannot widen or change their scope without prior permission.[12] Furthermore, they are required to have a board of members of a minimum of four, including at least a president, vice president, treasurer, and secretary (El-Daly 2006). At the time of our fieldwork, some of these new youth organizations were not (yet) registered as formal NGOs. This could also have been a more or less deliberate strategy in order to avoid control and possible harassment by the state. "Youth groups" and other such diffuse associations are more difficult to control because they locate themselves in other spaces and practices less easily regulated through traditional instruments of power (El-Rouby et al. 2007). Generally speaking, the youth organizations of our study must accept two rather broad conditions: first of all, they must stay completely out of formal politics and, secondly, although religious in nature, they had to downplay their "Islamic rationale" in order not to resemble the model of an Islamic modern that has been the core of the ideology of the Muslim Brotherhood.

According to the NGO law, state authorities can immediately dissolve civil society organizations if they become involved in political activities. In fact, by accepting the obligation to stay away from politics, organizations were pretty much safe from all the other infringements on their activities for which the NGO law actually provides (Ibrahim 1996). Our interviewees were all very much aware of this condition. In an interview, the president of one of the organizations expressed this quite openly, and he assured us that they make this point clear to all their members:

> We don't have political aspirations and we cannot have political aspirations. It is dangerous. If we had these aspirations, we would not have this meeting and we would not do all the work we do. (...) You will find groups who believe that it is their duty to do political work. But we cannot do this. (...) We cannot work in politics. We know that it is dangerous.

In this statement, our interview partner touches upon the second, more implicit condition given by the regime, namely, that the Islamic rationale of the organizations should not be too visible. For many Egyptians, the label "Islamic" has been closely linked to this dangerous field of politics. Islamic had the connotation of Islamist and consequently the new youth organizations were afraid to be prosecuted by the regime for raising the banner of Islam too high. This apprehensive approach was clearly reflected by a male volunteer among our informants:

> I think that most people working in charity and development are afraid to announce that they are Islamic. The government places restrictions on any group that has an Islamic name. I think that this makes them say that their motives are not Islamic, but consciously or subconsciously they are aware that their real motives inside them are Islamic. They have a mission or a role in developing their society, but they are not willing to announce that their motives are Islamic. They are not comfortable to announce so after the incidents here in Egypt in the 1980s and early 1990s, when Islamic groups were involved in some terrorism and something. I think that people have that idea that the government will restrict or even harm any groups that belong to Islam.

Most social welfare organizations, including the youth organizations studied here, preferred to register under other categories than that of cultural, scientific, and religious association, precisely because of the suspicion and harsher treatment that the state often reserved for Islamic organizations

(Abdel-Rahman 2004, 122). According to an Egyptian journalist, only two kinds of organization could maintain a good relationship with the state: secular organizations and Muslim organizations that managed to stay completely out of politics, that is, whose organizational rationales fell fully into the field of modern religion as oriented toward the transcendental world.

CONCLUSIONS

In Egypt, the state has constantly tried to dominate and control religious communication; however, at the same time, state authorities have encouraged employing religious traditions in societal negotiation beyond the functional demarcations of the religious field. The religious movement of which Amr Khaled is one of the most famous representatives has used this discursive space and has challenged both state control of religion and the hegemonic oppositional Islamic project of the Muslim Brotherhood. The religious discourse characterizing this movement differs significantly from both the official Islam of the state and the political Islam of the Muslim Brotherhood, and this alone left the regime with a feeling of uneasiness. Furthermore, the movement made an inroad into parts of the country's previously secularly defined nationalist elite.

While the state has dominated and controlled religious communication when approached from a macro-sociological level of analysis, organizations and social movements are the primary bearers of religious communication at the organizational level. In other words, religious organizations provide the answer to the question about the forms in which religious authority appears in contemporary societies. Organizations together with social movements are essential for giving form to new interpretations of religious traditions or for turning variations in already existing ones into concrete social phenomena (Beyer 2006, 107–109). The new youth organizations are concrete manifestations of this relationship between religion and organizational development in Egypt. As the next chapter will show, they represent a continuation of a long tradition of Islamic charity and religious ethics and morals, on the one hand, and a new way of understanding and practicing religion by combining traditional Islamic concepts and ideas with neoliberal values and a specific youth responsibility, on the other. On the basis of publicly accessible material and interviews with the leadership, we try to analyze their self-image and organizational rationale within the power coordinates of Egyptian society.

New Youth Organizations in Egypt: Charity and the "Muslim Professional"

Religious social welfare organizations in Egypt have a long tradition, and from the beginning they have been critically observed and have stood in competition with policies of poor relief made by the Egyptian state (cf. Ener 2003). The first Muslim and Coptic charitable associations appeared in the nineteenth century,[1] and in the twenty-first century this religious part of Egyptian civil society comprises a broad variety of organizations, ranging from small-scale charities related to local mosques and community-based associations to large national organizations with branches all over the country. In addition, there are numerous *zakat* committees, religious schools, health clinics, orphanages, women's organizations, and so on.[2] In 1939, the state established the ministry of social affairs, bringing the state back into the center of charity and countering responses to the needs of Egypt's poor made by the Muslim Brotherhood and leftist movements (Ener 2003, 134). In their activities, self-image and discursive representations, the new youth organizations very much draw on this tradition and its interlacement in state affairs. However, they also differ in more than one respect from Egypt's traditional religious social welfare organizations. These differences have been manifested in four new trends.

First of all, they are established and led by young people, taking Egypt's youth as their major human resource. This stands in sharp contrast to the overwhelming majority of religious charities that only to a limited extent engage youth and largely exclude them from leadership and decision making. Most Islamic charitable associations resemble Egyptian organizations and institutions in general, in being led by middle-aged men who see youth more as a target group that needs help and guidance than a resource in itself (El-Rouby 2007). Secondly, as already indicated in the previous chapter, the new youth organizations evolved together with and were inspired by a new Islamic movement. Related to the major themes of this movement, they have been organizing themselves around a specific understanding of Islamic morality with youth voluntarism and strategies for individual improvement, as well as peculiar ways to call for social responsibility. Third, the majority of volunteers in these organizations are young women. This distinguishes them remarkably from Egypt's traditional charitable associations, as well as from other civil society organizations in the country, including nonreligious ones, in which women tend to be clearly underrepresented (El-Daly 2006, 189). Finally, in comparison to the average civil society organization in Egypt, these youth organizations strongly rely on the use of new media. In professionally using the Internet, mobile phones, and satellite television for internal communication as well as providing information to donors and the general public, they actively take part in the digital technological revolution that is a characteristic feature of the infrastructure of second modernity. Thus, although standing in historical continuation of Egypt's traditional Islamic charitable associations, these youth organizations nevertheless represent a new phenomenon in the realm of Islamic social welfare provision. Due to a specific combination of youth participation and a contemporary approach to social Islam, they provide social sites for Egypt's religiously minded young middle class to engage in society on their own terms. They offer this constituency a meaningful religious framework to pursue their interests outside of the organized models of Egypt's official Islam and the Islamist ideology of the Muslim Brotherhood.

The organizations in our study were all established around 2000 or later, and the majority of them started out as student initiatives at universities in Cairo. This is no coincidence when looking at the modern history of Egypt, in general, and the role of Islamic actors, in particular. Student activism at the universities played a major role in the emergence and development of new ideas and movements within Egyptian civil society and politics throughout the twentieth century. During the politically turbulent years between the two World Wars, for instance, Cairo University was an important site for the struggle between various political parties such as the national-liberal Wafd, the Communists, the Muslim Brotherhood, the National Party, and Young Egypt (cf. Mitchell 1969, 37–52). Later, in the 1970s and 1980s, Islamic student associations at different Egyptian universities served as the training ground for a new generation of Islamist leaders, and it was from among university students that Islamist groups recruited their followers (cf. Wickham 2002). In comparison to these historical examples, however, the aims and forms of activities of the new youth organizations in our study are not overtly political in the conventional understanding of the term. They address social questions through a religious vocabulary that at least on the surface seems to respect the distinct functional spheres of religion and politics, differentiating themselves visibly from the holistic religiopolitical rhetoric of Islamist groups.

In the following section, we will briefly describe the selective sample of organizations in our study. We look at their organizational structures, economic background, recruitment patterns, and their use of media. What is the rationale behind these organizations, which problems do they identify in Egyptian society, and what are they aiming at? The second section analyzes the ways in which they try to tackle these major societal problems and formalize communication among their members. We discuss their attempts to bring about social change by promoting voluntarism, development and social entrepreneurship. Moreover, we present the normative ideal type of a "Muslim professional" that serves as a model for youth empowerment by combining Islamic morality with neo-liberal elements of management sciences. Finally, we explore the interplay between three central mobilizing forces—religion, nationalism, and friendship—which have been crucial in the successful establishment of these youth organization.

RELIGION AND DEVELOPMENT: THE RATIONALE OF CONTEMPORARY YOUTH ACTIVISM IN EGYPT

When visiting the Heliopolis branch of Resala for the first time in 2007, we found it located in a massive five-storey concrete block similar to many of the residence buildings in the area. When this branch opened in 2005, the building provided plenty of space for volunteers, staff, and related activities. Yet like many other Resala branches, the Heliopolis branch has witnessed a rapid increase in both the numbers of volunteers and the scale and variety of activities. Some of the work in Heliopolis, therefore, used to be carried out in the open-air yard as well as in small side-buildings and lean-tos besides the main building. This goes for the clothes sorting, the paper recycling, and the extra-curricular and literacy lessons. As a consequence of its growth, in 2012 the branch eventually moved into a newly constructed, much larger and more luxurious building in the neighboring lot. This twelve-storey building, white-painted and with decorated balconies, clearly symbolizes the success of the Resala Association for Charity. The price of land is expensive in Cairo, in particular, in upper-middle-class areas like Heliopolis. From 2000 to 2011, Resala grew from 1 to 63 branches spread over Egypt's 29 governorates, of which eight are located in expensive Cairo neighborhoods. In addition, Resala runs a hospital, a primary school, and several second-hand clothes stores.[3] This bears witness to the increasing amounts of money that have been donated to Resala. Other obvious signs of Resala's success are the commercials on radio and TV, as well as the meter-high billboards on the Ring Road and other main roads in Cairo. In 2011, Resala had a total number of more than 98,000 volunteers. The Heliopolis branch alone disposed over more than 8,000 volunteers and 580 formally employed staff. On the financial side, the total amount of in-cash donations to Resala was about 193 million Egyptian pounds in 2011 for the Resala association as a whole, and 34.8 million Egyptian pounds for the Heliopolis branch.[4]

Resala is the oldest and largest of the organizations in our sample. It once started as a student initiative at the Faculty of Engineering at Cairo University in 1999. Initially, its activities were blood donation, college services, and visits to orphanages, nursing homes, and hospitals. In 2000, a rich businessman donated a piece of land to the organization, and the members decided to register Resala as a formal NGO. In 2009, it had grown into the largest voluntary organization in the Arab world. Compared to Resala, most of the other new youth organizations are much smaller in size and reach, but they share many features of this pioneer organization when it comes to their organizational structures, forms of activities, and membership patterns. In total, we included nine youth organizations in our fieldwork. These are Alashanek Ya Baladi, Bayan, Al-Boraq, Mazeed, Misr Shoryan al-Ataa, Resala, Sama, Sunaa al-Hayah, and Zedny.[5] Apart from Alashanek Ya Baladi, the names of these organizations clearly display their religious background. Al-Boraq, for instance, is the name of the creature on which the Prophet made his ascension to the seven heavens. The name Zedny means "increase for me" and it is taken from a Koranic verse. Resala translates as "message," relating to God's revelation conveyed through the messenger Muhammad. Bayan, to give a last example, refers to the idea of empowering people to express themselves, an idea inspired by two specific verses from the Koran (27/4 and 4/138). Given the very common religious notions of these traditional Islamic references, they position these organizations in the mainstream religious field without associating them with Islamist ideologies that transgress the limitations of religious communication.

While the youth organizations share their roots in Egypt's new religious movement, they differ in form and degree regarding their individual organizational structures. Some of them are relatively well-established associations that are formally registered with the ministry for social solidarity. They have institutionalized boards, comprise various organizational committees, and carry out an extensive range of clearly defined programs and projects with deliberate strategies for their implementation. Yet another group of them resembles more what was termed "youth groups," rather informal groups of young people with a shared vision who meet regularly to service the community in different fields (El-Rouby et al. 2007, 9). In comparison to the older and formally established organizations, these youth groups are more open, decentralized, flexible, and nonhierarchical in their structure. Despite these differences, however, they advocate the same understanding of Islamic morality that characterizes the new Islamic movement, in general, and their organizational rationales revolve around similar issues such as youth voluntarism, individual improvement, and social responsibility.

In most organizations, the chairperson is also the president. Together with the other board members and the program directors, the president is responsible for the daily management and running of the organization. Other members are the volunteers and the regular members who participate in the activities and sometimes pay an annual membership fee to the organization. Most of the organizations have small headquarters from which they plan and organize their activities. The majority of these headquarters are found in the neighborhoods of their members and volunteers, often middle- or upper-middle-class residential areas such as Nasr City and Heliopolis. Alashanek Ya Baladi is an exception. Although most of its members and volunteers are from the upper middle class, the headquarter is in a very poor neighborhood in Old Cairo. Two of the organizations in our sample, Zedny and Bayan, work through larger and more traditional mosque-related Islamic charitable associations, which provide them with offices and lecture facilities.

Most organizations work within an area we can label as social welfare provision. Some are specialized in fields such as medical assistance, micro finance, or human development, while others direct their efforts to the development of specific geographical areas where they carry out projects and activities of very different kinds. Generally speaking, they all address two social groups, poor families and young people. In some cases, the target groups are poor families in general, but most organizations try to direct their efforts toward particularly vulnerable groups such as women, orphans, students, the disabled, or the elderly. Bayan and Zedny are again somehow special cases. Their beneficiaries are not particularly poor people, but young students and college graduates, primarily from the middle class, who lack the necessary extra skills to enter the labor market.

In economic terms, most of the organizations rely primarily, if not solely, on donations from individual Egyptians, many of which are given in line with the Islamic tradition of *zakat al-fitr* during Ramadan.[6] Furthermore, revenues from activities such as attendee fees or from the sale of second-hand clothes represent an important source of income for these organizations. Yet, most activities do not require large funds. All organizations rely almost solely on voluntary labor; only half of them dispose over salaried staff, and in most cases, these employees constitute only a tiny minority of the total number of people engaged. Moreover, most of the material needs such as food, clothes, and books are also covered by in-kind donations. In fact, these organizations receive many in-kind donations, and because of the many restrictions and extensive bureaucratic procedures related to all monetary aid in Egypt, some organizations even prefer in-kind to in-cash donations.

The professional use of new media such as the mobile phone and the Internet is crucial to the efficiency and daily functioning of the organizations. To a large extent, information to members and potential volunteers, as well as to donors and the general public, is communicated through websites, e-mail lists, text messages, blogs, Facebook, and chat rooms. Out of the nine organizations in this study, five have their own websites, two in Arabic, one in both Arabic and English, and two in English.[7] These websites contain information on their organizational background, mission and vision, activities, members, and staff. For example, on the websites of Zedny and Bayan you will find announcements of new courses for prospective students. Resala organizes the collection of donations through its website, which also functions as an essential space for communication and registration of new volunteers. Furthermore, text messages are a common way of communication among members and volunteers, for example, by reminding volunteers of particular events and activities. Finally, many members and volunteers are connected through the social networking website Facebook. This intensive and often sophisticated use of new media in information and mobilization clearly distinguished the new youth organizations from the average civil society organization in Egypt, and it is likely that their extensive use of new media is one of the reasons behind their rapid growth.

When it comes to the organizational rationale, the website of Zedny gives us a representative statement: "Our goal is to work together toward a promising future, and our achievements would be changing our country to a better place."[8] In a similar voice, Alashanek Ya Baladi combines its slogan "The path for a better country," with a call to the empowerment of marginalized youth and women.[9] The young activists want to take part in and contribute to development and social change in their country. They are aiming at building foundations for their own future and the future of Egyptian society in general. "We cannot wait for others to come and build this future," as the president of Mazeed put it; he continued: "Our slogan is 'Our Future, Our Decision!'" Most of our interlocutors referred to societal change and development in very general terms. Apparently, they did not have a specific model of a social order in mind when promoting their ideas of social change. Only one board member stressed that in his opinion the organization should strive for the establishment of a social order in which Islam would play a greater role. However, as will be discussed in detail below, the primary concern of these youth organizations is not the formation of any kind of Islamic government but rather to contribute to the transformation of Egyptian society through making a difference on the levels of the individual and the local community. Thus, they position themselves against the ideas of the developmental state, whether in its Nasserist secular or in its Islamist version as propagated by the Muslim Brotherhood. Instead, they revive classical bourgeois ideas of social improvement by morally autonomous selves whose Islamic versions once were advocated by nineteenth-century reformers such as Muhammad Abduh.

During our fieldwork, our interviewees repeatedly emphasized two types of problems as their primary concerns. The first is related to the poor and underprivileged classes in Egyptian society. Despite recent improvements, living standards in Egypt are extremely low by international standards. According to United Nations figures, around 20 percent of the population live below the poverty line, and 29 percent of the population are illiterate (UNDP 2008). Furthermore, national health services are poor and far from being able to provide even a minimum level of medical care for the population (Clark 2004, 48). Like many other social welfare organizations, the youth organizations identify poverty and poverty-related problems such as illiteracy, unemployment, and illness as the primary complex of problems in Egyptian society. According to Alashanek Ya Baladi, "Egypt suffers from poverty, illiteracy and health hazards, which keeps it underdeveloped all the way."[10]

The second core concern of our informants was the present state of Egyptian youth. Similar to Alashanek Ya Baladi, they perceive Egypt's youth as marginalized and lacking the necessary skills for contributing to societal development. They criticize young Egyptians for a lack of awareness with regard to their social environment, being preoccupied with a host of trivial things. Egypt's youth is "simply oppressed and lost."[11] This diagnosis holds strong empirical credibility and central salience for the primary target group of the new youth organizations, namely, formally educated middle-class youth (cf. Benford and Snow 2000). Egypt has been going through a period in which the numbers of young people have increased significantly compared to other age groups. According to statistics of the UN population division (2008), in 2005, 22 percent of Egyptians were between the ages of 14 and 24. For the majority of young Egyptians, prospects for the future are bleak. Despite a number of governmental and private initiatives, unemployment and underemployment remain widespread among young graduates from higher education institutes, colleges, and universities. The general unemployment rate in Egypt is about 25 percent, while 80 percent of the country's total number of unemployed is in the youth bracket. Among those who have a job, 69 percent do not have formal contracts and 49 percent are underemployed in temporary jobs (Herrera 2011, 128).

One of the reasons for this high level of unemployment among Egypt's youth is that their formal qualifications do not match those that private companies and the labor market in general would require from them. This is mainly critical for young people from the lower and middle strata of the middle class. Unlike the upper middle class and the elite, they cannot afford private universities and do not have the connections necessary to obtain access to jobs in the private sector. The lack of income opportunities together with the urban housing crisis means that many young people are not able to gain economic independence from their parents and create families of their own. In this sense, the socioeconomic condition of the country deprives them of a central field of modern subjectivity formation: intimacy in the form of the nuclear family. Furthermore, opportunities for Egyptian youth to participate in civic life and to influence important decision-making processes are scarce, as evidenced by university policies toward student activism. In sum, Egypt's youth continues to be the most disadvantaged group in society in terms of education and training, higher rates of unemployment, potentials for forming families, and channels for exercising citizenship (Assaad and Barsoum 2007; Ibrahim and Wassef 2000). Evidently, they feel excluded from core fields of modern subjectivity formation: They face severe problems in constructing meaningful selfhoods as working subjects, as responsible citizens in public life and through intimate family relations.

Viewing the problem partly as a result of this structural marginalization of young Egyptians, the youth organizations directly address the state of indifference and apathy that has spread among Egyptian youth. Instead of victimizing them, however, they appeal to youth as a societal resource: "Our youth waste time doing nothing instead of helping their society," as the head of one of Resala's branches put it. This criticism is especially directed toward educated and resourceful young people from the middle and upper classes. For example, the founder and chairwoman of Alashanek Ya Baladi lamented the "increasing passivity of the fortunate, who can really help (. . . ,) who can really educate (. . . ,) and who can really defend the rights of the powerless."[12] This judgment was underpinned by a survey among Egyptian youth, which documents a widespread apathy and lack of initiative. Youth have "little faith that their own voices and that their efforts might be appreciated, heard or considered" (UNDP 200; cf. Assaad and Barsoum 2007). In the perception of our youth organizations, the social exclusion of young people by state institutions and the older generation has been enhanced through their own disengagement and social apathy.

Finally, there was a strong tendency among our interviewees to link poverty-related problems and phenomena of youth exclusion and apathy to an alleged absence of religious ethics and morals in Egyptian society. According to the leadership of several organizations, everyday life and ordinary experiences are not addressed properly by the sheikhs and imams of religious institutions. Official Islam has failed to play a beneficial social role. Again echoing the social diagnosis of the classical Islamic reform movement of the nineteenth century, they see it as an important element of their work to improve this situation by providing Egypt's youth with religious role models. In the global context of second modernity, they closely relate the successful modernization of Egyptian society to issues of religious reform. According to them, the moral development of society and the individual must go hand in hand.

In sum, the new youth organizations wish to contribute to the development and change of their country by addressing problems concerning poverty, youth exclusion, and apathy. Due to the impeding social, economic, and political structures of the country, the organizations identify the mental origin of these problems in religious terms as a general lack of religious ethics and morals in Egyptian society. Their mission is therefore twofold but intertwined: They aim to develop and change their country by assisting poor and underprivileged people in society, and they wish to engage and morally educate young Egyptians in this process. Apparently, they manage to link two "ideological congruent but structurally unconnected frames" within the field of social welfare (Benford and Snow 2000, 624). Furthermore, they articulate a perceived general decline in religious morals, which is seen as one of the reasons for problems facing Egyptian society today. Implicitly, this decline is associated with the performance of Egypt's religious establishment, as well as with the violent degeneration of political Islam, the alternative Islamic modern of the Muslim Brotherhood. Within the structural constraints of about 60 years of authoritarian rule, challenged by a no less authoritarian version of an Islamic modern, these youth organizations express the desire of a revivalist religious movement aiming at the construction of a new model of an Islamic modern. This new model includes both elements of the rather conservative form of limited liberalism of classical bourgeois society and features of the postmodern, more pluralist social imaginary that has been a central pattern of second modernity. From this perspective, they are clearly part of the new *al-nahda* movement epitomized in the phenomenon of lay preachers such as Amr Khaled. The specific directions to pursue on this general path to social change certainly vary within the movement. For the group of new youth organizations studied here, two overall strategies stand out: one is a combination of youth voluntarism, development, and social entrepreneurship; and the other is a new role model combining Islamic morality and behavior with neoliberal business and management science. What these strategies have in common is an insistence on Islam as an important frame and guideline. They are embedded in an Islamic worldview, in a religiously guided apprehension of the modern world. Consequently, our interviewees want to "inspire people" to follow religious instruction whether they play the roles of beneficiaries or activists in their projects.

Changing Society: Voluntarism, Social Entrepreneurship, and Development

The new youth organizations deal with Egyptian youth as a resource to achieve social change. According to Alashanek Ya Baladi, the right way to bring about change is to "mobilize youth and give them the needed skills to solve problems in Egypt."[13] At this point, the concept of voluntarism is also introduced. The organizations in our study unanimously perceive voluntarism as a key to tackling both poverty-related problems and problems of indifference and apathy among young Egyptians. Furthermore, many of our interlocutors agreed on the advantages of relying on a voluntary workforce instead of recruiting salaried staff. The chairman of Resala was very explicit about this point: "Volunteers somehow do it better. (. . .). So why should we pay for human effort that people are ready to exert to please God?" According to him, volunteers do a better job because they "do this work from their heart, so it reaches the hearts of its recipients." In promoting voluntarism, most of the organizations refer to the Islamic institutions of *zakat* and *sadaqa* usually associated with voluntary work, in-kind contributions, or free services. In this way, the linkage to Islamic traditions bestows contemporary forms of social action with the necessary authenticity. The idea of voluntarism is placed within an Islamic framework, which also offers nonmaterial rewards. Later on, Resala's chairman continued by giving an example of their work with orphans:

> Imagine the impact on him [an orphanage child] when he finds people that truly love him and call themselves his brothers and sisters—people who take care of him, visit him and take him out. Do you think they would have a better effect if they were volunteers or if they took some monetary compensation for it? They MUST be volunteers! The child won't be truly convinced that they love him unless they are volunteers.

Voluntarism lies at the heart of Resala's organizational structure, where fewer than five percent of the members are salaried staff. All activities are based on voluntary work, be it the preparation of "food bags" by housewives for distribution in poor areas, the private tutoring programs for poor children, or the organizing of big events such as Mother's Day and Orphan Day.

The very large proportion of volunteers among members is one of the decisive features in distinguishing the new youth organizations from other Egyptian civil society organizations, whether religious or not.[14] Many youth organizations do not have any salaried staff. Others have a handful or even fewer to take care of routine administrative and financial tasks. In fact, a voluntary workforce is fundamental for these youth organizations. Naturally, the leaders try to make the volunteers' conditions as good as possible. The head of one of Resala's branches put it this way:

> Here we use the youth and open the doors for them. Our environment makes it easier for them. Other NGOs don't have the space. We have space and we are expanding. We have phones so the volunteers can call the families. You develop yourself to be able to do your job better.

In addition, the equality and similarity of employees and volunteers and the image of a community of peers were often emphasized, this time by a board member in Sunaa al-Hayah: "Here there is no difference between being an employee or a volunteer. We are all the same." All the board members we talked to interpreted the high proportion of volunteers in the organizational structure as being one of the major strengths of the new youth organizations. According to them, the voluntary aspect of participation entails that no one is there for the money and very few for the prestige alone. This is in sharp contrast to the rest of Egyptian civil society organizations in which staff often is looking for the scarce resources of salary and prestige. A board member of one of the more traditional Islamic charitable associations acknowledged this to be a widespread problem. In her eyes, organizations relying on badly paid staff do not really serve society; they are actually rather inactive and useless. Voluntarism is, therefore, perceived to be the appropriate way to involve young people and make social welfare work both more cost effective and more sincere.[15]

While voluntarism is seen as an essential condition for the existence and functioning of new youth organizations, for the majority of them, developmental strategies, social entrepreneurship, and modern management sciences are considered the most important tools through which they can achieve their mission of pursuing social change. With the exception of Resala, all the organizations examined explicitly promote more development-oriented approaches, replacing the traditional and short-term almsgiving and service provision with longer-term achievements and self-sustainability for the people involved.[16] As they see it, charitable activities are not enough to solve the problems facing Egyptian society. Instead they "just fulfill the needs of people" without addressing the roots of the problems. Some organizations went so far as to claim that, in the words of the president of Zedny, "charity is creating passive communities." The new youth organizations clearly see a need for a different approach aiming at long-term and sustainable development. Alashanek Ya Baladi, for instance, explicitly claims to seek a transformation of "the community through empowerment and knowledge, not charity and instant aid."[17] Along similar lines, a board member at Misr Shoryan al-Ataa stressed the difference between traditional charitable activities and activities of a more developmental character, such as those of most new youth organizations:

> Charity is just fulfilling the needs of people who are in need, like people who don't have a stable financial situation, people who need care, either medical or

social—they are fulfilling it, without any idea of the origin of that need and what the problems are. The other level, the sustainable development concept, is searching for the reason. Why are these people in need?

Evidently there is general agreement on the positive connotations of phrases such as "capacity-building" and "sustainable development." More specifically, board members and volunteers frequently mentioned vocational training, micro finance, and human capital development as some of the activities that foster long-term development. In relating these buzzwords of the global development industry to stories about the Prophet or to Amr Khaled's message of faith-based development, our informants usually bestowed them with a legitimating Islamic authenticity.

However, what distinguishes the new youth organizations from other actors within the field of social welfare is not so much this emphasis on development instead of charity, but its combination with voluntarism. In fact, since the late 1990s and early 2000s, many Egyptian social welfare organizations, religious or not, have adopted the global discourse of development-oriented approaches, and a number of new local development organizations have emerged (Atia 2008).[18] What is new about these youth organizations is the way in which they combine this developmental approach with voluntarism as their principle recruitment basis and the spirit of social entrepreneurship we could find among them. Social entrepreneurship is understood here as innovative and sometimes risky enterprises carried out by individuals, groups, or organizations aimed at creating social value (see, e.g., Peredo and McLean 2006). It having become a developmental buzzword during the past two decades, a consistent and mutually accepted definition of social entrepreneurship does not exist (Hill et al. 2010, 6). The literature on social enterprises discusses various forms of organizations that blend their economic and profit-making activities with objectives concerning social, environmental, or health issues (cf. Nyssens 2006), at the same time propagating "the provision of public goods away from the state" (Nicholls 2011, 2). Clearly, the concept combines some central patterns of the postmodern type of the modern subject as a creative entrepreneur with a social mission.

The social entrepreneurship we detected in the new youth organizations has two sides. First of all, the youth organizations are important innovators to implement new ways of helping poor and underprivileged people to break out of the poverty circle. For example, Resala has introduced the so-called Big Brother/Big Sister project aimed at giving orphans social and emotional support and reintegrating them into society.[19] Resala runs several orphanages all over Egypt, which in this case all have salaried staff responsible for the primary care of the children. The brothers and sisters project connects young Resala volunteers with the orphans, giving them "brothers" and "sisters" who can help them with their homework and take them on trips outside the orphanage. When the children reach school age, they are in most cases adopted by the families of the volunteers. Another example is the large "credit program" run by Alashanek Ya Baladi. Among other things, they offer micro loans to women and young girls in order to establish "micro-enterprises needed to create sustainable income." Furthermore, Alashanek Ya Baladi aims at contributing to institutional sustainability by leveraging its resources through social ventures.[20] Like Alashanek Ya Baladi, the groups engaged in social entrepreneurship often combine nonprofit with for-profit organizational features and conclude partnerships with businesses and academic institutions. In this way, they blur the boundaries between the public, private, and nonprofit sectors, presenting hybrid models of for-profit and nonprofit activities (Johnson 2000; cf. Peredo and McLean 2006, 64). This is again a strong parallel to Amr Khaled's appeal to young people to establish private social enterprises (Mandaville 2008).

On the surface, projects like those mentioned above do not seem to be shaped by a particularly Islamic approach. Nevertheless, Islamic ethics and morals still seem to occupy a central place in the implementation of concrete activities when activists and beneficiaries meet. In the eyes of many activists, the majority of Egypt's poor are ignorant and do not know "true Islam." Instead of only providing basic services, the youth organizations therefore wish to help people to break out of their poverty by changing and improving their attitudes and behavior. In other words, they consider the improvement of their morals and ethics through religious education as a central element in breaking the poverty cycle: "We need to change the way people think. We need to change them from sitting and waiting for someone with a solution to trying to create their own solution to their own problems. (...) We want to change people themselves, the way they think." However, sometimes the focus on changing individuals' attitudes and behavior has a patronizing ring to it, reflecting the underlying conviction that they alone possess the right interpretation of religious traditions in order to give guidance for moral behavior.

There is a strong intention to "inspire" poor people to behave according to the organization's own interpretations of Islamic moral precepts whether it concerns the upbringing of their children, relations between the opposite sex, or neighborliness. Clearly, the feature of an organized society comes here in. Our interlocutors tend to distinguish between what is correct religious behavior and what is not by judging the behavior of their beneficiaries in terms of what they themselves consider to be morally "good" and morally "bad." This judgment becomes the standard for society as a whole. By being good role models and displaying the right ethical and moral behavior, these young people believe they will remedy social ills that they relate to a lack of religious ethics and morals in society. Furthermore, they believe that poverty will decrease because people will take more responsibility for themselves and their families. Following Asef Bayat, this wish to influence others in their beliefs and behavior is a sign of a new form of "active piety," where the actively pious judge their social environments on their values and behavior (Bayat 2007, 150). Again, the ideological roots of this activism can be traced back to the ideas and concepts of reformers such as Muhammad Abduh, who in a similar way propagated the transformation of society through the education and improvement of individual Muslim citizens. Thus, our interviewees interpret religious traditions in order to get moral guidelines for how to be a good person, how to do good, and how to live a good life. In short, they make their interpretations of Islamic traditions a moral point of reference in the construction of successful modern selfhoods.

Many of the youth organizations in our study combine their engagement in assisting and helping the poor at community level with the provision of what could be termed human and career development courses. While the engagement in social welfare activities is motivated by a wish to fight poverty in general, these courses are directed toward more specific problems of middle-class youth such as unemployment, apathy, and the poor quality of higher education. This engagement is animated by a "spirit of social entrepreneurship." According to the leadership of our youth organizations, social entrepreneurship among young Egyptians is what society needs. Thus, they perceive it to be one of their finest tasks to educate and train young professionals and social entrepreneurs who can contribute to the development and change of Egyptian society. These potential social entrepreneurs must meet specific norms as to appearance and behavior. More specifically, the youth organization's career development courses are guided by the idea of the "Muslim professional." This normative ideal type of a Muslim professional, a morally upright and well-trained businessman, fuses concepts from neoliberal economic theories and management sciences with a specific kind of Islamic morality, representing a role model for the construction of modern Muslim selves. Clearly, the concept of the Muslim professional tries to reconcile authenticity with contemporary global economic hegemony; it merges the *homo islamicus* with the *homo economicus* in one type. Thus, the Muslim professional represents a peculiar combination of two contemporary hegemonic projects: neoliberalism as an encompassing set of global social practices and "Islamism" as an authentic form of Muslim modernity.

In particular two organizations, Zedny and Bayan, have specialized in this field of career development, employing the normative ideal of the Muslim professional. Bayan, for instance, wants to "bridge the gap in the Egyptian employment market between what the youth is taught and what is actually needed."[21] On the website of Zedny, its mission is stated as being "to design and implement intensive, comprehensive training programs for the youth, delivered by professional trainers at very competitive prices that would help equip them with the skills needed to face the current global challenges."[22] Through up-to-date courses in human and career development offered at a price affordable to most middle-class youth, they aim at preparing young Egyptians, especially students and graduates from public universities, for their professional careers and adult lives. Highly respected university professors and successful managers of multinational companies teach courses in topics such as leadership, coaching, problem solving, time management, and presentation and communication skills. While in Zedny the aim is to reach as many young people as possible and several hundred young people are often taught in the same course, Bayan prefers teaching in workshops that only comprise groups of 20–30 students.

The central administration of Zedny was located on the third floor of the Raba'a Adawiyya Association, a large mosque-related complex including a *zakat* committee and the Islamic medical centre in Nasr City. Zedny's offices differed significantly from the rest of the rooms and offices in the building, as well as from those of all the other Islamic charity associations that we visited during our fieldwork in Cairo. Visiting Zedny's headquarters was an exercise in observing the interlacement of social practices of an interactive and a material nature. The furniture and decoration was strikingly similar to that of Western European and North American business firms. The large reception room was furnished with comfortable chairs and a fashionable desk with a huge flatscreen on top. The walls were painted in a warm orange color, and all the walls separating the reception from the offices and lecture halls were made of glass. Furthermore, the premises seemed to be perfectly outfitted with the latest kinds of IT and communication equipment available. In short, Zedny's premises boldly represented the material culture of the neoliberal and postmodern dimension of the Muslim professional.

At least at first sight, neither Zedny nor Bayan seem to make any reference to Islam and the religious nature of their organizational rationale. The curricula of their courses were clearly influenced by North American business and management sciences, and the chairman of Zedny claimed that the organization was "managed like any multinational company," using tools and concepts such as "strategic objectives and directions," "brand manual," and "outcome." Furthermore, a diverse range of celebrities and legends were quoted in the course material, including North American sports stars, politicians and writers, and legendary historical figures and philosophers such as Gandhi and Aristotle. However, in our conversations with the leaders and organizers of Zedny and Bayan, it soon became clear that Islam does play a significant role in the self-conception of these two organizations. In fact, Islam and modern management sciences are mutually reinforcing elements of their discourses, and religious commitment and practice is expected from the members and volunteers in these organizations. On a very concrete level, Zedny and Bayan, like all the other youth organizations that we visited, made sure to leave time for common religious prayers and lectures in an otherwise tight schedule. "It's something natural to pray together, to refresh our minds with something related to our ideology," as the president of Zedny explained to us. In addition, similar to most of the other organizations, both Zedny and Bayan practiced gender segregation in their activities and courses: "We're trying to keep to the rules, and we're proud of it." For example, in both organizations, male and female course participants were seated separately on each side of the aisle of the lecture hall. Moreover, in their services for the poor during the holy month of Ramadan, Zedny and Bayan paid close attention to separating male and female volunteers in their activities.

In the normative logic of their ideal of a Muslim professional, the practices and strategies of an effective businessman are complementary rather than a contrast to the values and morals of a good Muslim. The Muslim professional dresses in the right way, works efficiently, and has high moral standards, perfectly combining bodily, social, and material discursive practices of a certain type. In short, this ideal type represents a whole set of technologies of the self derived from a number of religious and non-religious discourses. The lecturers and board members act as role models for the volunteers and the students who attend the offered courses. The courses themselves convey the necessary technologies for the self-fashioning of the students according to the model of a Muslim professional. Thus, the corporate identity of these organizations as a whole is promoting this ideal of the Muslim professional. The following statement from a founder and board member of Bayan perfectly illustrates this approach:

> My point of view is that we don't need to speak about Islam in how to do and what to do. We need to act. We need to show the other face—be good role models. So we try not to preach to people but to do something. We don't talk, we do. (...) We deal with the Islamic path but we don't preach it. For example, appointments: When I say that the lecture starts at six, at six-O-one you are late. When I say that you have to attend three out of four lectures to pass, if you only attend two, you have failed. There are no excuses. This is what it takes to be a Muslim professional. What do I mean by professional? Keep your commitments, try to know with what you're working, take care of the way you look, dress and present yourself. We are role models. I am not preaching perfection, but I am teaching total project management.

There is no doubt that individuals are themselves a part of this total project management that represents a hybrid combination of elements of the managerial ideal of peer-group-oriented subjectivity with the postmodern type of a creative entrepreneur. In line with the message of Amr Khaled, the Muslim professional does not know any contradiction between religious commitment and personal success. Quite to the contrary, in their aim to educate entrepreneurially minded subjects, the teachers and organizers of the courses themselves serve as concrete examples of the close relationship between Islam and personal success. One of our interviewees put that as follows:

> One of our members is very good at IT, and he's a very good Muslim as well. So the students say that they really want to be like Ahmed. He works in a multinational company, regularly goes to prayer and sticks to Islamic rules, while he is simultaneously free and liberal.

Clearly, the Muslim professional takes inspiration from globally acknowledged patterns of successful contemporary subjectivity formation, making them authentic through their relationship to Islamic traditions. This combination of global entrepreneurial imaginary with Islamic traits is also reflected in the dress style. Many leaders and organizers wear elegant business clothes. When we paid our first visit to Zedny, a clean-shaven young man with short hair and in an elegant suit was waiting for us at the reception. He was the personal assistant to the president and chairperson, and his appearance was very similar to the rest of the young men we could observe at Zedny and Bayan. Thus, the postmodern values of creative business were an integral part of the organization's body politics. These values were taught through bodily examples by teachers and administrative staff who simultaneously offered role models in religious lifestyle and observance of prayer. There is no doubt that in their successful combination of professional careers with being good and active Muslims they serve as peers for the slightly younger volunteers and the attendees of the career courses. Wickham refers to this peer role as "the efficiency" of agents or "social carriers" in social movements (2004, 238–9). In a similar vein, Benford and Snow underline the "credibility of the frame articulators" as one of the central factors determining whether a collective action frame has resonance among a specific target group (Benford and Snow 2000, 620–1). The lecturers and board members in organizations such as Zedny and Bayan are important role models for the young people due to their professional status and expertise and because they speak from a similar socioeconomic background. Embedded in the broader new Islamic movement, they become central social carriers for a specific, religiously defined form of contemporary Muslim selfhood.

The success of this movement is closely connected to the demonopolization of religious authority and therewith to the fundamental religious reorganization once initiated by the nineteenth-century Islamic reformers. The above examples show how lay people with perceived expertise in the religious field manage to gain support from the young generation in particular (cf. Starrett 1998). Even more important, their religious authority is inseparably connected to their being versed in contemporary neoliberal management techniques. They derive their authority by relating to globally acknowledged patterns of successful modern subjectivity formation, as well as to generally hegemonic discourses on development, project management, or human rights. In short, religious and nonreligious discourses clearly reinforce each other. In the process, the religious part conveyed to the young Egyptians in our study is not so much about rituals and theological doctrine. Instead religion bestows these global discourses with the necessary authenticity and moral autonomy. Islamic traditions provide our interlocutors with moral guidelines for constructing authentic modern identities. Again, we can see the role of the moral back-up code in the application of religious communication. While core ritual performances and religious sermons occupy a rather restricted space, religious morality and the ethics of a shared conception of the good life are central in the religious communication of the organizations in our fieldwork (cf. Mandaville 2008). By reinterpreting Islamic traditions through a framework of neoliberal norms and structures (Atia 2008), they offer social sites for the construction of new types of modern Muslim subjectivities that appeal to religiously minded young Egyptians from the middle class.

Forces of Mobilization: Religion, Nationalism, and Friendship

The target group of the new youth organizations is Egyptian youth in general, and according to the leadership of all the organizations we talked to, they are open for both Muslims and Christians. Reportedly, Resala has some Christian volunteers, although we were never introduced to any of them during our fieldwork. One could imagine that at least in some of the organizations, Christians would feel some discomfort because of the prevalence of Islamic vocabulary and practice. Furthermore, as some of our interviewees pointed out, Christians have their own sites for charity and social engagement.[23] Given the pronounced Islamic religious character of the organizations, they do indeed seem not to be very appealing to both practicing and nonpracticing Egyptians of Christian background. While there did not seem to be any official restriction on the kinds of people who were recruited as volunteers and ordinary members, it was different with regard to board members. At least at Bayan, commitment to the general outlook of the organization, including the candidate's religious values and behavior, seemed to be of great importance when the leadership was looking for new board members:

> We do very strict interviews. It is not a matter of just wanting to be a member. (...) The interviews are based not only on ability but on the willingness to do something for the society. If they have the willingness, they will definitely have the ability, and some very good behaviors. For example, one of the very good things I ask for is whether they pray the *fajr*,[24] because I think that this shows if he is willing or not.

Generally speaking, Islam plays a significant role in the motivational framing of most of our youth organizations. Religious values and Islamic rhetoric are used as a way to mobilize members and volunteers. To which degree, however, varies among the respective organizations. Obvious examples of this religious framing are the names chosen for the organizations, as briefly referred to at the beginning of this chapter. In providing a moral justification for involvement by referring to a higher truth, religion is a powerful tool for mobilization. Leaders make use of religious framing to touch people in their moral self-understanding and social responsibility. One example is found at the introduction of the letter from Alashanek Ya Baladi's chairperson, which even alludes to Judgment Day and the risk of going to hell: "Did you ever think why God created you? Did you ever know the value of life? Did you ever imagine that this world will vanish someday and you will be asked about what you have done to the people around you?"[25] Clearly, here the primary code of religion seems to be a powerful way to mobilize contemporary young Egyptians to engage in their society. This is certainly due to a number of national and transnational reasons, prime among them the role that Islamic traditions have played in the construction of modern authenticity in the Muslim world. When trying to recruit new volunteers for his organization, for instance, the founder and chairman of Resala propagated charity and volunteering on the basis of Islamic sources. In so doing, he applied relatively classical religious argumentation at the same time fusing it with contemporary notions about voluntary work. The following quotation is taken from one of his recruitment speeches in which he neatly combines the moral code of good and bad with the religious core code of blessed and cursed. We present this quote in its full length in order to show the character of religious arguments put forward by the leadership of this largest and most influential among Egypt's new youth organizations:

> Why is volunteering the right thing to practice religiosity? Finish the Sura to the end "do you see those who deny this religion."[26] In this Sura you see how God compares those people who're not believers in the first place to those who treat the orphans badly and who do not ensure that the needy get their food. So what do you think is the description of the true believer? The true believer should treat orphans well and make sure that the needy get their food. And those words, to be sure, are very beautiful. They have lots of volunteering in them. Let's get those people their food, let's get them blankets, let's buy them covers and something to shelter them in the winter, let's collect donations for them. That's what a true believer is, someone who is always making sure it happens, always moving and spreading the word, always exerting an effort and giving to all that's good.
>
> In other parts of the Koran there are descriptions of those who are in hell. What do you think are the reasons for them going to hell? There are two crimes. What do you think they are? They didn't believe in the mighty God, and they didn't work on letting the needy get their food. Those two crimes were enough for them to go to hell. The crime of not believing is a major crime and it truly leads to hell, and most people acknowledge that. The other crime that could make you go to hell, and most people are not aware of that, is not making sure that the needy get their food. You cannot but have a role in this. You have to participate, and you have to work on it, tell people about it, collect donations, deliver blankets, cook, you should do lots of things. You *should* have some role in ensuring that the needy get their food. You must do something. You can't ignore this and not help in any way. It might lead to you going to hell. You should participate because that's the heart of the religion and that's what God wants his people to do.

This quote perfectly illustrates the complex interrelationship of religious communication with discourses on volunteering, social activism and poverty relief. It demonstrates the way in which religious social action and personal strategies to achieve salvation are knitted into different "worldly" purposes. Most often, this kind of mobilization speeches are performed by the leadership themselves, but sometimes they also draw on external religious resource persons. At Zedny, for example, a representative of the religious establishment was sometimes invited to talk to the volunteers about Islam and why voluntary activities should be taken up: "Just to motivate people to go," as the president put it. In the passage above, Resala's chairman presents charity and voluntarism as obligatory in Islam, and the failure to meet this obligation might result in the person going to hell. Thus, it seems that religious arguments are also used to frighten young people with the consequences that their actions in this life could have for their life in the hereafter. The core binary code of religion (blessed/cursed), therefore, is not entirely absent in the religious communication of these organizations. However, in line with the general language of the new Islamic movement in Egypt, leaders most often employ the moral communication of the secondary code and use carrots rather than sticks to attract new members. One common way to motivate young Egyptians was to talk about the possible rewards given by God. In return for paying *zakat* and/or doing voluntary work to help the poor, many Muslims believe that they will receive rewards from God (*thawab*). They can come in this life or the afterlife, and the rewards materialize in everything from rather tangible things, such as wealth and professional success, to more intangible things, such as improved health, fertility, or merely happiness. In short, they relate in Weber's terms to issues of this-worldly and other-worldly forms of salvation. In his recruitment speech to potential volunteers, the chairman of Resala gave several examples of how volunteers in his organization had been rewarded by God. One, for instance, had been given a pay rise the day after he volunteered for the first time. Another no longer suffered from migraine. A third suddenly became pregnant after several years of trying. If we place these statements within the framework of Weber's theory of religious social action, Resala's chairman is mobilizing potential volunteers in terms of communication with the supernatural while offering this-worldly rewards.

By framing their engagement in religious terms, however, the organizations often walked a tightrope. As discussed previously, they had to be careful not to raise the religious banner too high. There was an upper limit to the degree to which the leadership could use Islam to mobilize Egyptian youth if they wanted to stay out of the regime's spotlight. Only one of the nine organizations in our study characterized itself as "Islamic." All other organizations objected to this labeling.[27] Furthermore, some pointed out that when it comes to religious talks and discussions, they have to restrict themselves. One of the leaders told us:

> We are not used to talking about this [the role of Islam], not because we fear it, but because we fear that people fear it. People appreciate it inside, but they are afraid of the political consequences. It is safer to talk about the social aspects than the religious ones.

In applying religious vocabulary, they had to stay within the discourse of social welfare and avoid crossing the boundaries of politics by resembling the political language of Islamist ideologies. More concretely, this perspective implies a focus on social problems such as poverty, suffering, and immorality detached from the institutional language of politics. Any association with Islamist political rhetoric would without doubt have resulted in a government crackdown. This might also be the reason why all the youth organizations in our study not only refrained from becoming involved in politics directly but also avoided supporting or collaborating with political groups, for example, the Muslim Brotherhood or its more liberal offspring the al-Wasat Party.[28]

Despite this core role of religion in the organizational rationale of our youth organizations, Islam is far from being the only significant frame for mobilization. In the effort to obtain a comprehensive understanding of the new youth organizations, it is important to contextualize religion as one among many potential frames of reference for collective action. Equally important seems to be patriotism. The love of and devotion to their country is another important element in the mobilization of Egyptian youth. Apart from a tendency toward passing references to the global Muslim *umma* and the sufferings of Muslims in Palestine, Iraq, and Afghanistan, most of the organizations closely think within the borders of the Egyptian national state. Their explicit mission is to change and develop *Egyptian* society. This is most explicit for Alashanek Ya Baladi, which means "for the sake of my country." Yet the leader of Resala, the probably most classical religious organization in our sample, also argues in his recruitment speech that "love for one's homeland" together with the religious obligation of charity should be incentives enough for people to volunteer for social welfare. Furthermore, many of our interviewees strongly expressed a wish for self-sustainability, for a strong Egypt free from foreign aid: "We don't need the foreigners to help our children. We can help them ourselves, and help them even better than they ever would," as the founder and chairperson of Resala lectured us. These are clear examples of Egyptian "nativism," the fact that religious loyalty has not replaced nationalist sentiments (Bayat 2007).

However, this strong reference to the Egyptian nation as a frame for mobilization does not amount to supporting the regime in power. Nation is here understood primarily as the total of all Egyptian citizens with no reference to the state or a particular form of rule. Only very few of our interlocutors expressed a conflicting relationship with state authorities; in fact, they often emphasized their good relations with officials from the ministry of social solidarity. Furthermore, some of our interviewees advocated enhanced communication and cooperation between them and the government. They wanted officials to acquire a better impression and understanding of them and their work.[29] While the close association of religion and nationalism in the worldview of these youth organizations indicated that they subscribe to the political idea of an Egyptian Islamic modern, they did so without antagonizing the then incumbent regime. Again, we can observe the rise of a new type of the Islamic modern in Egypt between the power coordinates given by the historically secular nature of the Egyptian state and its Islamist counterpart the Muslim Brotherhood.

Finally, we should not underestimate the social dimension of the work in these organizations. This dimension partly refers to the more global standards of identification with consumer lifestyles, as well as to deficiencies in the realm of intimacy due to the problems of young Egyptians in establishing their own nuclear family relations. An important element in the mobilization of young people is the emphasis on friendship, fun, and happiness, which comes out of this engagement. Many organizations arrange social activities and events, such as country trips, games, and picnics, for the volunteers. During our fieldwork, for instance, we participated in a whole-day trip to Alexandria arranged by the leadership of Misr Shoryan Al-Ataa. The purpose of this trip was to "shake together" the group of volunteers through shared sightseeing, a picnic, and games at the beach. At Resala, the founder and chairperson explained the rationale of these activities:

> Everyone is searching for happiness, and this search for happiness is the axis around which their lives revolve. That's why they travel in the summer, take walks in days of fine weather, and watch television. It's happiness they're seeking; they want to have a nice time. We just want them to try a different and more effective kind of happiness and that's why we raised another slogan saying: "If you want a genuine, true smile, go to Resala!"

Conclusions

Like Amr Khaled, the leaders acknowledged in our interviews that their primary target group, the upper middle-class youth, is not ready to give up fun, entertainment, and friendship when engaging in social welfare activities and community work. Clearly, they are all taking part in a more global consumption- and leisure-oriented culture. In shaping new modern Muslim citizens, the organizations must acknowledge this cultural framing of their volunteers, which clearly cuts across national and religious borders. A broad range of social and entertaining events are, therefore, closely knitted into attempts to convey technologies of the self for the empowerment and education of the volunteers themselves. The aim is to develop not only the beneficiaries, but also the personal skills of the volunteers. In the mobilization of volunteers, the leadership makes an effort to underline the social dimension of the work as well as the emotional rewards and individual empowerment of social assistance and development activities. They depict the organizations as social sites for the construction of modern identities combining the dimensions of working subjects with consumption-oriented selves. Moreover, they offer a certain sphere of intimacy as an alternative to marriage and nuclear family life for which so many young Egyptians are longing.

These specific frames of mobilization not only work in the process of persuading individual actors to sign up as members and volunteers but provide an enduring framework for the identity construction of the staff in the organizations. The next chapter will show that in moving to the micro level, we will explore how distinctive emotional and behavioral expectations and values are transferred to and enacted by the young people after they have become members of the organizations. Moreover, when observing the individual level, we got the impression that social welfare often is a means rather than an end of this new form of Islamic activism. From the perspective of the individual members, engaging in social welfare provides an opportunity to develop necessary skills and technologies of the self for the construction of meaningful modern selfhoods as working subjects. The youth organizations offer alternative sites for these social processes in a society in which the access of young people to the fields of politics, labor, and intimacy has been heavily constrained.

CHAPTER 9

Leaders, Organizers, and Volunteers: Encountering Idiosyncratic Forms of Subjectivities

During our fieldwork, we had the opportunity to attend a celebration of Mother's Day that was jointly organized by three local branches of Resala in Cairo. Like Orphan's Day, Mother's Day is one of the major annual events for many Egyptian social welfare organizations and an excellent occasion to see our new youth organizations and their volunteers at work. Resala had invited hundreds of mothers from Cairo's poor suburbs to come to the Cairo Stadium in order to treat them with drinks, food, and entertainment. Approaching the stadium area, we found ourselves in the midst of a honking crowd of minibuses that were transporting the mothers to the event. The entrance hall of the stadium was turned into a big indoor marketplace. The whole area was flooded by groups of young volunteers in red, white, and blue t-shirts with "Resala" printed on them in English and Arabic. We saw undoubtedly more Resala volunteers than visitors. The young people shouted and laughed as they tried to sell us Resala merchandise products and souvenirs made in specific Resala handicraft projects. A group of girls approached us. While one wanted us to sign up as volunteers, another one asked us for donations. We gave her twenty pounds and she returned a receipt as a proof of our donation. We also bought a few souvenirs from the stands around.

Entering the stadium arena, we were met by a wall of noise. It was a mix of shouting crowds, loud music from bad speakers, and the distorted voices of people making announcements through micro phones. The name "Resala" was continuously shouted and people joined in and clapped. It was almost impossible to understand each other's voices. We eventually found a seat from which we could watch the show. The stadium was decorated overall with balloons and banners. There was a huge stage in the middle of the arena. During the three hours we were there, DJs, mothers, and different official people appeared on this stage and gave brief speeches to the audience. There must have been thousands of young volunteers all in their blue, white, or red t-shirts. Many of them looked like teenagers. On a number of reserved chairs, a few hundred mothers were seated. They watched the show and at some point they all received plastic bags with food and drinks. Some of them were smiling and clapping, but others looked rather confused and seemed to be out of place. The mothers were surrounded by a sea of young people—girls and boys—running around in circles and constantly shouting "Resala! Resala! Resala!" These young people were apparently having a great time. Yet, was this not a party for the volunteers rather than for the "poor mothers"?

In a nutshell, Resala's celebration of Mother's Day epitomizes the argument of this chapter. According to our observations, the mothers seemed only to play the role of extras at this event. First of all, Resala was celebrating itself through practices strongly reinforcing its own corporate identity. From this perspective, Mother's Day primarily served as social training ground for upcoming Muslim professionals, while the provision of goods to poor mothers was secondary in meaning. The volunteers participated in an event with hundreds of peers representing through bodily practices and public performances a specific kind of Islamic activism that closely reminds us of patterns of the consumption-oriented culture of the salaried masses. The event could be read as a collective social practice offering the participating volunteers a collection of meaningful tools to construct and affirm personal identification within a group of peers. To be sure, while the participants resembled the peer-group type of organized modernity in form, as they combined fun, entertainment, and merchandising activities, this event also alluded to features of second modernity in content. In this sense, the event shows the factual idiosyncratic nature of these organizations. Furthermore, the Mother's Day is a perfect example of the previously mentioned description made by Asef Bayat that Amr Khaled's ideological recipe was a marriage of faith and fun. This content also distinguishes the discursive practices of Resala remarkably from the peer-group model of the Muslim Brotherhood. Nevertheless, looking at the organization's volunteers, it is rather social adaptation than individual creation that dominates the imaginaries of these young people. Yet this does not apply to all of Resala's members. At the individual level, we can observe clear variations regarding the types of modern subjectivities to which our interlocutors relate.

Usually we find three types of members in the youth organizations being considered here: board members (including the president or chairperson), experienced organizers, and volunteers. While most tasks at Resala's Mother's Day were carried out by volunteers, the overall planning, organization, and coordination of the event were the responsibility of a few experienced organizers, either employees or volunteers who had been members of Resala for years. The members of the youth organizations are normally in their twenties, and the majority of them are college students or recent graduates of mainly public universities in Cairo. They usually come from the broader stratum of Cairo's amorphous middle class, best defined by their educational background of being graduates from national universities such as Cairo University and Ain Shams University, which are generally known for their middle-class intakes. In our sample, only Alashanek Ya Baladi is an exception in this regard. This organization was founded at the private and very expensive American University in Cairo (AUC), which caters for Egypt's higher middle and upper class. The majority of the volunteers at Alashanek Ya Baladi are still AUC students or graduates.

The educational background of the volunteers very often reflects the particular activities and fields of engagement of the respective organization in which they work. For example, Misr Shoryan al-Ataa offers services in the field of health care, and naturally many of the volunteers are students and graduates of medical and pharmaceutical faculties. Less specialized organizations, however, might recruit volunteers from all possible backgrounds, as far as university education is concerned. The board members tend to have been in the organization for a long time—they might even be its founders. In comparison to the average volunteer, they are often slightly older, and many of them already have a professional career besides their work for the organization. Yet again, they are still extraordinarily young when compared to board members in Egyptian civil society organizations in general. According to a survey of 60 civil society organizations published in 2004, 74 percent of all board members in Egypt were more than 50 years old (Abdel-Rahman 2004, 158).

Another distinctive feature of the new youth organization is their gender composition. Women constitute a very large proportion of the volunteers and experienced organizers. In our sample, they make up a minimum of 65 percent, and in Alashanek Ya Baladi they even come close to 90 percent. However, they are not as well represented in the leadership as in the rank and file. Out of the nine organizations in our sample, only Alashanek Ya Baladi had a female chairperson. This is also the only organization where more than 50 percent of the board members were women. The remaining organizations had none or one to three women among their ten board members.[1] In terms of leadership, the same pattern is generally found among civil society organizations in Egypt, where the gender gap is even larger when it comes to the field of Islamic charities. According to a recent study, there is a serious gender gap in Egyptian civil society organizations. In a nationwide survey of 1,048 civil society organizations, male membership was twice as high as female membership. In addition, women are more likely to participate in organizations engaged in conventional mother–child care service (El-Daly 2006, 28). To a certain extent, the leadership of our youth organizations expressed its willingness to change this situation. Several board members remarked that young women participate more regularly in the activities of the organizations, and many of them described the female volunteers as "more dedicated" and "responsible." Moreover, several board members acknowledged the importance of having women in the leadership.

Not only is the rising importance of female membership visible in the clear predominance of women among the regular volunteers, but young women also make up a large proportion of the midlevel management. Women are working as team leaders, coordinators, and PR agents in the youth organizations. From a historical perspective, the significance of women in this new

Islamic movement actually seems to follow a broader tendency in the modernization of Egypt. In the latter decades of the nineteenth century, women began to participate in shaping the social imaginaries of modern Egypt through the typically bourgeois medium of literacy by engaging in the writing of poems, novels, or essays (cf. Hatem 2011). In the twentieth century, then, the competing forms of first modernity in Egypt were accompanied by women expressing their agency in individual and collective forms of activism employing the ideological tropes of Islamic reform and Arab nationalism (Badran 1995). This chapter will also show in which ways our female interlocutors justify the construction of their selfhoods in a similar way as these predecessors within the discursive formation of a new Islamic movement.

In the following, we take a closer look at the role of these youth organizations in the subjectivity formation of their three respective types of members. The first section examines the leaders with regard to their own position and the vision that is guiding their attitudes toward the volunteers. What kinds of modern Muslim identities do they claim for themselves and for Egypt's youth more generally? Then we move to the middle-level management and take a closer look at the predominantly female experienced organizers. In which ways do these young Egyptians make use of the modern youth organizations in shaping their own meaningful patterns of modern selfhood? Finally, we come back to the ordinary volunteers and try to understand how they negotiate their identities in reference to both the postmodern imperatives of creative entrepreneurship and the peer-group-oriented framework of collectively resembling the imaginary of a Muslim professional. In so doing, we treat these organizations as designed by youth for youth. At the micro level, we can discern that the aim to change the conditions for Egypt's youth and thus those for one's own life clearly supersede the developmental aim of poverty relief. Indeed, there are different rationales at work when analyzing the macro, meso, and micro levels.

Leadership with Vision: "It Is not Enough to Just Worship God"

Most leaders[2] of the new youth organizations we met were between 25 and 40 years old. They had different educational and professional backgrounds, but they were all university graduates with degrees in well-reputed fields such as engineering, pharmaceutics, and medicine. While two were about to complete their MA degrees, the others had full-time careers as well, either working in private business, at a hospital, or in academic fields. Out of the nine leaders we interviewed, only two were women. Before taking part in establishing one of the new youth organizations, many of these leaders had volunteered in other charitable or developmental organizations. On the basis of this previous experience, they developed a vision in which religious aspects play an important but not the only important role.

There is, for example, Mohammad Omar, the president of Zedny, who has been working in the "charity community" since he was 15. Omar has previous experience from working at Resala and Al-Boraq, and he volunteered for several years in the scout division. Therefore, he convincingly considered himself to be "one of the civil society members here in Egypt." His long-term engagement in the field has led him to quit instant aid activities in favor of activities aimed at more sustainable and long-term development. This is also the reason why in 2004 he and two of his friends decided to establish Zedny as an organization that aims at improving the skills and qualifications of young Egyptians by applying ideas from human development discourses. A slightly different story was told to us by Sherif Abdel-Azeem, who is the founder and chairperson of Resala. During a period of residence in the United States and Canada, he became aware of how many foreigners were engaged in charitable and developmental activities that aim at helping poor and unprivileged people in developing countries like Egypt. In particular one story about an American lady supporting the education of a poor Egyptian boy through monthly in-cash donations moved him: "When listening to her story, I felt deep pain. Although she had every right to be proud of herself, I was still in pain, why? It is the feeling that this good came from foreigners while the capable people who actually live in this country are not taking any action." Abdel-Azeem decided to return to Egypt. While holding a professorship at the Faculty of Engineering at the American University in Cairo, he also served as chairman of one of the largest social welfare organization in Egypt and the largest voluntary youth organization in the Arab world.

Representing the educated and rather privileged part of Egypt's middle class, Omar, AbdelAzeem, and the other leaders we interviewed expressed not only religious motivations, but also nationalist sentiments and great social responsibility with respect to their society. The desire to contribute to social change and development in Egypt through poverty relief was certainly an important issue for them. Yet, when asked about the most significant and urgent problems to address in Egyptian society, they unanimously pointed to the complex of youth-related problems we discussed earlier. They specifically identified poor education, unemployment, "ignorance," and a general lack of civic engagement as those areas in which they saw the most urgent need for action. While considering the provision of food and shelter for the poorest communities a necessary task, their real mission was seemingly to help Egyptian middle-class youth in finding the right track for life, leading to professional and personal success. Through education, training, and instruction, that is, the transfer of contemporary technologies of the self, they wanted to empower young people, making them capable of solving their own problems. For example, to improve their chances of obtaining an appropriate job, the leaders encouraged them to advance their language and computer skills, and they instructed them in the writing of convincing CVs. To shape a dynamic and skilled middle-class youth in Egypt is the real vision of these leaders, as this statement made by a founding board member of Bayan explains: "I will educate them and train them and give them some very good level of income. What will happen is that society will be forced to see them from another point of view. This is the way I see it."

This vision of the leadership of Egypt's new youth organizations is a direct reaction to the widespread feeling of exclusion and marginalization, which has taken hold of Egypt's young middle class. Due to a lack of appropriate qualifications, a general tendency to give preferential treatment to more senior people in Egyptian society (in particular men) and the need for an established network for patronage, the majority of young Egyptians have major difficulties in finding appropriate employment. In short, they are deprived of the most important social arena for establishing modern subjectivities: they are prevented from constructing themselves as working subjects. Even worse, without a job it is almost impossible to get married and to found a family. Thus, many young Egyptians are also deprived of the most crucial field of intimacy for shaping meaningful selfhoods. Indeed, the crucial fields of working subjects and intimacy are closely knitted together. In order to overcome these social constraints, many leaders perceive a call to activism as one of their preferential tasks. They lament the widespread "ignorance" or the lack of knowledge and interest in society that seemingly characterizes Egypt's youth. Establishing new youth organizations, therefore, is a means of raising social awareness and getting more young people involved: "The solution is to encourage youth to work in NGOs and contribute to the community." Therefore, part of their mission is to recruit young men and women for their organizations and convince them to invest time and energy in activities for the sake of the broader community, which in the end should contribute to solving the problems of the young volunteers themselves.

This mobilization of Egypt's middle-class youth in the name of charity is with no doubt of a highly political nature. Yet it is political activism outside the confines of formal politics. The structural straight jacket of Egyptian politics excluded the possibility of pluralist societies to organize themselves in interest groups that would articulate the specific problems of Egyptian youth in more political ways. Given the entrenched tradition of Islamic charity, the foundation of religious organizations with a charitable purpose seemed to be a viable alternative. The leaders, therefore, emphasized the religious background of their activism. To help the poor is a religious obligation and brings the individual believer "closer to God." A representative of Bayan's board explained to us: "This is about religion. I do this to be in a state of wellbeing with Allah. This is my motive." His colleague, the chairman of Mazeed, affirmed this position: "Our motive and the main reason we work for is God." The leaders here are participating in a general discourse regarding the individual motivation of members of the new youth organizations, whether board members, managers, or ordinary volunteers. They unanimously state that charitable and voluntary work for the benefit of the community will return tenfold in the form of God's rewards. They apparently hope that if they strive hard enough, eventually, they will go to paradise: "We work for the greater good. All of us want to go to paradise." Thus, they put their social engagement in a frame of religious action, communicating with God and aspiring for redemption. To be sure, this is not to put the sincerity of the religious motivation of these leaders in doubt. The people we met are not mere utility maximizers who employ religious communication as an instrumental tool. Rather, we observe a specific compatibility of structural contexts with individual agency that might explain why the sociopolitical and socioeconomic problems of Egypt's middle-class youth have been most successfully articulated by a new Islamic movement. The religious motivation of activists and the power configurations of Egyptian society have been conducive to the emergence of religiously framed youth organizations engaged in social welfare projects.

This peculiar confluence of interests and ideas is also visible in the leaders' tendency to present themselves as role models for the young people. First of all, their own biographies provide success stories for the volunteers. This is a way to motivate more young people to improve their formal skills and qualifications and encourage them to use the field of Islamic charity as a social training ground to prepare them for future jobs. However, our interviewees perceive formal skills and qualifications as not being sufficient to have success. In order to be successful on the labor market, these young middle-class people also have to improve their bodily practices. They must work on their general appearance, developing the ways they talk, interact, and present themselves in public. By teaching these technologies of the self, religion too plays an important role in both justification and content. In the eyes of the leadership, success is in the hands of God. The achievement of worldly gains, therefore, also depends on the observance of religious obligations. Moreover, religious norms and practices provide useful guidelines for social interaction in Egyptian society.

The set of applicable technologies of the self is embodied in the normative ideal of the Muslim professional. To a certain extent, the leadership and the midlevel management of the organizations want to serve as role models of this normative ideal type through exemplary behavior. A board member of Bayan put it this way: "I know that I have knowledge. I see the mentality, so it is my role to change it." This position can easily be justified in religious terms. Referring to the Islamic principle of *amr bil maaruf wal-nahi an al-munkar* (to enjoin others in doing good or right, and the forbidding of evil or wrong), playing the role model can be firmly embedded in Islamic traditions. Being good role models and thereby encouraging others to be good Muslims is thus a mobilizing source that closely links contemporary youth organizations to the legacy of Islamic reform, according to which a new generation of modern Muslim subjects must be cultivated to change individuals by means of scientific and religious education (cf. Haj 2009, 119).

In real life, however, the perceived role models still share many of the problems that confront the ordinary volunteer. Leadership responsibility not only entailed many hours of hard work, but also a greater risk of government harassment. In the context of the political contestation between Egypt's secular state and visions of an Egyptian Islamic modern, leading one of the new youth organizations often meant walking a tightrope. The president of Misr

Shoryan al-Ataa was among the youngest of the leaders in our interviews. Like other young men, he wanted to marry and was looking for a good career to support his family. Holding a degree in medicine, he certainly belonged to the more privileged stratum among Egypt's youth. Nevertheless, the road to professional success and marriage was also still long and difficult for him. In our interview, he clearly expressed some worries about combining both his career and his responsibilities in heading an organization: "Now we're all young. Our parents support us. We have the time and energy. But later we will spend our time supporting our own families. (. . .) I cannot spend all my time here. What about my life?" The quote reflects the essentially lifecycle relevance of engaging in such a youth-dominated charity organization. As the actors get older, the social training ground increasingly comes into conflict with the career ambitions and dreams of a meaningful and successful personal life.

In addition, this threat was enhanced by the fact that the leaders were well aware of being under the supervision of the regime's security apparatus. They would have been the first to be detained by the police if one of their volunteers crossed the often barely visible red lines. Rumors went round that the president of one of the organizations had been arrested because of his close ties with Amr Khaled. Consequently, most leaders avoided talking about politics and refused to admit to any political agenda whatsoever when asked about the effects of the organization's work in the political scene. In fact, they did not seem to have any interest in being recognized as agents of change in what they perceive as the political field. Directing our discussions toward the Muslim Brotherhood, the silence among the leaders was even more apparent. One board member told us:

> I have nothing to say about them. They have a different agenda. They want to change society, we want to change the individual. For a better life, a better job, a better family. If you don't understand yourself, you won't be able to help others.

This statement indicates to which extent religious communication in Egypt under Mubarak represented both an opportunity and a constraint. The field of Islamic charity and religious communication provided opportunities for social engagement and activities in which young Egyptians could compensate for their exclusion from fields of politics, intimacy, and the labor market. However, this opportunity immediately became a constraint if they left the restricted domains of religious communication. This happened when referring to the idea of an Islamic modern as propagated by the Muslim Brotherhood. Then the emphasis was not on individual salvation but on social change through political action. The security policies of the Egyptian regime apparently applied standards of functional differentiation in its judgment as to who posed a threat or not to its authoritarian rule. From our perspective, there is no doubt that the youth organizations strive for social change. Yet unlike the Muslim Brotherhood and other political actors, religious or not, they claim to aim at social change through the improvement and development of the individual. Their aspired social order is not framed as a result of collective political action, but as the eventual outcome of the moral betterment of individuals. This peculiar blending of liberal and Islamist ideas the leaders of our youth organizations share with the broader stream of Egypt's new Islamic movement. The idea of an Islamic modern as manifested in this movement combines elements of the classical bourgeois type of restricted liberal modernity with more postmodern elements related to the ideal type of second modernity. Together with strategically sober leadership, this idea of achieving an Islamic modern was tolerated by the Mubarak regime, and most of the organizations have in this way avoided any direct confrontation with state authorities.

THE EXPERIENCED FEMALE ORGANIZER: "WOMEN HAVE MORE TIME"

While most of the top leaders of our organizations were men, a large percentage of the midlevel management was made up of young women. The majority of them were in their twenties and most were graduate students or recent graduates. Almost all of them were volunteers, apart from a few regular employees. Mona was one of these volunteers, working for Bayan.[3] At the time of our fieldwork, she was 28 years old and a graduate in English Language and Literature from Ain Shams University. She was employed as an instructor at one of Egypt's private universities while at the same time working on her MA. At Bayan, she was the marketing leader who is responsible for most of the course advertisements, as well as for communication and correspondence with instructors and students. Furthermore, Mona was involved in the planning and organization of the English lessons. She had been a member of Bayan almost from the beginning, attending one of the first Bayan lessons at Sedik Mosque in Heliopolis in 2004. Not much later, she already participated in organizing the next course. Mona was, without a doubt, a very dedicated and devout volunteer who spoke warmly about the founders and instructors of Bayan, whom she clearly admired.

Heba is another good example of the same type of female organizer. She too is a university graduate, and at the time of our fieldwork she was in her mid-twenties. During her college years, Heba had the opportunity to do field research in one of Cairo's poor suburbs. This experience was an eye-opener for her: "I couldn't believe how people were living, and I wanted to help." Consequently, she started to volunteer in several charity organizations. She collected donations from wealthy Egyptians and distributed money, food, and clothes to poor families. However, she still felt that something was missing. A few years later, Heba attended one of Zedny's courses in human development. Right from the beginning, Zedny's approach convinced her: "I started to see the value of these things in myself. I started to wonder why I did not work on something like that and try to change other people." When we interviewed Heba, she had already been working for Zedny for more than two years. Together with others, she was meanwhile responsible for preparing and designing programs for Zedny's course attendees.

Most of our male and female interlocutors explained the predominance of women among the volunteers by referring to rather stereotypical representations:

> I think that the reason is that girls and females have more time to spare. Boys are always looking for jobs to gain money in order to start building their future. Women have more time. That's why they can go and help in society. They don't have to work in a profit-making company.

In line with general stereotypes about the nature of females, many women themselves pointed to the more empathetic and emotional character of women, which made them particularly suited to conducting social welfare activities. According to the vice president of one of the organizations, "girls are more emotional. Boys say that it is their problem. Girls want to help. Girls feel more responsibility towards problems in society. They are more positive." These quotes clearly underpin Brock's reasoning about social welfare activities, which she views to be often ascribed to feminine qualities attached to the female body (Brock 2008, 86).

Despite these gendered representations, however, the motivational background of the female organizers does not differ significantly from those of the mainly male leaders. At the center of their concerns, there is a strong wish to make a difference for other young people. They are aware of and grateful for the opportunities they could enjoy in gaining knowledge and experience throughout the past years. This led them to feel an obligation to help young people whom they consider to be in a less privileged situation than their own. They know, however, that this is a long and difficult process. For many young Egyptians, future perspectives are bleak. Given the mere amount of social constraints, also after the Arab Spring, decisive and quick changes should not be expected. Nevertheless, our interviewees remained rather optimistic:

> We can see the little things: The woman who is trying to raise her children the right way and teach them and give them all that they need for their future. And the young man who manages to get the right job because he knows his abilities and his way.

For some women, the youth organization provides the only social site for constructing meaningful identities with reference to the modern idea of a working subject. In their voluntary work, they see opportunities for both making use of their university education and acquiring other kinds of skills that cannot be obtained through formal education but through working practices alone. Such skills include project planning and management, communication, and organizational work. Important to note is that these women value the organizational work, in particular, the responsibility, the teamwork, and the striving toward a common goal. One of the female organizers told us emphatically:

> It's really amazing how we are dealing with each other. At work people are good with each other, but they are not doing something where they see the value. Here we are working together, and we see the value of what we are doing.

The opportunity for self-empowerment, that is, the successful acquisition of meaningful technologies of the self, was a clear common thread running through the interviews that we conducted with these female organizers. For Mona, for instance, it was obvious that the organizations are places where young people develop themselves: "We not only develop the people we help, but also the people working with us. The volunteers themselves develop skills." Mona's remarks have strong autobiographical traits. She began as a regular course participant and at the time of our fieldwork she had progressed to being a marketing leader. Thus, for the female volunteers with responsibility for the planning, organization, or communication of activities, the engagement in organizations like these is personally empowering and a way to obtain recognition from others. They learn technologies of the self, which they then reconvey to the next generation of volunteers. In this transmission process, the new youth organizations become central stages for the construction of meaningful selfhoods.

Among the female organizers, the search for an Islamic modern is also stressed by referring to religion as the primary factor of motivation. Like the leaders, these women seem to believe in divine rewards for their efforts:

> I do voluntary work because it is obligatory, not just because I have free time. It is part of being Muslim. There is a quote: you have to give out part of your money in *zakat*, but when it comes to knowledge you have to spread out a hundred percent of your knowledge.

In this statement, Heba touches upon two very important dimensions of the religious motivation, namely, the qualification for religious salvation and the promotion of others' religious devotion. In line with their leaders, the religious motivational background of the female organizers is twofold and intertwined: Helping others in need and showing them how to live according to Islamic codes of conduct is both a motivation in itself and a religious confirmation for the volunteer to achieve salvation through God's grace. Yet religion was not necessarily always the primary reason for doing voluntary work. Basma was a volunteer in Sama where she was responsible for PR and communication. She recalled her earlier experiences, and those of other young women, with organizational work:

> Five years ago some of us were members of Rotary, Caritas and other organizations. Because of political and economic reasons, however, young people got depressed and therefore they turned toward God. Before we did not have any

limits. We went to parties and camping with boys and girls. But why not do charity and be close to God? People are doing what they used to do but from a religious example.

Basma mentioned further that in the beginning she flirted with secular Western organizations. In fact, she once used to volunteer in a women's rights' organization. "I was going to become a Western feminist at university," Basma said, indirectly referring to the sharp contrast she saw between herself and "Western feminists." In her eyes, a Western feminist is a nonbeliever who parties and goes camping with boys, while a Muslim activist like herself wears the *hijab* and adheres to Islamic traditions on gender segregation: "Most of us don't shake hands. It is not a regulation, but we don't do it because our Prophet never did it." Basma expressed that a clear shift in orientation for many women has occurred. While voluntary work for the benefit of the community was not new to them, the reasons for their social engagement had changed. Religious communication seemingly infiltrated the developmental discourse and gradually superseded it. In the course of this transformation, the increasing importance of religion in all aspects of their lives found its bodily expression in a change in appearance and social practices, especially in relation to the opposite sex. What they regard as good and bad, respectively, is now very much influenced by the discourse on morality of Egypt's new Islamic movement. Through references to the Islamic traditions, they achieve the necessary sense of authenticity in constructing their selves.

Consequently, for these women, the construction of meaningful modern selfhoods is also a process of religious and spiritual development. Many of them describe a shift that has occurred in their religious understandings and practices. They put on the *hijab* and started to pray and read the Koran. In their self-representation, religious observance became an intimate part of being an authentic modern Muslim. They wanted to reach a deeper understanding of Islam. Depending on the individual story, different political events and changes in their personal lives represent triggering factors in their turn toward religion. However, common to most of them is the idea of a move forward to something better and truer. This idea and experience of religious and spiritual development and progress is similar to that of the pious Shiite women in Lara Deeb's study on gender and public piety in Lebanon (Deeb 2006). Like the women in her study, our informants, both women and men, refer to a particular religious knowledge and awareness that led them to strive continuously to improve themselves. Furthermore, they distinguish their religious practices from the "traditional" understanding of other Muslims, as well as from their own understanding of Islam before their personal shift toward religion occurred. A female organizer at Misr Shoryan al-Ataa explained to us: "The difference between us and the other Muslims is that we go to the roots. (. . .) We look more in-depth. We try to reach a deeper level of meaning instead of following the rituals." The stories of our female organizers are specific manifestations of a much broader movement of piety and new forms of female Islamic activism among young Muslim women that has also impacted on a good part of Egypt's middle and upper middle-class women (cf. Christiansen 1998, 2003; Mahmood 2005; Hafez 2011). Through instruction and exemplary behavior, they hope to inspire both women and men to contribute to their society while at the same time developing and improving themselves, professionally and spiritually.

This new piety movement and the attempt to establish true meaning with respect to Islamic traditions by female religious laity reflects a major process of religious reorganization that has captured Islam as a whole. Once initiated by the Islamic reform movement in the nineteenth century, its trajectory has been conditioned and shaped in close interaction with the development of other societal subsystems, not least with the historical institutionalization of the political system through national states. For the young people in our field study, the ability to articulate their own experiences independently through means of religious communication is in fact something recently learned in Egypt. The new Islamic movement around lay preachers such as Amr Khaled has been the social vehicle for this learning process, while the decades-long power struggle between the Egyptian state and the Muslim Brotherhood provided the structural frame within which this religious reorganization achieved its institutionalized forms. The new religious youth organizations and their organizational rationales based in Islamic charity traditions are one form of this institutionalization process. In this process, the relative importance of religion for Egypt's young middle class is also an unintended consequence of state policies to control the religious field. The educational policy of religious socialization in public schools must be seen as a case in point (cf. Starrett 1998). While the Brotherhood—so far—has not been able to transform Egyptian society according to its model of an Islamic modern, the struggle between state and Brotherhood has strongly impacted on the religious field in Egypt. The leaders and female organizers follow the Muslim Brotherhood in imagining contemporary Egypt in terms of an Islamic modern. However, they do so in deviating from the specific organized form of first modernity that has captured the social imaginary of the Brotherhood for decades. They are a clear expression of the struggle within the Islamist camp, challenging the relative hegemony of the Brotherhood's model by incorporating new elements of a postmodern conceptualization of Muslim subjectivities in combining them with elements of rather traditional gender roles. From this perspective, the youth organizations are both a post-Brotherhood phenomenon and a part of a new Islamist movement.[4]

THE REGULAR VOLUNTEER: "YOU CAN ALSO ENJOY YOUR TIME"

While board members, organizers, and representatives of the midlevel management might have been active in civil society groups before this wave of new youth organizations emerged, for most of the ordinary volunteers, their involvement is an entirely new experience. Many of these volunteers were initially inspired by Amr Khaled's call for social engagement. The number of regular volunteers in the organizations of our sample varies from around 50 for smaller, more recently established organizations such as Mazeed and Sama to Resala's tens of thousands of volunteers.[5] Although a relatively motley crowd, most volunteers are in their early twenties, are students or recent university graduates with a middle-class background, and young women constitute more than two-thirds of them. At Resala's Mother's Day celebration, we could see them in action. While most of them had joined Resala more recently, some volunteers at Mother's Day, the voluntary organizers of the event, had been members of Resala for some years. They were responsible for one or two specific activities such as the second-hand clothes project or the computer and English-language lessons. Some of these long-term volunteers spent most of their spare time in the organization, whereas others came once a week or a couple of times each month by assisting the more ordinary volunteers.

A good example of an ordinary volunteer is Reem. She was 26 years old and a recent graduate in English translation from Cairo University. She taught Arabic at a private language institute in the center of Cairo. Reem volunteered for Resala once in a while during Ramadan, where she assisted more experienced volunteers in the distribution of food, blankets, and garments. She described this work in very positive terms and praised Resala's mission and the efforts of its leaders, organizers, and volunteers. Before graduation, she used to volunteer every Friday and Saturday, but since she had started working she had difficulties in finding the time to volunteer regularly. "But I try to come from time to time; and I try to bring some food or some medicine," Reem said apologetically. According to the leadership, the commitment of volunteers sometimes causes problems and many organizations must face great variations in the number of volunteers depending on the time of the year.

For volunteers like Reem, the religious obligation to do charity and the striving for God's rewards seem to be strong parts of their motivational background, as it is for leaders and female organizers. Very often the ordinary volunteers mentioned the inspiring role of Amr Khaled and other lay preachers. A female Al-Boraq volunteer in her early twenties explained her motivation as follows: "It is not enough to just worship God. We are responsible for the people." In fact, a small survey that we carried out among volunteers at one of Resala's Mother's Day events proved that the religious obligation to do charity is the primary motivational factor. In line with Brock's findings (2008), however, we could observe that the social aspect of the work and the opportunity to meet like-minded young people outside conventional places such as school or university are also important incentives to join a youth organization. It might also be one of the reasons why especially young women find this work so appealing. Before volunteering for the organizations, many of them spent most of their spare time at home or at university. Big events such as Resala's Mother's Day or the annual distribution of food and blankets among poor communities during Ramadan are opportunities for hundreds, maybe thousands, of young people to meet.

For some volunteers, such events might also be a forum to meet a future husband or wife, although most organizations try to limit the interaction between the sexes. Thus, the social networks acquired through the activism are significant outcomes and an essential motivating factor for the engagement of ordinary volunteers. They experience working as a team and being a part of a network of "likeminded" people. In Heba's words, "You can also enjoy your time. There are many people to know, you have many experiences to gain." Similarly to Rebecca Anne Allahyari's study of voluntary workers in two charitable organizations in Sacramento, California, for young Egyptian volunteers, sociability also seems to work as an "unspoken, underlying reward" to sustain their work (Allahyari 2000, 128). In short, in trying to construct meaningful selfhoods, these volunteers clearly imagine themselves with respect to the generalized behavior of a peer-group-oriented culture.

Through participant observation, we could detect the ways in which these organizational forums become essential social sites for the internalization of specific sets of values, ideals, and bodily practices. Framing processes and exemplary behavior are some of the most effective ways to convey the ideological outlook of an organization to its members. The Mother's Day event of Resala is a very good example of this process. Before the actual event, new volunteers were instructed in what to say and how to approach beneficiaries and potential donors. This is usually done by one of the more experienced volunteers. Furthermore, throughout the day, the volunteers heard and shouted the slogans again and again, and they listened to speeches praising Resala and its efforts to help Egypt's poor. Youth voluntarism and community engagement are the crux of the matter at Resala, and leaders and organizers encourage volunteers to use their energy and enthusiasm to spread and promote this message especially among other young people. They do this with enthusiasm and dedication. Furthermore, the ideal of the Muslim professional promoted by many leaders seems to gain resonance among the ordinary volunteers. The volunteers in our interviews were polite, respectful, and decently dressed. They clearly expressed a desire to become like their leaders, both in personal and professional terms. Many seemed to strive to conform to the religious commitment and practice expected and encouraged by the leadership. For these young volunteers, being an active member of Resala was an essential part of constructing their own identities as modern Muslims in reference to a given normative ideal type.

In this process of forming meaningful selfhoods, the youth organizations transfer distinct "emotional and behavioral expectations" to the volunteers and thus make them part of a specific moral discourse (cf. Allahyari 2000, 3–4). In trying to meet these moral expectations, the volunteers internalize specific codes of conduct and discursive practices; they learn applicable technologies of the self. A good case in point is the moral ideal of the equal worth of the poor. Treating the poor equally and like any other person is a central normative expectation of the youth organizations, as we learnt on various occasions. Embedded in the organization's religious discourse and behavioral practices, this norm serves as an effective moral frame. With reference to Islamic traditions, the volunteers learn that poverty is not a punishment by God. Rather, poverty represents a trial that can come upon anybody. Therefore, we must treat the poor with equal respect and dignity. The poor have the right to share of the meal of those who are well fed (Benthall 1999, 36). While participating in Mazeed's monthly second-hand "clothes exhibition," we could observe the way in which these moral expectations are transmitted through social practices. Before the actual clothes sale, the organization had spent weeks collecting, sorting, and cleaning clothes that had been donated to Mazeed by individual Egyptians. The clothes exhibition, then, took place in the poor neighborhood Ezbet El Hagana on the outskirts of Cairo.

After almost an hour of driving through the narrow, dusty, and garbage-filled streets of Cairo's poor suburbs, we arrived at our destination, which was a local charitable association in a three-storey building connected to a small mosque. The building was buzzing with activity; people were everywhere, especially crowds of children, running up and down the stairs. On the second floor, a group of about 15 girls was reciting the Koran together with a woman from the association. When we entered the third floor of the building, we were met by the local organizers ready to help unpacking and arranging the clothes. Rasha, one of the young women from Mazeed, showed us how to arrange the bags, and she instructed us about prices and what to say to the customers. Rasha concluded: "The prices are fixed—three pounds for one bag!"

After everything was prepared, the people of the neighborhood were let into the room. They had been waiting for a long time behind a barrier at the entrance, which was put up by the folks from the local organization. In groups of about 20, they were allowed to enter the room. Most of them were women with their children. They rushed to the tables and stands, eagerly searching through the piles of clothes and shoes. Each group was allowed to stay in the room for about 20 minutes. Then, a young woman dressed in black from top to toe shouted from the middle of the room that now the time was over and they had to pay and leave the room. When they had left, the next group was let in. It went on like this for more than three hours.

We were observing Rasha while she was serving the poor women. Like the usual street peddlers in Cairo, she presented potential bags for the women, putting them directly into their hands. We got the impression that she was really exerting herself to find exactly the right bag for each individual customer. Only when it came to the price was she unyielding. She played her role as a friendly but determined seller really well. It was interesting to see how she was perfectly able to switch roles: she was now the humble peddler advertising her goods, while the poor women represented the respected customers she had to please. Apparently, she unconsciously combined the religious norm of equality with those of economic market exchange. At least in this situation, the religious and economic rationales of the Muslim professional were elegantly fused in a certain social practice.

With regard to the clothes exhibition project, the volunteers explained this fusion of the two different but mutually reinforcing rationales by emphasizing that they "want to give the people the opportunity to choose what they like—feeling that he or she is buying like any other normal person." The switching of roles, whereby the volunteer plays the role of a street peddler and the beneficiary a customer, is an example of how a moral ideal becomes embodied in social practice. It is an example of how volunteers learn and refine the moral discourse on which the rationale of the organization relies. However, some of the Egyptian volunteers occasionally face difficulties in conforming to this moral ideal. Guided by the leaders' and organizers' application of distinct Islamic moral ideals concerning the right and dignity of the poor, the ordinary volunteers are engaged in a process of moral self-improvement through voluntary community engagement. They first have to learn to turn the normative ideals and social practices of the organization into an individual routine. This observation brings us back to Amr Khaled. The idea of moral self-improvement through voluntary social activism very much resonates with the message of Amr Khaled and the broader movement he epitomizes. This new Islamic movement promotes community service and social responsibility as a way to attain personal moral improvement as well as God's blessings. Here, the moral improvement of the self through religious practices is synonymous with the learning of a morally imbued technology through which young Muslims are able to construct meaningful selfhoods according to an authoritative model.

In fact, self-improvement is a significant aspect of the volunteers' involvement. Religious values and Islamic symbols play a significant role in the recruitment and mobilization of ordinary volunteers. As previous examples illustrate, leaders and female organizers also make use of religious communication about hell and paradise to touch people in their moral self-understanding and social responsibility. However, as the following statement suggests, references to the religious dimension of salvation are more than handy tools in motivating new volunteers. Reflecting on his work at Sunaa al-Hayah, a male volunteer concluded: "We were focused on helping others. In the process, we found out that we had become better Muslims. We thought that we were already good Muslims." According to Saba Mahmood, fear and hope can be an integral aspect of the pious action itself (Mahmood 2005, 140). Considering the practices of women involved in the piety movement in local mosques in Cairo, she argues that, for example, "repeated invocations of fear, and practices that evoke and express that fear, train one to live piously" (2005, 143). Thus, for the volunteers, the fear for God's punishment and the hope for God's rewards are an integral part of self-fashioning, of a learning process of technologies of the self which combine specific activities aimed at helping society's poor with the search for the formation of meaningful forms of modern selfhoods.

So the society is benefiting, and those needy are benefiting even more, but do you know who benefits the most in all this? It's not the society and not the needy, it's the volunteer himself. Our biggest slogan at Resala is "Don't forget that the one benefiting the most from your volunteering is YOU." In all this we're only talking about the rewards in the afterlife. But is the reward only in the afterlife? The rewards are in this life as well! What is the reward that God gives in this life as well? Success! Self-Satisfaction! People's love!

With these words, Abdel-Azeem, the founder and chairman of Resala, highlights our argument that in Egypt's new youth organizations, the youth is also strongly engaged in promoting its own interests through forms of religious social action. These organizations represent social sites at which leaders, organizers, and ordinary volunteers engage in constructing meaningful selfhoods. Within Egypt's particular power configuration, these youth organizations have offered young people opportunities to fashion themselves according to the imaginary of the Muslim professional, a peculiar mixture of technologies of the self, generating a religiously minded working subject in between competing social imaginaries associated with first and second modernities. Confronted with a repressive political system, a closed labor market, severe restrictions on intimacy and a social fabric of stifling patriarchal seniority, Egypt's new youth organizations offer a crucial space for the learning of discursive practices among peers, which can successfully be employed as modern technologies of the self. As Hisham El-Rouby, the chairperson of the Youth Association for Population and Development, frankly stated: "This is an opportunity for volunteers to develop themselves."

Conclusions

Our analysis of three types of members in these youth organizations has shown the ways in which individual identity constructions revolve around the ideal type of a Muslim professional. Yet this general orientation toward the normative ideal of a Muslim professional certainly does not exclude variations in the ways in which individuals construct their identities. While the self-image of the leadership withers between the rather elitist moral autonomy of the bourgeois subject and the postmodern idea of a creative entrepreneur, the ordinary regular volunteer, at least at first glance, seemingly wants most closely to represent the extroverted average type of an individual whose practices resemble the binding forms of behavior of a group of peers. In this process, the female organizers help them to learn these practices through the activities conducted by the organizations. Many of the organizers combine the desire for creative work of second modernity with the ideal of efficient working coordination of the managerial type represented by first modernity.

When it comes to religion, these three types of members seemingly share a religious worldview. In this attitude, trends in society at large and individual preferences seem to meet. Putting personal interests, as well as discursive elements of function systems other than religion, into an Islamic framework, the members of these organizations follow the path of the Islamic reform movement in transforming the language of religious traditions into the vernacular of an authentic Islamic modernity. Moreover, in their search for true Islam by interpreting Islamic traditions without relying on established religious authorities, they are an integral part of the ongoing trend of religious reorganization in the Muslim world. In the representative words of Mai, a volunteer at Mazeed, "our religion is misunderstood." The new youth organizations undoubtedly represent one of the crucial building sites of a contemporary form of the Islamic modern in Egypt. They do so within the structural framework of Egyptian state building in which the Islamic modern has always been an alternative to different forms of essentially secular rule. It will be interesting to observe future developments after the Arab Spring and whether a process toward the democratization of the country will bring about the establishment of an Egyptian Islamic modern or the continuation of an Egyptian modernity in which the rationale of the state essentially remains founded in secular grounds.

Conclusions

This book has aimed to explore the ongoing social transformation in the Middle East, which we assume to be behind the revolutionary events of the so-called Arab Spring. We suggested undertaking this exploration in a conversation between social theory and Islamic and Middle East studies. In this effort, we made Islamic charities and youth organizations the social sites of our investigation, putting our focus on the intersection between political structures, civil society organizations, and the formation of individual selfhoods. In particular, we have investigated the relationship between global social imaginaries and the reinterpretation of Islamic traditions in the construction of various types of social order and forms of modern Muslim subjectivities. We assumed that in the Muslim world also, social orders and identities have evolved in close relationship with globally relevant imaginaries. These imaginaries we have tried to capture with the help of theories on successive modernities and modern subjectivity formation. Fruitful analytical tools for our interpretation of social change in the Middle East were, on the one hand, the distinction between forms of modern social orders designated as restricted liberal, first and second modernities, oscillating between an emphasis on the modern autonomy of collectives versus individuals. On the other hand, we introduced three ideal types of subjectivity formation designated as classical bourgeois, peer-group-oriented, and postmodern subjectivities.

Through these conceptual lenses, we interpret the Arab Spring to be initially characterized by the uprising of a heterogeneous and predominantly young protest movement advocating pluralist elements of second modernity. In retrospect, the scenes from Cairo's Tahrir Square at least partly corrected the picture of the quietist, apathetic, and marginalized status of Egypt's contemporary youth that was frequently conveyed to us by our interviewees. In the course of events, however, the features of second modernity visible in this initial youth protest were superseded by patterns of organized society increasingly characterizing the current political reorganization of Egypt. In the subsequent negotiations of social orders, the collectivist Islamist worldview of the Muslim Brotherhood seems to play a significant role. In the aftermath of the Arab Spring, in Egypt, and to a lesser degree in Tunisia, ideas of an organized Islamic modern at first have taken the lead in defining the postrevolutionary social imaginary of national politics. Yet these imaginaries of an Islamic modern have not remained uncontested. They find themselves in contestation from within and without. Moreover, the initial spirit of civil disobedience has not disappeared. In summer 2013, on the occasion of Egyptian President Muhammad Mursi's first anniversary in office, it vehemently erupted again in massive demonstrations against the President and the ruling position of the Muslim Brotherhood, leading to the removal of President Mursi from office by the July 3rd military intervention. When Field Marshal Abdel Fattah al-Sisi announced the deposition of Mursi, he was surrounded by key figures of the liberal and secular opposition, as well as religious leaders of the al-Azhar and the Coptic Church. Since then, a military-led interim government has ruled the country without an electoral mandate, replacing the Islamist model of an organized society by a nonreligious version of authoritarian rule that has closely reminded us to the prerevolutionary regime. In their concrete institutional forms, the authoritarian regimes of Presidents Mubarak and Ben Ali have lost their legitimacy. In societies at large, however, it appears as if imaginaries of an organized first modernity with their respective collectively defined forms of subjectivities still prevail, whether in Islamist or secular forms. At the point in time we concluded this book, the pluralist elements of second modernity seemed to have almost disappeared from the political scene in Egypt that, then, was characterized by the fierce clash between Islamist and non-Islamist imaginations of a state-organized society, in which allegedly liberal forces supported the military at the expense of democracy.

In our theoretical language, the party organizations of the Muslim Brotherhood movement try to employ Islamic norms and practices first of all as a technology of domination. The ideas of control of first modernity still capture the political worldview of the Muslim Brotherhood. The majority of Islamist groups address the problems of modern contingency not through the regulative regimes of autonomous individuals but by means of a state-centered implementation of collectively binding rules. However, this vision of an organized Islamic society is not necessarily endorsed by the heterogeneous group of supporters of an Islamic modern as a whole. This is apparent in light of the different visions and self-representations of the socially active interlocutors of our study. The leaders, staff members, and volunteers with whom we talked in our fieldwork presented us with utterly hybrid images of the Islamic modern. While sharing the reference to Islamic traditions in principle, they have been constructing collective and individual identities by combining religion with various elements related to our ideal types in idiosyncratic ways. Moreover, our findings show that the Muslim Brotherhood organizations in both Jordan and Egypt have felt compelled to ideologically integrate and Islamize global discourses on development, democracy, and human rights, while still advocating a state-centered collective model of first modernity. In this way, the cultural conflict about the very nature of the Islamic modern has become an inherent part of the Islamist movement itself and has the potential to fragment the religious political camp. This trend toward fragmentation is probably discernible in the conflicts among Muslim Brothers and Salafists in Egypt and Tunisia. From a historical perspective, the relationship between the Jordanian regime and the Muslim Brotherhood has already witnessed these inbuilt contradictions of conflicting interests and visions, a hybridity that has characterized the evolution of the Islamic modern from its beginnings.

The hybridity of the Islamic modern becomes even more pronounced when we look at the micro level. The ideal type of the Muslim professional, for instance, selectively builds on globally relevant patterns we can associate with postmodern imaginaries of the self. Revolving around the key concept of social entrepreneurship, this normative role model for the activists of our Egyptian youth organizations combines the neoliberal features of the creative, project-oriented, and self-reliant entrepreneur with a kind of a morally grounded, social awareness narrated in an Islamic idiom. To a certain extent, this type fuses patterns of both the classical bourgeois and the creative entrepreneur, deriving its authenticity through a certain framing within Islamic traditions. At the same time, however, the organizations in our study, by using the authoritative role model of the Muslim professional, aim at a generalization of behavior through collectively binding social practices. Many of them tend to imagine an Islamic social order closely resembling the managerial organization of the mass society of first modernity. On the basis of patterns of bourgeois and postmodern subjectivities, the Muslim professional serves these youth organizations as a role model for an, in principle, rather peer-group-oriented collectivity. Similar idiosyncratic constructions could be observed among our young interlocutors of the ICCS in Jordan. While they felt comfortable in an organization with a relatively strong collective framing of Islamic discourse and body politics, they simultaneously appreciated the postmodern conditions of creative and individualized work. The participant observations of our fieldwork underpin the claim of poststructuralist theory that we should not perceive successive forms of modernity and types of modern selfhoods in terms of a linear relationship of consecutive replacement. Rather, they represent mutually contested frames of reference in an ongoing cultural conflict about the legitimate representation of modernity.

This conflicting and hybrid combination of different bodies of knowledge and social practices is also clearly visible at the organizational level. With respect to the meso level, we based our study on a heterogeneous group of welfare and youth organizations in Egypt and Jordan. In treating them as social sites for both ongoing negotiations about legitimate forms of social order and for the individual construction of successful modern selfhoods, we go beyond discussing Islamic charities as fronts for political groups or caterers to the interests of a pious middle class alone. With regard to their self-representation, our sample reflects organizational identities relating to various elements of both first and second modernities. These identifications, for instance, find their material expression in the different architectural features of their premises. While JOHUD and Zedny provide their staff with a rather postmodern working environment, ICCS' or Resala's offices reminded us more of the formalized bureaucratic coordination of action that is a characteristic feature of first modernity.

Given our specific interest in the role that religion plays in the construction of modern collective and individual identities, the selection of our social sites has certainly been skewed in favor of particularly Islamic organizations. Only in the case study on Jordan did we include with JOHUD a nonreligious welfare organization for reasons of comparison and due to the very significance of this kind of royal NGO in the Jordanian setting. Yet due to the specific nature of social organizations, transgressing and undermining the macro-sociological constructions of communicative systems, it is actually not clear-cut what defines an organization as predominantly religious. Drawing on Weberian tradition, we suggested measuring the religious character of an organization according to the religious communication it employs, defined by communication with supernatural actors according to a code of blessed/cursed. However, as we have seen in the example of JOHUD, some nonreligious organizations also address donors and beneficiaries in religious language. They apply an Islamic idiom when collecting donations in the holy month of Ramadan and promote their humanist values and social programs in an Islamic vernacular. Therefore, we defined the religious character of an organization exclusively according to whether or not religious communication was at the core of its organizational rationale and self-representation.

Explicitly Islamic organizations, then, are characterized by a discourse of religious duties and awards at the organizational level. Thereby, however, we can observe a constant fusion of religious and nonreligious discourses. In Jordan, for instance, the Zakat Fund and ICCS promote different versions of an organized Islamic society as the legitimate social order. As a governmental organization, the Zakat Fund works toward the stabilization of the political status quo, whereas the ICCS follows the discursive language of the Muslim Brotherhood movement and advocates the transformation of the social order along Islamist lines. In Egypt, most of our youth organizations distanced themselves from the collectively binding representations of both Egyptian state Islam and the Islamist ideology of the Muslim Brotherhood. Instead they adhered to the discourse of a new Islamic movement, emphasizing individual piety and fusing religious language with concepts of social empowerment, democracy, and basic human rights. Generally speaking, all these organizations continue in their own ways the approach of the Islamic reform movement in Islamizing modern nonreligious discourses, practices, and institutions. Yet in this process, the interpretation of Islamic traditions seems to be subject to the discursive power of global imaginaries, which often give them their specific meanings.

Zooming into the individual level, however, the specifically religious rationale of an organization does not necessarily tell us something about the role religion plays among its members. On the one hand, we met with people in religious organizations where Islam was not the central motivator but rather a convenient facilitator for achieving utterly worldly goals such as employment, social status, friendships, and access to various material resources. This observation underlines again that in societies characterized by a hegemonic Islamic vernacular the application of religious language alone should not be taken as a straight expression of religiosity. In addition, the choice of a particular organization for social engagement often depended on the ethnic, ideological, tribal, or local networks of which our interviewees already had been an integral part. Also in this case, religion might not have been the prime mover in joining an Islamic organization. On the other hand, we talked to pious individuals who were "following the path of God" in consciously joining a nonreligious organization. A good example is Hanin, one of our informants among JOHUD's members. In our conversations, Hanin perfectly combined discourses on religious traditions with developmental ideas and elements of the pluralistic and individualized imaginary of a postmodern form of subjectivity. For her, it was precisely the nonreligious nature of JOHUD that gave her room to conduct work as a consciously practicing Muslim. To construct a meaningful selfhood as a modern pious Muslim, Hanin does not need a specifically Islamic working environment in order to realize herself as a modern working subject. She defines herself as a sincere believer not in aiming at matching the "average type" of an Islamic group of peers, but through the individual interpretation of her work and behavior through the prisms of religious traditions. In doing so, Hanin was very different from many of our interlocutors at ICCS or Resala, who often emphasized the explicitly religious organizational rationale of these charities. In their case, the identification with a collectively organized group of peers apparently held a central place in the construction of meaningful selfhoods.

In analytical terms, we would, therefore, suggest distinguishing between Islam as a hegemonic discourse and as a means of collective and individual religious identification. The gradual rise of the Islamic modern into relative hegemony has tended to blur this distinction by making references to Islamic traditions an almost necessary but empty signifier. At the beginning of the twenty-first century, claiming authenticity without referring to Islam has become a difficult task. In the past decades, most parts of the Muslim world have experienced a wave of "religious awakening." Islamic language has increasingly penetrated public life, political debates, and individual social practices. This religious awakening has reinforced the hegemonic status that Islam has achieved in representing Muslim societies at a global level. For both observers and the observed, the reference to Islam has become a discursive nodal point in the general representation of modern Muslim life. Yet hegemonies are historical and not substantial in their character.

In 1956, for instance, Egyptian President Gamal Abd al-Nasser announced women's right to vote, cheered by a group of women in front of the presidential palace (see the picture in Kamrava 2011, Figure 7, 95). In striking contrast to today, not a single of the Egyptian middle-class women in this picture was wearing a headscarf or was dressed in "pious" garments. Taking female bodies as a site for individual self-actualization, this picture strongly resembles the classical peer-group model of the American middle class rather than any form of the Islamic modern. Since then, however, Egyptian society has experienced a profound "Islamization." This not only is apparent in public spaces, but also impacts on the norms and values of individuals. Our informants from Egypt's new youth organizations have been molded by this increasingly more religiously defined social environment around them. Under the general religious awakening of Egyptian society, a substantial number of the younger generation of Egypt's middle class have reconsidered the values of their parents and made references to Islamic traditions a major pattern of the formation of their selves. For them, societal reform, educational achievements, professional careers, and Islamic morals are together central points of reference for the successful establishment of individual modern selfhoods.

In our analysis of this religious awakening, however, we should avoid treating Islam as an independent variable. On all three levels of analysis, our study has shown the contingent ways in which Islamic traditions play a part in complex processes of collective and individual identity constructions. In Jordan, Egypt, and elsewhere, the currently hegemonic imagination of an Islamic modern is deeply molded by historically individual trajectories of national state formation. At state level, the multiple versions of the Islamic modern express a strong path dependency. This multiplicity in shaping Islamic modernities is also mirrored in the self-representations of the social-welfare and youth organizations of our study.

The organizational rationales and Islamic outlooks of the organizations in our sample have developed in an inseparable connection with the state and nation building of their respective countries. Thus, the Islamic character of an organization in Jordan has always been embedded in a certain notion of the Islamic nature of the Jordanian state. Only with the increasing rift between regime and Brotherhood, Islamic charities in Jordan had to navigate more carefully with regard to what kind of Islam they represent. In Egypt, by contrast, Islamic organizations have often walked a tightrope. As long as they were not representing Egypt's state Islam, they had to carefully distance themselves from the Muslim Brotherhood movement and its Islamist alternative to the state's imagination of the Egyptian modern. It has been in this narrow space between state Islam and Brotherhood that Egypt's new Islamic movement and the youth organizations of our study have evolved.

In addition to the specific national contexts, the organizational rationale of welfare and youth organizations also relates visibly to broader global discourses and imaginaries. Many of them are part of the globally hegemonic discourses on sustainable development, democracy, and human rights. On a more abstract level, we can discern various elements of our ideal types of social order and subjectivity formation as figuring in their otherwise historically specific imaginations. In this context, social stratifications seem to make a certain difference as to which model of an Islamic modernity these organizations and their members advocate. In light of our findings, we tentatively would argue that the more affluent middle classes express a tendency to combine Islamic traditions with the pluralistic and individualized set of values of second modernity, whereas the lower middle classes rather identify with the peer-group-oriented model of organized modernity that, for instance, is represented by the mainstream of the Muslim Brotherhood and the ICCS. Yet, as we have seen in the case of ICCS, these dominant imaginaries have also been contested from within, in particular, through the different attitudes of individual members.

This observation finally brings us back to the micro level. Here, we could observe a number of idiosyncratic ways to blend traits of the classical bourgeois with peer-group behavior and the social imperatives of the creative entrepreneur. Combining these with Islamic traditions apparently serves both their social justification in light of the hegemony of the Islamic modern and their individual incorporation into religious life styles. While it is difficult for the observer to judge individuals unambiguously according to this distinction, both ways show the unquestionable compatibility of religious traditions with modern imaginaries. Of course, with our specific case studies, we were only able to shed light on very small and particular segments of Middle Eastern societies. Concerning the role of global imaginaries in shaping multiple modernities, our book must be considered as a tentative and rather limited first step. The theoretical approach suggested here needs more empirical application, which must also go beyond religious contexts. Yet despite these limitations, through our particular analytical framework, we can clearly discern that contemporary negotiations about social orders and modern forms of subjectivities in Muslim societies can be understood with the help of concepts that social theorists derived from and tend to reduce to the European historical experience. We can understand the ongoing transformation of Middle Eastern societies in terms of a cultural conflict among different forms of globally relevant social imaginaries. Apparently, the ownership of these social imaginaries is not restricted to Europe alone. Employing them in the study of non-European histories, we can facilitate comparative research that goes beyond an understanding of cultural differences based on fundamental binaries such as between Western and non-Western societies. Taking the horizon of globally shared social imaginaries seriously might be another way to contribute to "provincializing Europe" (Chakrabarty 2000), to promoting the abandonment of the still influential equation of modernization with Westernization.

Notes

Introduction "We Have a Collective Vision to Build Our Society"

1. A couple of years before the Arab Spring, Asef Bayat already suggested that authoritarian regimes might be able to suppress political movements, but meet their limits in stifling the daily lives of their ordinary citizens (Bayat 2007, 202).

2. To a certain extent, the argumentation of this book and its theoretical framework is constantly questioning and critically reflecting on the rather homogeneous notions of Islam and of the West. However, for the mere sake of convenience, it is almost impossible to avoid these terms entirely when writing on a subject such as we do in this book. Therefore, we hope that conceptual purists among our readers will excuse the rather loose application of these terms in some instances.

3. See, for instance, Cooke and Lawrence (2005); Deeb (2006); Haenni (2005); Hefner and Zaman (2007); Hirschkind (2006); Juul Petersen (2012); Mahmood (2005); Peterson (2011); Salvatore and Eickelman (2004); Shehabuddin (2008); Soares and Otayek (2007); and Sparre (2013).

4. Also the Muslim world knows the tension between Islam and other functionally circumscribed areas of society. Although never forming a "church," Islam has been highly institutionalized, went through various processes of orthodoxification, and has a universal claim. Regarding the individual believer, the Day of Judgment and therewith the quest for salvation play a central role in religious action. There would be much fewer similarities with regard to Eastern religions such as Buddhism or Hinduism in comparison to Islam.

5. Being aware of the limitations of the validity of data from interviews, in particular, with respect to the authoritarian political nature of both countries, we tried to ensure in our fieldwork to conduct them in a safe, open, and trusting environment, guaranteeing all interviewees anonymity if desired. Most of the names in our case studies are, therefore, not the original names of our interlocutors. Only if they explicitly granted us permission to disclose their real names, we have used them. The interviews were organized around relatively open themes rather than specific or even suggestive questions, facilitating free and open conversations. Our interlocutors seemed to speak with ease and confidence, not being afraid to talk about Islam in relation to social welfare activities.

6. In September 2005, the Danish newspaper *Jyllandsposten* published a number of cartoons about Prophet Muhammad. What was the local provocation of an internationally insignificant newspaper developed into a fierce international

dispute about the limits of freedom of speech during which Danish embassies in Beirut, Damascus, Islamabad, and Teheran were attacked and set on fire.

I Theoretical and Analytical Framework: Understanding Islamic History with the Help of Social Theory

1. This normative and emic application of the modern has played an important role in Muslim contexts. In Turkey, for instance, the Kemalist state elite justified its state-centered authoritarian rule by invoking a modernizing mission against the resilient forces of religiously inspired traditionalism. Since the second half of the nineteenth century, modernity has developed into a central term in Ottoman and Turkish political discourses, more recently applied in Alevi revivalist movements (Erdemir 2006). Islamic reformist scholars such as Fazlur Rahman (1984) or Tariq Ramadan (2008) developed modernist theologies in order to place Islam right in the center of contemporary society. In their efforts to better the life of their communities, even movements of public piety apply the classical distinction between tradition (*taqlid*) and modernity (*hadara/hadith*) in their interpretation of Islamic traditions (cf. Deeb 2006).

i Modernity, Successive Modernities, and the Formation of the Modern Subject

1. See Dirlik (2003); Eisenstadt (2000); Therborn (2003); and Schmidt (2008).
2. Theoretically, we subscribe to this open and all-encompassing concept of society that—in principle—defines society as world society. However, as a matter of convenience, we will use the term "society" throughout the text also with respect to particular communities such as Jordanian society, Muslim societies, European societies, and so on. In this usage, however, society does not represent an analytical concept.
3. *Provincializing Europe* is the title of Dipesh Chakrabarty's wholesale critique of the Eurocentric character of the social sciences. According to him, European imperialism and Third World nationalism participated in the construction of the narrative of modernization as Westernization. Therefore, Chakrabarty advocates writing a new history of modernity in which its own ambivalences, contradictions, and repressive practices are visibly inscribed (1992, 19–21).
4. Unfortunately, there is a difference in the numbering and consequently naming of the three types of successive forms of modernity that might confuse the reader. In Wagner's typology, the first type refers to the bourgeois society of the nineteenth century, which does not play a role in the theories of Beck and Giddens who only talk about first and second modernities with respect to the organized mass society and its postmodern follower of reflexive modernity. In fusing these concepts, in our analytical framework, first and second modernities are preceded by what Wagner called restricted liberal society. These three sequences then also fit in relation to Reckwitz's three types of modern subjectivity formation, which we introduce in the third section of the chapter.
5. There is a strong tendency to equate the modern state with liberal democracy and representative forms of government. While we can indeed observe a move toward democracy after the Second World War, modern state formation in the twentieth century was equally characterized by the formation of authoritarian and totalitarian polities, forms of rule that still have not been abandoned in many parts of the globe.

6. In this chapter, we will deal exclusively with the macro and micro levels. The meso level will be discussed with a specific emphasis on religious organizations and social movements in the second chapter.

7. Haj's critique is thereby directed against the very influential study by Albert Hourani (1962). For other examples, see, for instance, Deeb (2006) and Mahmood (2005).

8. In combining Reckwitz's three ideal types with the three types of successive modernities, we adopt his perspective of a relative hegemony of these types in the historical course of modernity. However, the previous types are not entirely replaced but continue to play a role in the negotiation about legitimate social orders. Thus, we do not endorse the view of Ulrich Beck that an epocal rupture, a fundamental separation between first and second modernity has taken place. Rather we can observe cultural conflicts about hegemony between elements of all three types of successive modernities.

9. For the second type, which Reckwitz calls *Angestelltensubjekt*, we borrow the term of the "salaried masses" from Siegfried Kracauer's book of the same name in which he critically described the lifestyle of Germany's new middle-class employees.

10. Putting his focus on American mass culture, Reckwitz deliberately neglects two alternative forms of subjectivity that play a significant role in the period of first modernity: fascism and communism. He underlines that a comparative study of American peer-group society with fascist and communist societies could not only show differences and similarities among these social orders, but also contribute to a new understanding of multiple modernities within the West (2006, 29).

11. Reckwitz only refers to religion briefly in the introduction, declaring it together with other social fields such as politics, law, or education as a potential arena for the analysis of the construction of modern selves (2006, 29).

12. Throughout this book we normally apply the term "Islamist" instead of the also frequently used term "fundamentalist," which serves much more comparative purposes than the first.

2   Modern Religion, Religious Organizations, and Religious Social Action

1. There is a difference between autonomy and independence. While a system has to be autonomous in its internal operations in order to establish the necessary boundaries between system and environment, the environment—including other functional systems—certainly impacts on the system. In this sense, we do have an interdependent relation among functional systems. However, in its relation to the environment, a system has to transform every element from outside into the internal logic of its own operational mechanism. In order to exist as a system, it has to maintain its autonomy in the sense of operational closure, and this makes systems autonomous but not independent.

2. In defining the religious code in this way, Beyer tries to circumvent the "Christian bias," which is implicit in Luhmann's (transcendent/immanent) or Durkheim's (sacred/profane) dichotomies.

3. In our reading, Beyer does not understand these religious programs as static, in the manner of the cultural programs of those theories of multiple modernities that found our critique before. Yet choosing the term "program" has a tendency to imply that.

4. This return to Max Weber's theoretical approach certainly does not mean that we endorse the results of his fragmented study on Islam. On the basis of a selective reading of the findings of the Islamic studies of his time, Weber's image of Islam found severe criticism and must be considered as almost entirely outmoded (cf. Jung 2011, 149–53).

5. The rationality of magic, however, is of a different type than the formal rationality of modernity.

6.. From the perspective of social action, Weber's definition of religious action based on the interaction (communication) with transcendent actors supports the systemic definition of modern religion as a specific system of communication by Luhmann and Beyer.

3   ISLAMIC REFORM AND THE CONSTRUCTION OF MODERN MUSLIM SUBJECTIVITIES

1. This does not mean that references to religion are completely absent in East Asian modernities. Yet these references to Buddhism or Confucianism have never achieved the role of a core signifier as in Islamic modernities.

2. For a critical discussion of this label in Western scholarship, see Lauzière (2010).

3. In this process, Islamic reformers closely followed the interpretative paths of non-European intellectuals. They first pictured Islam as an integral part of civilization in universal terms, before applying it in its narrower ethnic meaning as Islamic civilization among other civilizations. Similar to developments in Asia, Muslim intellectuals began to use the authoritative meaning of civilization against the West and denounced the destructiveness and vices of Western civilization (see Aydin 2007; Duara 2004, 90–5).

4. By associating the Brotherhood with this type of the modern salaried masses, we have made two restrictions. The first relates to the consumptive attitudes of this kind of modern subjectivity, which demand a level of economic development that Egypt had certainly not achieved. Second, the Muslim Brotherhood and other movements in the region also displayed elements that we can attribute to the fascist and socialist alternatives, which we have mentioned only briefly. In our opinion, however, fascism and socialism do not necessarily appear to be opposing forms of subjectivity to the peer-group-oriented type. Rather we would view them as alternatives within this type, expressing very different modes of organizing modernity and shaping modern subjects.

5. Michel Foucault indicated the mutual interconnectedness of these two modern disciplinary methods, which together are characteristic of modern governmentality (1988, 19).

6. In this attitude, however, they also follow specific authoritative types of second modernity as given by the structures of a successfully achieved ideal of postmodern subjectivity.

II   POLITICS OF MUSLIM SUBJECTIVITIES IN JORDAN

1. See, for example, Abu Rumman (2007); Adams (1996); Boulby (2000); Brown and Hamzawy (2010); Ghanem and Mohanad (2011); Moaddel (2002); Robinson (1997); Rubin (2007); Schwedler (2006); and Stemman (2008).

2. This general lack of knowledge of political parties was documented by a survey of the Center for Strategic Studies in Amman in which 30 percent stated that they knew of the IAF, while the other parties were known by 13 percent or less of the interviewees (Moaddel 2002, 114).

3. There are no official statistics on the number of Islamic organizations as compared to non-Islamic. According to Wiktorowicz (2001, 84), the number of Islamic NGOs in 1995 was 49, or six percent of all NGOs. However, this figure remains unclear since he does not define the term "Islamic." Judging from our fieldwork experiences, we estimate the number of organizations with an Islamic orientation to be much higher.

4. Despite their importance, they have received little academic attention in analyses of Jordanian society; see Wiktorowicz (2001); Clark (2004); Harmsen (2008); and Sparre and Petersen (2007).

4   State and Islam in Jordan: The Contested Islamic Modern

1. If not quoted otherwise, we rely with respect to the historical data in this chapter on the works of Abu Rumman (2007); Anderson (2005); Harmsen (2008); Robinson (2004); Salibi (1993); Schwedler (2006); and Wiktorowicz (2001).

2. On the various dimensions of this claim of "Islamic legitimacy," see also Brand (1999) and Valbjørn (2005).

3. This quote is taken from Wiktorowicz (2001, 49).

4. "Islam is the religion of the State and Arabic is its official language," art. 2.

5. The Constitution of Jordan, available at http://www.kinghussein.gov.jo /constitution_jo.html (accessed September 22, 2012).

6. These courts have exclusive jurisdiction on matters of personal status (e.g., marriage, divorce, and inheritance), Islamic endowments (*awqaf*), and cases concerning blood money (*diya*) (Constitution of Jordan, Article 10). Religious judges appointed by the state administer these cases. Only Muslims are subject to these courts. Non-Muslims have the right to establish religious tribunals for their own communities. Beside personal status law, civil and special state courts administer justice (Article 99). Until 1976, tribal disputes were settled on the basis of tribal customary laws.

7. The Jordanian National Charter, Chapter 1, fifth principle.

8. www.ammanmessage.com (accessed June 23, 2012).

9. Some argue that the foundation of this close relationship goes back to King Hussein's college years, when he studied at the Islamic College, established by Haj Abdullatif Abu Qura, who was the leader of the Muslim Brotherhood. However, these relations were also marred by conflict at times. For instance, King Hussein was highly skeptical toward the Brotherhood's pronounced anti-Zionism, which he saw as a contrast to his own policy of compromise and cooperation. He kept a close eye on the organization, and Abu Qurah was, in fact, arrested several times (Harmsen 2008, 138). For an analysis of the relationship between the Muslim Brotherhood and the kings of Jordan between 1945 and 1993, see Boulby (2000).

10. However, the regime has not only fought against secular political ideologies, but also banned Islamist groups that do not endorse the general vision of the monarchy's Islamic modern and its dynastic rule. Hizb al-Tahrir, for instance, although not officially admitted as a political party, could muster a

substantial following during the 1950s and 1960s and with its transnational-ist Islamist ideology challenged the very territorial integrity of the Jordanian state (Taji-Farouki 1996). Other examples are the various Salafist movements that have appeared more recently on Jordan's Islamist political scene (Wiktorowicz 2000, 2001).

11. Martial law was lifted the year after, only to be reintroduced in 1967 during the war with Israel (Wiktorowicz 2001, 11). On the developments leading to the declaration of material law, see Robinson (2004, 94–102) and Salibi (1993, 190–5).

12. In 1984, King Hussein decided to hold elections for eight seats in the Lower House. Muslim Brotherhood members won two of these seats.

13. There are, however, signs that this influence might be waning. In 2009, the Jordan Bar Association elected an independent candidate for president, ending a decade of Brotherhood dominance of the association. Likewise, in April 2009, the Medical Association elected a candidate from the left wing, also replacing a Brotherhood candidate (*Jordan Times* April 12, 2009).

14. The government promoted policies of good neighbourhood with Israel and tried "to sell" the peace treaty by promising future foreign investment and economic benefits for the whole of the country. However, these peace dividends turned out to be a mere fantasy (Scham and Lucas 2003).

15. Certainly, this is not only a response to the increased power of the Muslim Brotherhood alone, but just as much due to the increasing strength of Salafist groups, as well as a response to international demands for a moderate Islam.

16. Speech held by King Abdullah II at the Catholic University of America, September 13, 2005 (www.jordanembassyus.org/hmka09132005.htm, accessed September 22, 2012). Other examples of this discourse can be found in various speeches and publications, including, for example, the Jordan Human Development Report, in which the king states: "We are proud to be seen as a model of Arab and Islamic tolerance and enlightened vision" (UNDP 2004, iii).

17. The extent and intensity of poverty among Jordanians has increased since the 1980s, and today, 23 percent of all households and 31 percent of all individuals have an income below the poverty line, according to the Jordanian Department of Statistics and the Ministry of Social Development (Loewe et al. 2001, III). While the concrete figures about poverty are contested, all surveys seem to agree on the fact that the poverty rate has been increasing in the past decades. Given the country's poor economy and demographic developments, most studies make the high rates of unemployment and underemployment responsible for this rise in poverty (Loewe et al. 2001, 16f).

18. The law has been subject to severe criticism by international and Jordanian organizations, and in 2006, a coalition of organizations presented a draft of new law to the ministry of social development. In October 2007, however, the cabinet proposed a new law that did not take into account any of the provisions of the draft, and which many civil society organizations claimed was even more restrictive than the current law. This law, named Law on Societies (Law 51 of 2008), was enacted in 2008, but was amended in 2009 as a partial response to the criticism (Law 22 of 2009); see NGO Law Monitor (2012).

19. Law no. 33 of 1966, Article 2.

20. However, GUVS cannot always live up to regime expectations. In September 2006, the government decided to install temporary management at the

headquarters of GUVS, and in June 2007, at the Amman branch of GUVS (Human Rights Watch 2008).

21. This does not mean, however, that the regime does not act against secular organizations as well. In 2002, the Jordanian Society for Citizen's Rights was dissolved, officially because of failure to provide annual reports on finance and activities and refusing to allow ministerial officials to enter their premises. Unofficially, it was related to the organization's outspoken criticism of oppressive state policies toward Palestinian citizens (Harmsen 2008, 168).

22. Paradoxically, however, some also said that the suspicion of Islamic organizations on the part of the regime had led more Jordanians to support them, and that the loss of international donors was, thus, balanced out by the increase in national ones.

5   CHARITIES AND SOCIAL WELFARE ORGANIZATIONS IN JORDAN:
     NEGOTIATING THE ISLAMIC MODERN

1. Although JOHUD does not define itself as an Islamic organization, we have included it for three reasons. First, it represents a major player in the field of social welfare provision, deeply involved in the societal negotiations that have been going on in this field. Secondly, while not religious at organizational level, some members of JOHUD claim religious motivations for their engagement in the organization. Thirdly, in analyzing not only organizations with a distinct religious rationale, we try to avoid the bias toward pious organizations as strongly criticized, for instance, with regard to the work of Mahmood (Bangstad 2011; Schielke 2009).

2. The independent organizations constitute a very varied group in size and ideological outlooks. They also include organizations that are connected to parties and movements other than the Brotherhood, for example, Nawal al-Faouri's Al-Aqsa, which is connected to Hizb al-Wasat.

3. Beside *zakat*, the institution of *sadaqa* (voluntary alms) also plays an important role in the Islamic approach to social welfare.

4. These are the creed (*shahada*), the five daily prayers (*salah*), the *zakat*, fasting during the month Ramadan (*saum*), and the pilgrimage to Mecca (*hajj*).

5. The organization is divided into a number of centers and initiatives, including the Queen Zein al-Sharaf Institute for Development (training of staff and volunteers), the Small Business Development Center (training, capacity building, and advisory services), the Princess Basma Youth Resource Center (education and training of young people), Beit al-Bawadi (creative enterprises), Radio Farah al-Nas, the Goodwill Campaign, and the Queen Alia Social Work Competition.

6. The first was the Young Muslim Women's Association, established in 1974. The YMWA was followed in 1977 by Queen Alia Fund for Social Development (since 1999, the Jordan Hashemite Fund for Human Development), the Noor al-Hussein Foundation in 1985, the Jordan River Foundation in 1995, the King Hussein Foundation in 1999, and Tkiyet um Ali, established in 2004. Beside the royal charities, the royal family has established and chairs a number of organizations and institutions in other areas of society, for example, the Royal Institute for Interfaith Studies and the Royal Aal al-Bayt Institute for Islamic Thought.

7. However, there are differences between the royal organizations, in particular, between the Jordan River Foundation and the other organizations. Chaired by Queen Rania, this NGO receives more public funds than others and its staff gets higher salaries, at least according to members of JOHUD.

8. *Jordan Times* December 10, 2000.

9. http://www.style.com/vogue/feature/2009_March_Queen_Rania / (accessed April 15, 2009).

10. Advocacy work is conducted by NGOs that understand themselves as specifically advocating political issues such as human rights, environmental protection, or women rights.

11. According to an interview with an anonymous resource person.

12. www.johud.org.jo (accessed September 19, 2012).

13. www.johud.org.jo (accessed September 19, 2012).

14. In 1978, the then Queen Alia Foundation obtained a fatwa from the chief mufti of the country permitting Muslim citizens to pay their *zakat* through the Fund (Bint Talal 2004, 118).

15. www.johud.org.jo (accessed September 19, 2012).

16. We will deal more with this organization and Amr Khaled in the following chapter.

17. www.tkiyetumali.org (accessed September 22, 2012).

18. *Jordan Times* October 22, 2006.

19. Interview with director of the Zakat Fund.

20. In an interview, the secretary general of the Ministry of Religious Foundations even said that the ministry plays a daily role in supervising the committees (www.humanityvoice.net/news_details.php?id=1170, accessed September 22, 2012).

21. Brochure from the Zakat Fund, own translation.

22. Brochure from the Zakat Fund, own translation.

23. Interview with director of Zakat Fund, April 9, 2007.

24. For instance, the *Jordan Times* October 10, 2006, *King Abdullah Announces Plan to Build Al Aqsa 5th Minaret*: "The King [. . .] emphasised the importance of the Zakat Fund in alleviating the suffering of the poor and strengthening social solidarity. He reiterated his support for this fund." This article further mentions the king's plans to build a new minaret at Al-Aqsa Mosque and to create a special fund for the support and protection of holy sites and shrines. Another article, *King revisits Jordan Valley town to check on progress in development projects*, tells of the king visiting *zakat* committees in Deir Alla, donating 50,000 JD to the committees (October 11, 2005, retrieved from www.kingabdullah.gov.jo, accessed September 22, 2012).

25. The Koran lists eight categories of *zakat* beneficiaries: "Alms are for the poor and the needy, and those employed to administer (the funds); for those whose hearts have been (recently) reconciled (to truth); for those in bondage and in debt; in the cause of Allah; and for the wayfarer" (9, 60). The question of whether *zakat* benefits non-Muslims or not is frequently discussed among Muslim scholars. While the majority insists that *zakat* cannot be given to non-Muslims, an increasing number of people have been challenging this view. They argue, with the Jordanian scholar Abdul-Azziz Al-Khayyat, that the first category of beneficiaries listed in the Koran (*al-fuqaraa*) should be translated into "all the poor," thus including non-Muslims (Benthall and Bellion-Jourdan 2003, 10).

26. This is according to ICCS management. According to Hammad (1999), in 1998, the ICCS branch in Amman had a budget of approx. three million JD, the Mafraq branch a budget of 150,000 JD, and the Zarqa branch 1 million JD. He does not provide figures for the branches in Irbid and Ramtha.

27. The ICCS runs 55 community centers, 52 schools and kindergartens, 15 health clinics, 3 colleges and universities, and 2 hospitals.

28. The ICCS is very active in Palestinian camps and the Muslim Brotherhood recruits most of its followers among the country's Palestinian population; see Abu Rumman (2007, 16, 39).

29. According to ICCS management, the clinics treat approx. 140,000 people annually, more than 15,000 students are enrolled in the schools, 13,000 orphans receive support, and 25,000 families use the services of the community centers.

30. A large number of our data results from interviews with leaders and members so that we often can not provide direct references. Their reliablity should therefore not be taken as given.

31. According to a spokesperson from the Muslim Brotherhood, the ICCS is the only organization formally under the authority of the Brotherhood, but a number of other organizations are connected to it and the IAF through personal ties, strategic alliances, and convergence of persons in management positions.

32. Although promoting this image, the ICCS is, in fact, largely concentrated in the predominantly Palestinian areas around Amman, Zarqa, and Irbid, and has no centers in the tribal south (Clark 2004, 99).

33. Interview with Egbert Harmsen in 2003 (Harmsen 2008, 228).

34. www.queenrania.jo/content/modulePopup.aspx?secID=&itemID=1690 &ModuleID=press&ModuleOrigID=news (accessed December 1, 2008).

6   CHARITY AND THE CONSTRUCTION OF MODERN MUSLIM SUBJECTIVITIES IN JORDAN

1. On top of the general problems with unemployment, many Palestinians face additional difficulties in finding a job in the public sector, which has historically been reserved for citizens of Transjordanian origin whose loyalty to the state was rarely questioned (Clark 2004, 89).

2. As a general feature of Jordanian society, employment in all types of organization also strongly relies on personal patronage (*wasta*) and networks based on ethnic, tribal, and family affiliations.

3. Cf. personal correspondence with Janine Clark, May 2009.

4. Information from website and interviews.

5. However, the director of Tkiyet um Ali was a man.

6. We will present a more detailed account of this new Islamic movement in the following case study on Egypt, where it has its origins.

7. Quote from website, www.johud.org.jo (accessed December 2, 2008).

8. *Jordan Times* September 9, 2008.

9. Clark (2004) argues that doctors in the Islamic Hospital and health clinics are in fact paid relatively well, especially when taking into consideration the various benefits they are offered (vacation, sick leave, working hours, equipment, etc.). However, compared to royal organizations, salaries are low.

10. Not all volunteers in independent organizations are wealthy—some are similarly placed as the ICCS constituency, coming from the lower middle classes.
11. We found this type also in the local *zakat* committees of the governmental Zakat Fund.
12. Khawla bint al-Azwar was a woman who fought against the Romans to rescue her brother who had been caught as a prisoner of war. That al-Netaqueen was the daughter of the prophet's best friend, and she used to bring him food when he was hiding from his enemies.

III   Politics of Muslim Subjectivities in Egypt

1. The term *daiyat* (sing: *daiya*) is often used to describe a recent movement of young women preachers who deliver religious lessons to other women in mosques (Mahmood 2005).
2. Galal Amin has emphasized that the enormous expansion of Egypt's middle class has fundamentally weakened its distinctive features. He associates the "Islamic revival" in Egypt with the ascent of lower classes into the middle class (Amin 2011, 85–100). We use the term in the following chapters as a vague category for urban, formally educated, and salaried people whose living conditions are well above poverty level but who are also clearly distinct from Egypt's new rich.

7   State and Islam in Egypt: Competing Models of Organized Modernity

1. Muhammad Ali received the title Viceroy of Egypt and the hereditary succession to this title by his heirs made official in 1841 by a degree of the Ottoman Sultan (Vatikiotis 1985, 68).
2. "Islam is the religion of the state, Arabic is the official language, the principles of the Islamic *sharia* shall be a chief source of legislation" (cf. Lombardi 2006, 125)
3. *Al-Ahram*, cf. Bayat (2007, 166–7)
4. Michel Foucault himself stressed the fact of this dialectic relationship between the technologies of domination of others and those of the self (1988, 19).
5. Saad Eddin Ibrahim (1988) argues that the conflict in the Brotherhood resulted in no less than four broad tendencies: the "apolitical Muslim Brotherhood," denouncing all political activity and dedicating itself to religious teaching, moral reinforcement, and the establishment of Islamic social institutions; the "mainstream Muslim Brotherhood," led by Hasan Ismail al-Hudaybi, committed to achieve its political objectives by nonviolent means; the antiregime Muslim groups, such as the Islamic Liberation Organization and the Jihad Organization, that by means of violence aimed at toppling the regime and bringing about an Islamic regime; and the "anti-society Muslim groups," such as Al-Takfir wa al-Hijra, that believed in breaking away from a society in moral decay in order to build a nucleus "community of believers" who could eventually overthrow the rulers and establish an Islamic state. In the following, the primary focus will be on the "mainstream Muslim Brotherhood" in contrast to the 'revolutionary' wing, encompassing both the third and fourth of Ibrahim's categories.

6. For literature about Sayyid Qutb, see Calvert (2010); Khatab (2006); Musallam (2005); and Shepard (1996).

7. See BBC News, "Divisive Egypt reforms approved"; retrieved June 4, 2009, http://news.bbc.co.uk/2/hi/middle_east/6498573.stm.

8. www.amrkhaled.net

9. Interview with *Al-Ahram Weekly*; cf. Wise (2006, 57).

10. www.amrkhaled.net.

11. On February 7, 2013, a new draft NGO law was presented by the Ministry of Insurance and Social Affairs. According to human rights observers, it is even more restrictive than the law currently in effect. According to Cairo Institute for Human Rights, it "demonstrates more hostility towards civil society than all NGO laws and bills drafted under Abd al-Nasser, Mubarak, and the Supreme Council of Armed Forces" (http://www.cihrs .org/?p=5875&lang=en, retrieved February 13, 2013).

12. The 13 categories of activity are as follows: social assistance; religious, scientific, and cultural services; maternity and child care; family welfare; special categories and handicapped welfare; old-age welfare; friendship among peoples; family planning; social protection; management and administration; prison inmates' welfare; literacy; and multiple services (Clark 2004, 49). One exception is the large group of the so-called Community Development Organizations, registered under a separate category at the ministry of social affairs. They are allowed to carry out a wide range of activities and services. Many have strong ties with the state authorities, they receive substantial subsidies from the government, and the staff is usually paid by the ministry of social solidarity (LaTowsky 1997).

8   New Youth Organizations in Egypt: Charity and the "Muslim Professional"

1. Among the largest were the Coptic Association dating from 1891 and the Islamic Charity Organization established in 1896 (LaTowsky 1997).

2. Al-Jamaiyya al-Shariyya, dating from 1912, and the more recent Mahmoud Mosque Association established in 1976 are among the largest and most influential.

3. Educational and medical services are free for poor beneficiaries, while others pay a small fee for tuition (see Clark 2004).

4. To this should be added various in-kind donations, of which some are sold and thus converted to monetary resources. In 2011, Resala Heliopolis was the largest branch in terms of the number of donors and the areas covered.

5. Although there were definitely more than nine such youth organizations in Cairo, in 2007, our sample represented the most famous among them.

6. *Zakat al-fitr* is a duty on every Muslim to pay a share of his or her wealth immediately after the holy month of Ramadan to bless his or her fast (El-Daly 2004, 55).

7. These are Alashanek Ya Baladi (www.ayb-sd.org), Bayan (www.bayan-online .org), Resala (www.resala.org), Sunaa al-Hayah (www.lifemakers.org.eg), and Zedny (www.zedny.org).

8. www.zedny.org (retrieved May 14, 2007).

9. www.ayb-sd.org (retrieved May 10, 2007).

10. www.ayb-sd.org (retrieved May 10, 2007).

11. www.ayb-sd.org (retrieved May 10, 2007).
12. www.ayb-sd.org (retrieved May 10, 2007).
13. www.ayb-sd.org (retrieved May 10, 2007).
14. A high percentage of Egyptian civil society organizations rely entirely or partially on paid staff; very few rely entirely on volunteers (Clark 2004, 62).
15. This argument stands in direct contrast to the view of some Islamic charitable organizations. In the Mahmoud Mosque Association, for example, they strive toward more salaried staff, which are seen as more reliable and committed to their work (Atia 2008, 179). As to the new youth organizations, some board members acknowledged that there are some disadvantages in not having permanent staff. Many of the volunteers are students or have a full-time job beside their work in the organization. They have a limited number of hours to spend and especially during exam periods most organizations have a serious lack of hands. Furthermore, volunteers are not always one hundred percent reliable; many volunteers participate in one or two activities, after which they either try another organization or stop doing voluntary work all together. Finally, many leaders acknowledge that some volunteers lack the necessary experience and qualifications. A few organizations offer basic training to new volunteers, but in most organizations, they just watch and learn from the others.
16. As Atia (2008) and Brock (2008) rightly observe, Resala is a special case. In contrast to many of the other organizations, the leadership and the volunteers characterize their activities as charitable rather than developmental, and they have no plans to change this approach.
17. www.ayb-sd.com (retrieved May 10, 2007).
18. For an analysis of the trend and transitional phase, see Atia (2008).
19. The primary inspiration for this project came from the Big Brothers/Big Sisters of America, a US nonprofit organization whose mission is to help children reach their potential through professionally supported, one-to-one relationships with mentors. However, according to Resala's leadership, they had to make a few adjustments in order to bring the project in accordance with their interpretation of Islamic *sharia*. For example, if a female volunteer wants to become a "big sister" of a boy, the boy is officially a "cousin" and not a "little brother" because certain rules of segregation have to be maintained.
20. One of these social ventures supported by Alashanek Ya Baladi is "Zaytoona." Zaytoona is a brand name given to the products manufactured at a vocational center in Old Cairo.
21. www.bayan-online.org (retrieved May 11, 2007).
22. www.zedny.org (retrieved May 14, 2007).
23. Many young Christians are engaged in the charitable activities of churches. Furthermore, there are several large Coptic charitable and developmental organizations such as the Coptic Evangelical Organization for Social Services (CEOSS).
24. The early morning prayer, conducted in the period between dawn and sunrise.
25. www.ayb-sd.org (retrieved May 10, 2007).
26. Surat al-Maoun in the Koran.
27. When exploring the role of religion in the organizations' mobilization process, self-definition is a good starting point. However, such an approach might also create problems, precisely because some organizations reject this label due to fear of government retaliation.

28. Because of the general status of the Muslim Brotherhood in Egypt, as well as some of the new youth organizations' reservations toward us and the research project, we almost abstained from asking questions about the relationship between the youth organizations and the Muslim Brotherhood or other Islamist political actors. However, it was our impression that few if any of these organizations had direct links to them. This observation is supported by several scholars in the field, for example, Bayat (2007, 14).

29. At the time of our fieldwork, Resala seemed to be among the organizations with the best relationship with the state authorities. One concrete manifestation of this relationship was a speech delivered by the Egyptian minister of organizational development at Resala's annual Mother's Day event in March 2007. Resala was founded by rich people, and because of the huge donations, it is able to attract from the public, and it has expanded beyond expectations. However, Resala also was subject to intense surveillance by the regime, and the closing down of all Resala branches at the Egyptian universities in winter 2007 was an indicator that the government regarded it as an increasing threat (Brock 2008, 79).

9 LEADERS, ORGANIZERS, AND VOLUNTEERS: ENCOUNTERING IDIOSYNCRATIC FORMS OF SUBJECTIVITIES

1. At Sunaa al-Hayah, three out of ten board members are women. At Zedny and Bayan, all the board members are male, and at Boraq only one out of ten seats is held by a woman.
2. Leaders are here defined as presidents, chairpersons, or board members.
3. Except for Mohammad Omar and Sherif Abdelazeem, all names are pseudonyms.
4. Heba Rouf, a researcher and an activist, described Sunaa al-Hayah as a "post-Ikhwan" phenomenon.
5. As mentioned before, most of Resala's activities are of a more charitable character compared to other organizations, and therefore also relatively easy to carry out for the inexperienced volunteer.

References

Abdel-Rahman, Maha. 2004. *Civil society exposed: The politics of NGOs in Egypt.* Cairo: The American University in Cairo Press.

Abu Rumman, Mohammad. 2007. *The Moslem Brotherhood in the Jordanian Parliamentarian Elections 2007: A Passing "Political Setback" or Diminished Popularity?* Amman: Friedrich Ebert Foundation.

Adams, Linda Schull. 1996. "Political Liberalization in Jordan: An Analysis of the State's Relationship with the Muslim Brotherhood." *Journal of Church and State* 38(3): 507–28.

Allahyari, Rebecca Anne. 2000. *Visions of Charity: Volunteer Workers and Moral Community.* Ewing: University of California Press.

Allardt, Erik. 2005. Europe's Multiple Modernities. In *Comparing Modernitites. Pluralism versus Homogenity. Essays in Homage to Shmuel N. Eisenstadt,* edited by Ben-Rafael Eliezer and Yitzhak Sternberg, 413–42. Leiden: Brill.

Alon, Yoav. 2007. *The Making of Jordan. Tribes, Colonialism and the Modern State.* London: I.B. Tauris.

Amin, Galal. 2011. *Egypt in the Era of Hosni Mubarak 1981–2011.* Cairo and New York: The American University in Cairo Press.

Anderson, Betty. 2005. *Nationalist Voices in Jordan—The Street and the State.* Austin: University of Texas Press.

Asad, Talal. 1993. *Genealogies of Religion. Discipline and Reasons of Power in Christianity and Islam.* Baltimore and London: Johns Hopkins University Press.

———. 1986. *The Idea of an Anthropology of Islam.* Washington, DC: Centre for Contemporary Arab Studies, Georgetown University.

Assaad, Ragui, and Ghada Barsoum. 2007. "Youth Exclusion in Egypt: In Search of 'Second Chances.'" The Middle East Youth Initiative Working Paper, Wolfensohn Center for Development and Dubai School of Government.

Atia, Mona. 2008. "Building a House in Heaven: Islamic Charity in Neoliberal Egypt." PhD Dissertation, University of Washington.

Atia, Tarek. 2005. "Amr Khaled: A Preacher's Puzzle." *Al-Ahram Weekly* 265. http://weekly.ahram.org.eg/2005/765/profile.htm, retrieved September 20, 2012.

Aydin, Cemil. 2007. *The Politics of Anti-Westernism in Asia. Visions of World Order in Pan-Islamic and Pan-Asian Thought.* New York: Columbia University Press.

Al-Azmeh, Aziz. 1996. *Islams and Modernities,* 2nd ed. London: Verso.

Badran, Margot. 1995. *Feminists, Islam, and Nation. Gender and the Making of Modern Egypt.* Princeton: Princeton University Press.

Balba, Jehan, Meredith Connelly, and Carrie Parrott Monahan. 2008. "Inspired by Faith. A Background Report "Mapping" the Social Economic Development Work in the Muslim World." *Berkley Center Reports.* Washington, DC: Berkley Center for Religion, Peace and World Affairs, Georgetown University.

Bangstad, Sindre. 2011. "Saba Mahmood and Anthropological Feminism after Virtue." *Theory, Culture & Society* 28(3): 28–54.

Barari, Hassan A. 2008. "Four Decades after Black September: A Jordanian Perspective." *Civil Wars* 10(3): 231–243.

Bayat, Asef. 2002. "Activism and Social Development in the Middle East." *International Journal of Middle East Studies* 34(1): 1–28.

———. 2007. *Making Islam Democratic: Social Movements and the Post-Islamist Turn*. Stanford: Stanford University Press.

Beck, Ulrich. 1992. *Risk Society: Towards a New Modernity*. London: Sage.

———. 1997. *The Reinvention of Politics: Rethinking Modernity in the Global Social Order*. Oxford: Blackwell Publishers.

Beckford, James. 2003. *Social Theory and Religion*. Cambridge: Cambridge University Press.

Benford, Robert D., and David A. Snow. 2000. "Framing Processes and Social Movements: An Overview and Assessment." *Annual Review of Sociology* 26(August): 611–39.

Benthall, Jonathan. 1999. "Financial Worship: The Quranic Injunction to Almsgiving." *Journal of Royal Anthropological Institute* 5: 27–42.

Benthall, Jonathan, and Jerome Bellion-Jourdan. 2003. *The Charitable Crescent*. London: I.B.Tauris.

Beyer, Peter L. 2006. *Religion and Global Society*. London and New York: Routledge.

Bint Talal, Basma. 2004. *Rethinking an NGO: Development, Donors and Civil Society in Jordan*. London: I.B. Tauris.

Bloch, Charles. 1972. *Die Dritte Französische Republik. Entwicklung und Kampf einer parlamentarischen Demokratie (1870–1940)*. Stuttgart: K.F. Koehler Verlag.

Bonacker, Thorsten. 2008. "Gesellschaft: Warum die Einheit der Gesellschaft aufgeschoben wird." In *Poststrukturalistische Sozialwissenschaften*, edited by S. Moebius and A. Reckwitz, 27–43. Franfurt a.M.: Suhrkamp Verlag.

Bonner, Michael, Mine Ener, and Amy Singer. 2003. *Poverty and Charity in Middle Eastern Contexts*. Albany: SUNY Press.

Boulby, Matthew. 2000. "The Muslim Brotherhood and the Kings of Jordan 1945–1993." *Arab Studies Journal* 32(3): 425–426.

Brand, Laurie A. 1998. *Women, the State, and Political Liberalization*. New York: Columbia University Press.

———. 1999. "Al-Muhajirin wa-al-Ansar——Hashemite Strategies for Managing Communal Identity in Jordan." In *International Dimensions of Ethnic Conflict in the Middle East*, edited by Leonard Binder, 279–306. Gainesville: University Press of Florida.

Breuer, Stefan. 2007. *Max Webers tragische Soziologie. Aspekte und Perspektiven*. Tübingen: Mohr Siebeck.

Brock, Katja Gregers. 2008. "Agents of Change? A Study of Why Young Egyptian Middle-class Women Engage in Voluntary Civil Society Organizations." Master Thesis, International Development Studies, Roskilde University.

Brown, Nathan, and Amr Hamzawy. 2010. "Jordan and Its Islamic Movement: The Limits of Inclusion?" In *Between Religion and Politics*, 47–78. New York: Carnegie Endowment for International Peace.

Calvert, John. 2010. *Sayyed Qutb and the Origin of Radical Islamism*. New York: Columbia University Press.

Chakrabarty, Dipesh. 1992. "Postcoloniality and the Artifice of History: Who Speaks for 'Indian' Pasts?" *Representations* 37(special issue, Winter): 1–26.

Christiansen, Connie Carøe. 1998. "Self and Social Process in Women's Islamic Activism: Claims for Recognition." PhD Dissertation, Institute of Anthropology, University of Copenhagen.

———. 2003. "Women's Islamic Activism: Between Self-practices and Social Reform Efforts." In *Modernizing Islam: Religion in the Public Sphere in the Middle East and Europe*, edited by John L. Esposito and Francois Burgat, 145–65. London: Hurst.

Clark, Janine. 2004. *Islam, Charity and Activism: Middle-class Networks and Social Welfare in Egypt, Jordan, and Yemen*. Bloomington and Indianapolis: Indiana University Press.

———. 2012. "Patronage, Prestige, and Power. The Islamic Center Charity Society's Political Role with the Muslim Brotherhood." In *Islamist Politics in the Middle East*, edited by Samer S. Shehata, 69–87. London and New York: Routledge.

———. 2006. "The Conditions of Islamist Moderation: Unpacking Cross-ideological Cooperation in Jordan." *International Journal of Middle East Studies* 38(4): 539–60.

Clark, Janine A., and Jillian Schwedler. 2003. "Who Opened the Window? Women's Activism in Islamist Parties." *Comparative Politics* 35(3): 293–312.

Clark, Janine, and Wacheke Michuki. 2009. "Women and NGO Professionalisation. A Case Study of Jordan." *Development in Practice* 9(3): 329–39.

Cohen, Amnon. 1982. *Political Parties in the West Bank under the Jordanian Regime, 1949–1967*. Ithaca and London: Cornell University Press.

Commins, David. 2005. "Hasan al-Banna (1906–1949)." In *Pioneers of Islamic Revival*, edited by Ali Rahnema, 125–53. London: Zed books.

Cooke, Miriam, and Bruce Lawrence, eds. 2005. *Muslim Networks from Hajj to Hip Hop*. Chapel Hill: University of North Carolina Press.

Dagi, Ihsan D. 2004. "Rethinking Human Rights, Democracy, and the West: Post-Islamist Intellectuals in Turkey." *Critique: Critical Middle Eastern Studies* 13(2): 135–51.

Davis, Natalie Zemon. 2003. "Conclusion." In *Poverty and Charity in Middle Eastern Contexts*, edited by Michael Bonner, Mine Ener, and Amy Singer, 315–25. Albany: SUNY University Press.

Dean, H., and Khan, Z. 1997. "Muslim Perspectives on Welfare." *Journal of Social Policy* 26(2): 193–209.

Deeb, Lara. 2006. *An Enchanted Modern. Gender and Public Piety in Shi'i Lebanon*. Princeton and Oxford: Princeton University Press.

Dirlik, Arif. 2003. "Global Modernity: Modernity in an Age of Global Capitalism." *European Journal of Social Theory* 6(3): 275–92.

Duara, Prasenjit. 1998. "The Regime of Authenticity: Timelessness, Gender, and National History in Modern China." *History and Theory* 37(3): 287–308.

———. 2004. *Sovereignty and Authenticity. Manchukuo and the East Asian Modern*. Lanham: Rowman & Littlefield.

Durkheim, Emile. 1995. *The Elementary Forms of Religious Life*. New York: The Free Press.

Eich, Thomas. 2003. "The Forgotten Salafi—Abu L-Huda as-Sayyadi." *Die Welt des Islams* 43(1): 61–87.

Eisenstadt, Samuel N. 2000. "Multiple Modernities." *Daedalus* 129(1): 1–29.

El-Daly, Marwa. 2006. *Philanthropy in Egypt: A Comprehensive Study on Local Philanthropy in Egypt and Potentials of Directing Giving and Volunteering Towards Development*. Cairo: Center for Development Studies.

El-Ghobashy, Mona. 2005. "The Metamorphosis of the Egyptian Muslim Brothers." *International Journal of Middle East Studies* 37(3): 373–95.

El-Rouby, Hisham, Manal Samra, Ghada Helmy, and Mohamed Refay. 2007. "Mapping Organizations Working with and for Youth." *Capacity Building & Partnership Program*, Cairo, May 2007.

Elbayar, Kareem. 2005. "NGO Laws in Selected Arab States." *International Journal of Not-for-Profit Law* 7(4): 3–27.

Ener, Mine. 2003. *Managing Egypt's Poor and the Politics of Benevolence, 1800–1952*. Princeton and Oxford: Princeton University Press.

Eppel, Michael. 2009. "Note About the Term *Effendiyya* in the History of the Middle East." *International Journal of the History of the Middle East* 41: 535–39.

Erdemir, Aykan. 2006. "Tradition and Modernity: Alevis' Ambiguous Terms and Turkey's Ambivalent Subjects." *Middle Eastern Studies* 41(6): 937–51.

Esposito, John, and Dalia Mogahed. 2007. *Who Speaks for Islam? What a Billion Muslims Really Think*. New York: Gallup Press.

Euben, Roxanne L. 1999. *Enemy in the Mirror. Islamic Fundamentalism and the Limits of Modern Rationalism*. Princeton: Princeton University Press.

Fischer, Johan. 2008. *Proper Islamic Consumption. Shopping among the Malays in Modern Malaysia*. NIAS: Nordic Institute of Asian Studies.

Foucault, Michel. 1988. *The Care of the Self*. New York: Vintage.

Frick, Werner. 1988. *Providenz und Kontingenz. Untersuchung zur Schicksalssemantik im deutschen und europäischen Roman des 17. und 18. Jahrhunderts*, Teil 1. Tübingen: Max Niemeyer Verlag.

Gershoni, Israel, and James P. Jankowski. 1986. *Egypt, Islam and the Arabs: The Search for Egyptian Nationhood, 1900–1930*. Oxford: Oxford University Press.

Ghanem, As'ad, and Mohanad Mustafa. 2011. "Strategies of Electoral Participation by Islamic Movements: The Muslim Brotherhood and Parliamentary Elections in Egypt and Jordan, November 2010." *Contemporary Politics* 17(4): 393–409.

Giddens, Anthony. 1991. *Modernity and Self-identity: Self and Society in the Late Modern Age*. Cambridge: Polity Press.

Graf, Friedrich W. 1987. "Max Weber und die protestantische Theologie seiner Zeit." *Zeitschrift für Religions- und Geistesgeschichte* 39: 122–47.

Guégnard, Christine, Xavier Matheu, and Musa Shteiwi. 2005. *Unemployment in Jordan*. Torino: European Training Foundation.

Haenni, Patrick. 2005. *L'islam de marché: l'autre révolution conservatrice*. Paris: Seuil.

Haenni, P., and H. Tammam. 2003. "Egypt's Air-conditioned Islam." *Le Monde Diplomatique* September 2003.

Hafez, Sherine. 2011. *An Islam of Her Own: Reconsidering Religion and Secularism in Women's Islamic Movement*. Cairo: The American University in Cairo Press.

Haj, Samira. 2009. *Reconfiguring Islamic Tradition. Reform, Rationality, and Modernity*. Stanford: Stanford University Press.

Hammad, Waleed. 1999. *Jordanian Women's Organizations and Sustainable Development*. Al-Urdun Al-Jadid Research Centre, Sindbad Publishing House.

Hanieh, Hassan Abu. 2008. *Women and Politics: From the Perspective of Islamic Movements in Jordan*. Amman: Friedrich Ebert Stiftung.

Harmsen, Egbert. 2008. *Islam, Civil Society and Social Work. Muslim Voluntary Welfare Associations in Jordan Between Patronage and Empowerment*. Amsterdam: Amsterdam University Press.

al-Hassan Golley N. 2004. "Is Feminism Relevant to Arab Women?" *Third World Quarterly* 25(3): 521–36.

Hatem, Mervat. 2001. *Literature, Gender, and Nation-Building in Nineteenth Century Egypt. The Life and Works of `A'isha Taymur.* New York: Palgrave MacMillan.

Hawthorne, Amy. 2004. "Middle Eastern Democracy: Is Civil Society the Answer?" *Carnegie Papers* 44. Washington, DC: Carnegie Endowment for International Peace.

Hayward, J. E. S. 1960. "Solidarist Syndicalism: Durkheim and Duguit." In *Emile Durkheim: Critical Assessments*, Volume IV, edited by Peter Hamilton, 128–44. London and New York: Routledge (reprint 1990).

Hefner, Robert W., and Muhammad Qasim Zaman, eds. 2007. *Schooling Islam: Modern Muslim Education.* Princeton: Princeton University Press.

Hegghammer, Thomas. 2010. *Jihad in Saudi Arabia: Violence and Pan-Islamism Since 1979.* Cambridge: Cambridge University Press.

Herrera, Linda. 2011. "Young Egyptians' Quest for Jobs and Justice." In *Being Young and Muslim: New Cultural Politics in the Global South and North*, edited by Linda Herrera and Asef Bayat, 127–43. Oxford: Oxford University Press.

Hill, T. L., Tanvi H. Kothari, and Matthew Shea. 2010. "Patterns of Meaning in the Social Entrepreneurship Literature: A Research Platform." *Journal of Social Entrepreneurship* 1(1): 5–31.

Hirschkind, Charles. 2006. *The Ethical Soundscape: Cassette Sermons and Islamic Counterpublics.* New York: Columbia University Press.

Hourani, Albert. 1962. *Arabic Thought in the Liberal Age 1798–1939*, reissued with a new preface 1983. Cambridge: Cambridge University Press.

Huff, Toby E., and Wolfgang Schluchter, eds. 1999. *Max Weber & Islam.* New Brunswick: Transaction.

Human Rights Watch. 2008. *Jordan Country Summary* (retrieved from www.hrw.org/legacy/wr2k8/pdfs/jordan.pdf, accessed September 22, 2012).

Hunter, Shireen, ed. 2009. *Reformist Voices of Islam. Mediating Islam and Modernity.* London: M.E.Shape.

Ibrahim, Barbara, and Hind Wassef. 2000. "Caught Between Two Worlds: Youth in the Egyptian Hinterland." In *Alienation or Integration of Arab Youth: Between Family, State and Street*, edited by Roel Meijer, 161–85. London: Curzon Press.

Ibrahim, Haslina. 1999. "Free Will and Predestination: A Comparative Study of the Views of Abu Al-Hassan Al-Ash'ri and Muhammad 'Abduh." Unpublished MA thesis, Kulliya of Islamic Revealed Knowledge and Human Sciences, International Islamic University Malaysia.

Ibrahim, Saad Eddin. 1996. "Anatomy of Egypt's militant Islamic groups: Methodological Notes and Preliminary Findings." *International Journal of Middle East Studies* 12(4): 423–453.

———. 1988. "Egypt's Islamic Activism in the 1980s." *Third World Quarterly* 10(2): 632–57.

Jeldtoft, Nadia. 2011. "Lived Islam: Religious Identity with 'Non-Organized' Muslim Minorities." *Ethnic and Racial Studies* 34(7): 1134–51.

Johnson, S. 2000. "Literature Review on Social Entrepreneurship." Canadian Centre for Social Entrepreneurship, Edmonton.

Jung, Dietrich. 2011. *Orientalists, Islamists, and the Global Public Sphere: A Genealogy of the Modern Essentialist Image of Islam.* Sheffield: Equinox.

Juul Petersen, Marie. 2012. "Trajectories of Transnational Muslim NGOS." *Development in Practice* 22(5–6): 763–78.

Kassim, Hisham, ed. 2006. *The Directory of Civil Society Organizations in Jordan.* Amman: Al-Urdun al-Jadid Research Center.

Kamrava, Mehran. 2011. *The Modern Middle East. A Political History Since the First World War*, second ed. Berkeley: University of California Press.

Khatab, Sayed. 2006. *The Power of Sovereignty. The Political and Ideological Philosophy of Sayyid Qutb*. London: Routledge.

Kornbluth, D. 2002. "Jordan and the Anti-normalization Campaign 1994–2001." *Terrorism and Political Violence* 14(3): 80–108.

Krämer, Gudrun. 2010. *Hasan al-Banna*. Oxford: One World.

Laclau, Ernest and Chantal Mouffe. 2001. *Hegemony and Socialist Strategy: Towards a Radical Democratic Politics*, second ed. London and New York: Verso.

Lapidus, Ira M. 2002 [1988]. *A History of Islamic Societies*, second edition. Cambridge: Cambridge University Press.

LaTowsky, Robert J. 1997. "Egypt's NGO Sector: A Briefing Paper." *Education for Development Occasional Paper Series* 1(4): 1–22.

Lauzière, Henri. 2010. "The Construction of *Salafiyya*: Reconsidering Salafism from the Perspective of Conceptual History." *International Journal of Middle East Studies* 42(August): 369–89.

Lincoln, Bruce. 2003. *Holy Terrors. Thinking about Religion after September 11*. Chicago: University of Chicago Press.

Livingston, John W. 1995. "Muhammad ʿAbduh on Science." *The Muslim World* 85(3–4): 215–34.

Loewe, Markus, Jens Ochtrop, Christine Peter, Alexandra Roth, Maja Tampe, and Arvid Türkner. 2001. *Improving the Social Protection of the Urban Poor and Near-Poor in Jordan: The Potential of Micro-insurance*. Bonn: German Development Institute.

Lombardi, Clark B. 2006. *State Law as Islamic Law in Modern Egypt: The Incorporation of the Shari'a into Egyptian Constitutional Law*. Leiden: Brill.

Luckmann, Thomas. 1963. *Das Problem der Religion in der modernen Gesellschaft*. Freiburg: Rombach.

Luhmann, Niklas. 1981. "Geschichte als Prozess und die Theorie sozio-kultureller Evolution. " In *Soziologische Aufklärung*, Band 3. Opladen: Westdeutscher Verlag.

———. 1989. "Individuum, Individualität, Individualismus." In *Gesellschaftsstruktur und Semantik. Studien zur Wissenssoziologie der modernen Gesellschaft*, Band 3, 149–258. Frankfurt a.M: Suhrkamp.

———. 1992. "Kontingenz als Eigenwert der modernen Gesellschaft." In *Beobachtungen der Moderne*, 93–128. Opladen: VS Verlag.

———. 1986. *Ökologische Kommunikation. Kann sich die moderne Gesellschaft auf ökologische Gefährdungen einstellen?* Opladen: Westdeutscher Verlag.

Lukes, Steven. 1985. *Emile Durkheim: His Life and Work. A Historical and Critical Study*. Stanford, CA: Stanford University Press.

———. 1971. "The Meanings of 'Individualism.'" *Journal of the History of Ideas* 32(1): 45–66.

Mahmood, Saba. 2005. *Politics of Piety. The Islamic Revival and the Feminist Subject*. Princeton and Oxford: Princeton University Press.

Mandaville, Peter. 2008. "Beyond Political Islam? Post-Islamism, Social Change and New Religious Movements in the Muslim world." Conference paper, University of Copenhagen, December 18, 2008.

———. 2001. *Transnational Muslim Politics: Reimagining the Umma*. London: Routledge.

Meyer, John W., John Boli, George Thomas, and Francisco Ramirez. 1997. "World Society and the Nation State." *American Journal of Sociology* 103(1): 144–81.

Mitchell, Richard P. 1969. *The Society of the Muslim Brothers*. London: Oxford University Press.

Moaddel, Mansor. 2002. *Jordanian Exceptionalism. A Comparative Analysis of State-religion Relationships in Egypt, Iran, Jordan, and Syria*. London: Palgrave Macmillan.

Moll, Yasmin. 2010. "Islamic Televangelism: Religion, Media and Visuality in Contemporary Egypt." *Arab Media & Society* 10(Spring): 1–27.

Musallam, Adnan. 2005. *From Secularism to Jihad. Sayyid Qutb and the Foundations of Radical Islam*. Westport and London: Praeger.

Nakash, Yitzhak. 1994. *The Shi'is of Iraq*. Princeton: Princeton University Press.

NGO Law Monitor. 2012. http://www.icnl.org/research/monitor/jordan.html, accessed September 22, 2012.

Nicholls, Alex. 2011. "Editorial: Social Enterprise—At the Forefront of Rethinking Business?" *Journal of Social Entrepreneurship* 2(1): 1–5.

Van Nieuwkerk, Karen. 2008. "Creating an Islamic Cultural Sphere: Contested Notions of Art, Leisure and Entertainment. An Introduction." *Contemporary Islam* 2(1): 169–76.

Noyon, Jennifer. 2003. *Islam, Politics and Pluralism: Theory and Practice in Turkey, Jordan, Tunisia and Algeria*. London: The Royal Institute of International Affairs.

Nyssens, Marthe, ed. 2006. *Social Enterprise. At the Crossroads of Market, Public Policy and Civil Society*. London and New York: Routledge.

Osman, Tarek. 2011. *Egypt on the Brink. From the Rise of Nasser to the Fall of Mubarak*. New Haven and London: Yale University Press.

Otterbeck, Jonas. 2008. "Battling Over the Public Sphere: Islamic Reactions to the Music of Today." *Contemporary Islam* 2(1): 211–28.

Pals, Daniel L. 1996. *Seven Theories of Religion*. Oxford: Oxford University Press.

Peredo, Ana Maríe, and Murdith McLean. 2006. "Social entrepreneurship: A Critical Review of the Concept." *Journal of World Business* 41(1): 56–65.

Peterson, Mark Allen. 2011. *Connected in Cairo. Growing up Cosmopolitan in the Modern Middle East*. Bloomington and Indianapolis: Indiana University Press.

Poggi, Gianfranco. 2001. *Forms of Power*. Cambridge: Cambridge University Press.

Rabo, Annika. 1996. "Gender, State and Civil Society in Jordan and Syria." In *Civil Society. Challenging Western Models*, edited by Chris Hann and Elizabeth Dunn, 155–77. London: Routledge.

Rahman, Fazlur. 1984. *Islam and Modernity: Transformation of an Intellectual Tradition*. Chicago: University of Chicago Press.

Ramadan, Tariq. 2008. *Radical Reform. Islamic Ethics and Liberation*. Oxford: Oxford University Press.

Reckwitz, Andreas. 2006. *Das hybride Subjekt. Eine Theorie der Subjektkulturen von der bürgelichen Moderne zur Postmoderne*. Weilerswist: Velbrück Wissenschaft.

———. 2008a. "Moderne: Der Kampf um die Öffnung und Schließung von Kontingenzen. " In *Poststrukturalistische Sozialwissenschaften*, edited by S. Moebius and A. Reckwitz, 226–44. Franfurt a.M.: Suhrkamp Verlag.

———. 2008b. "Subjekt/Identität: Die Produktion und Subversion des Individuums." In *Poststrukturalistische Sozialwissenschaften*, edited by S. Moebius and A. Reckwitz, 75–92. Frankfurt a.M.: Suhrkamp Verlag.

———. 2008c. *Subjekt*. Bielefeld: Transcript Verlag.

Roald, Anne Sofie. 1994. *Tarbiya: Education and Politics in Islamic Movements in Jordan and Malaysia*. Stockholm: Almqvist & Wiksell.

Robertson, Roland. 1992. *Globalization, Social Theory and Global Culture*. London: SAGE.

Robins, Philip. 2004. *A History of Jordan*. Cambridge: Cambridge University Press.

Robinson, Glenn E. 1997. "Can Islamists be Democrats? The Case of Jordan." *Middle East Journal* 51(3): 373–87.

Rock, Aaron. 2010. "Amr Khaled: From Da'wa to Political and Religious Leadership." *British Journal of Middle Eastern Studies* 37(1): 15–37.

Roy, Olivier. 2002. *L'Islam mondialisé*. Paris: Seuil.

Rubin, Barry. 2007. "Comparing Three Muslim Brotherhoods: Syria, Jordan, Egypt." *Middle East Review of International Affairs* 11(2): 107–16.

Sadowski, Yahya. 1993. "The New Orientalism and the Democracy Debate." *Middle East Report* 183(July–Aug.): 14–21.

Said, Edward W. 1978. *Orientalism*. New York: Vintage.

Salibi, Kamal. 1993. *The Modern History of Jordan*. London: I.B. Tauris.

Salvatore, Armando, and Dale F. Eickelman. 2004. *Public Islam and the Common Good*. Leiden: Brill.

Scaff, Lawrence A. 2000. "Weber on the Cultural Situation of the Modern Age." In *The Cambridge Companion to Weber*, edited by Stephen Turner, 99–116. Cambridge: Cambridge University Press.

Scham Paul, L., and Russel E. Lucas. 2003. "Normalization and Anti-normalization in Jordan: The Public Debate." *Israel Affairs* 9(3): 141–64.

Schatz, Klaus. 1992. *Vaticanum I, 1869–1870, Band I: Vor der Eröffnung*. Paderborn: Ferdinand Schönigh Verlag.

Schatzki, Theodore R. 2002. *The Site of the Social: A Philosophical Account of the Constitution of Social Life and Change*. University Park: Pennsylvania State University Press.

Schielke, Samuli. 2009. "Being Good in Ramadan: Ambivalence, Fragmentation, and the Moral Self in the Lives of Young Egyptians." *Journal of the Royal Anthropological Institute (N.S.)* (special issue 1): 24–40.

Schmidt, Volker. 2008. "Multiple Modernities or Varieties of Modernities?" *Current Sociology* 54(1): 77–97.

Schwedler, Jillian. 2006. *Faith in Moderation. Islamist Parties in Jordan and Yemen*. Cambridge: Cambridge University Press.

Sedgwick, Mark. 2010. *Muhammad Abduh*. Oxford: Oneworld Publications.

Sharot, Stephen. 2001. *A Comparative Sociology of World Religions. Virtuosos, Priests, and Popular Religion*. New York: New York University Press.

Shehabuddin, Elora. 2008. *Reshaping the Holy: Women, Islam, and Democracy in Bangladesh*. New York: Columbia University Press.

Shepard, William. 1996. *Sayyid Qutb and Islamic Activism. A Translation and Critical Analysis of Social Justice in Islam*. Leiden: Brill.

Singer, Amy. 2008. *Charity in Islamic Societies*. Cambridge: Cambridge University Press.

Singh, Ranjit. 2002. "Liberalisation or Democratisation?: The Limits of Political Reform and Civil Society in Jordan." In *Jordan in Transition 1990–2000*, edited by Georg Joffé, 66–90. London: Hurst.

Soares, Benjamin F., and Filippo Osella. 2009. "Islam, Politics, Anthropology." *Journal of the Royal Anthropological Institute* 15(s1): 1–23.

Soares, Benjamin F., and René Otayek, eds. 2007. *Islam and Muslim Politics in Africa*. New York: Palgrave MacMillan.

Sparre, Sara Lei. 2013. *A Generation in the Making: The Formation of Young Muslim Volunteers in Cairo.* PhD Dissertation, University of Copenhagen, Denmark.

Sparre, Sara Lei, and Marie Juul Petersen. 2007. "Islam and Civil Society: Case Studies from Jordan and Egypt." *DIIS Report 2007:13.* Copenhagen: DIIS.

Spickard, James V. 2003. "What is Happening to Religion? Six Sociological Narratives." Under www.ku.dk/satsning/Religion.

Starrett, Gregory. 1998. *Putting Islam to Work: Education, Politics, and Religious Transformation in Egypt.* Berkeley, Los Angeles and London: University of California Press.

———. 1995. "The Political Economy of Religious Commodities in Cairo." *American Anthropologist* 97(1): 51–68.

Stemman, Juan Jose Escobar. 2008. Islamic Activism in Jordan. *Athena Intelligence Journal* 3(3): 7–18.

Stephan, Maria S. 2009. *Civilian Jihad. Nonviolent Struggle, Democratization, and Governance in the Middle East.* New York and London: Palgrave Macmillan.

Sullivan, Dennis, and Sana Abed-Kotob. 1999. *Islam in Contemporary Egypt: Civil Society vs. the State.* Boulder and London: Lynne Rienner Publishers.

Taji-Farouki, Suha. 1996. *A Fundamental Quest: Hizb al-Tahrir and the Search for the Islamic Caliphate.* London: Grey Seal.

Tauber, Eliezer. 1989. "Rashid Rida as Pan-Arabist before World-War I." *The Muslim World* 79(2): 102–12.

Taylor, Charles. 2007. *A Secular Age.* Harvard: Harvard University Press.

———. 1989. *Sources of the Self: The Making of the Modern Identity.* Cambridge: Cambridge University Press.

Therborn, Göran. 2003. "Entangled Modernities." *European Journal of Social Theory* 6(3): 293–305.

Tripp, Charles. 2006. *Islam and the Moral Economy. The Challenge of Capitalism.* Cambridge: Cambridge University Press.

United Nations Development Programme (UNDP). 2008. "Egypt's Social Contract: The Role of Civil Society." *Egypt Human Development Report.* Cairo: United Nations Development Programme and Institute of National Planning.

———. 2004. "Building Sustainable Livelihoods." *Jordan Human Development Report.* Amman: Ministry of Planning and International Cooperation, United Nations Development Programme, Jordan Hashemite Fund for Development.

Valbjørn, Morten. 2005. "Hvor og hvad er Jordan. Jordansk stats-og nationsbygning." *Den Jyske Historiker* 110–111(special issue): 74–102.

Vatikiotis, P. J. 1967. *Politics and the Military in Jordan. A Study of the Arab Legion 1921–1957.* London: Frank Cass.

———. 1985. *The History of Egypt,* third edition. London: Weidenfeld and Nicolson.

Wagner, Peter. 1994. *A Sociology of Modernity: Liberty and Discipline.* London: Routledge.

———. 2001. *Theorizing Modernity. Inescapability and Attainability in Social Theory.* London, Thousand Oaks and New Delhi: Sage.

———. 2004. "Modernity: One or Many?" In *The Blackwell Companion to Sociology,* edited by Judith R. Blau, 30–42. Oxford: Blackwell.

———. 2010. "Successive Modernities and the Idea of Progress: A First Attempt." *Distinktion* 11(2): 9–24.

Waterbury, John. 1983. *The Egypt of Nasser and Sadat. The Political Economy of Two Regimes.* Princeton: Princeton University Press.

Weber, Max. 1948. *From Max Weber: Essays in Sociology*, edited by H. H. Gerth and C. Wright Mills, London and New York: Routledge (New Edition, 1991).

———. 1915. "Religious Rejections of the World and Their Directions." In *From Max Weber: Essays in Sociology*, edited by H. H. Gerth and C. Wright Mills, 129–56. London: Routledge (1991).

Wickham, Carrie Rosefsky. 2004. "Interests, Ideas and Islamist Outreach in Egypt." In *Islamic Activism: A Social Movement Theory Approach*, edited by Quintan Wiktorowicz, 231–249. Bloomington, Indiana: Indiana University Press.

———. 2002. *Mobilizing Islam: Religion, Activism, and Political Change in Egypt.* New York: Columbia University Press.

Wiktorowicz, Quintan. 2004. "Introduction: Islamic Activism and Social Movement Theory." In *Islamic Activism: A Social Movement Theory Approach*, edited by Quintan Wiktorowicz, 1–33. Bloomington and Indianapolis: Indiana University Press.

———. 2001. *The Management of Islamic Activism: Salafis, the Muslim Brotherhood and State Power in Jordan.* Albany: SUNY Press.

———. 2000. "The Salafi Movement in Jordan." *International Journal of Middle East Studies* 32(2): 219–240.

Wilson, Mary Christina. 1987. *King Abdullah, Britain and the Making of Jordan.* New York: Cambridge University Press.

Wise, Lindsay. 2006. "Amr Khaled vs Yusuf Al Qaradawi: The Danish Cartoon Controversy and the Clash of Two Islamic TV Titans." http://www.tbsjournal.com/Wise.htm.

———. 2003. "'Words from the Heart:' New Forms of Islamic Preaching in Egypt." M.Phil. Thesis in Modern Middle East Studies, Oxford University.

Wuchterl, Kurt. 2011. *Kontingenz oder das Andere der Vernunft. Zum Verhältnis von Philosophie, Naturwissenschaft und Religion.* Stuttgart: Franz Steiner Verlag.

Zaman, Muhammad Qasim. 2002. *The Ulama in Contemporary Islam. Custodians of Change.* Princeton: Princeton University Press.

Zeghal, Malika. 1999. "Religion and Politics in Egypt: The Ulema of Al-Azhar, Radical Islam, and the State (1952–94)." *International Journal of Middle East Studies* 31(3): 371–99.

Zollner, Barbara H. E. 2009. *The Muslim Brotherhood: Hasan al-Hudaybi and Ideology.* London: Routledge.

Zysow, Aron. 2008. "Zakat." In *Encyclopaedia of Islam*, 2nd ed.,11:409. Leiden: Brill.

Index